GREAT LAKES, GREAT NATIONAL FORESTS

A Recreational Guide
To The National Forests Of Michigan Minnesota, Wisconsin, Illinois, Indiana Ohio, Pennsylvania And New York

Also by Eric Freedman

*On the Water, Michigan: Your Comprehensive
Guide to Water Recreation in the Great Lake State*

Pioneering Michigan

Michigan Free

GREAT LAKES, GREAT NATIONAL FORESTS

A Recreational Guide
To The National Forests Of Michigan, Minnesota, Wisconsin, Illinois, Indiana, Ohio, Pennsylvania And New York

By Eric Freedman

PEGG LEGG PUBLICATIONS

Published by Thunder Bay Press
Production and design by Pegg Legg Publications
Editing by Christine Uthoff
Printing by Eerdmans Printing Company, Grand Rapids,
Michigan
Cover photo by U.S. Forest Service
Inside photography by Eric Freedman and Jim DuFresne
unless otherwise noted.

ISBN: 1-882376-13-7

Printed in the United States of America

95 96 97 98 99   1   2   3   4   5   6   7   8

Lansing, Michigan

For Mary Ann, Ian and Cara,
Who sampled the riches of the
national forests with me.

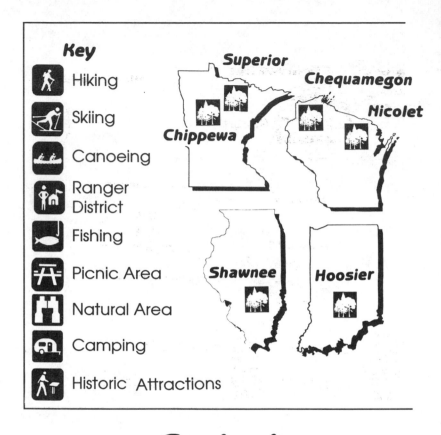

Key

 Hiking

Skiing

Canoeing

Ranger District

Fishing

Picnic Area

Natural Area

Camping

Historic Attractions

Contents

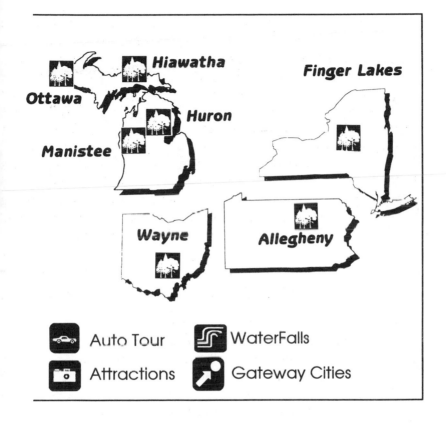

Ottawa · Hiawatha · Huron · Manistee · Finger Lakes · Wayne · Allegheny

🚗 Auto Tour   〰️ WaterFalls

📷 Attractions   🔍 Gateway Cities

Welcome To
The National Forests

Waterfalls and gorges, lakes and rivers, virgin timber and endangered wildflowers, hiking trails and canoe routes, trophy trout and waterfront campsites, sand dunes and mountains. All these and more are found in the 8.2 million acres of national forestland in the eight states - Wisconsin, Minnesota, New York, Michigan, Pennsylvania, Illinois, Indiana and Ohio - bordering the Great Lakes. They range from tiny Finger Lakes National Forest in New York to sprawling Superior National Forest in northeast Minnesota.

Collectively, they offer some of America's most pristine wilderness and some of America's premier recreational opportunities. Individually, each offers some of America's most diverse wildlife habitats, and are outstanding outdoor playgrounds.

Unlike the better known national parks, crowds are rare, even on summer holiday weekends. There are no entrance fees, and with the exception of developed campgrounds, most facilities and services are free.

Another major difference is that land within national parks is all generally owned by the federal government, with relatively few private in-holdings. By contrast, most national forests are scattered holdings or dispersed land, so there may be substantial private holdings, as well as county and state-owned land within their borders. On one hand, access to some public land may be restricted and national forest users must take care to avoid trespassing on private property. On the other hand, the often close proximity of state parks, state forests and county parks increases available recreation opportunities.

Ecotourism is booming in the United States, and national forests are ideal recreation and travel destinations for people who enjoy low-impact, environmentally conscious, "nature" tourism. Already, national forests across the country draw more visitors each year than any other federal lands and boast the nation's largest trail system, as well as more than 4,400 campgrounds and 1,300 picnic grounds. There is, literally, something for everybody in the 13 national forests of the Great Lakes:

Campers can tent in isolated backcountry places, use small waterfront campsites with the basic necessities available, or park their RVs at bustling campgrounds with hot showers and electrical hookups.

Hikers and walkers can select a half-mile boardwalk nature trail, an 8-mile day route or a weeklong expedition through remote, glaciar-scarred terrain.

Anglers can bring home trophy freshwater fish.

Canoeists can enjoy thousands of miles of rivers and streams, from gentle paddles to challenging whitewater, and cross portages once used by Native Americans, French voyageurs and early European settlers.

Boaters can sail, row or motor on thousands of inland lakes and rivers, or on the Great Lakes.

Cross-country skiers, snowmobilers and snowshoers can make the most of winter on extensive trail systems, unplowed forest roads and abandoned railroad grades.

Children can swim, participate in naturalist programs, pick wild blueberries and strawberries, spot deer and loons, and learn about the world around them on an interpretive trail.

Environmentalists can cherish a growing amount of acreage protected as wilderness, preserves or natural areas.

History buffs can visit archaeological digs, former Civilian Conservation Corps and logging camps, abandoned farmsteads, cemeteries and ghost towns, as well as museums and visitor cen-

National forests offer a wide range of hiking opportunities whether you're looking for a short nature trail or a four-day backpacking trek.

ters that interpret human and natural history.

Horseback riders, ATV users and mountain bikers can find appropriate trails and campgrounds for their activities.

Scuba divers can explore shipwrecks and stunning underwater formations.

Birders can spot hundreds of species, some rare and endangered, ranging from bald eagles and great blue herons to Kirtland's warblers and Canada geese.

Motorists can drive some of America's most beautiful roads in the national scenic byway system.

At the same time, the system of 155 national forests generates controversy, largely because Congress gives the U.S. Forest Service a multiple-use mandate in administering them. Public forestland combines wilderness, logging, recreation, scientific research, mineral exploration and historical projects, oil drilling, environmental protection and mining. Visitors to the 13 national forests in the Great Lakes states can see evidence of all those activities, although lumbering is the most obvious commercial use.

This official multi-use policy leads to inevitable conflicts among commercial, recreational users and environmentalists over logging areas, techniques and road building. There are debates over protection of habitats for threatened and endangered species, the acceptable scope of waterfront development, land acquisition policies, user fees and whether the federal government charges loggers and miners enough for publicly owned resources.

The national forests also confront budgetary pressures that affect recreational opportunities. Insufficient staff and financial resources create a maintenance and reconstruction backlog on national forest trails and developed recreation sites.

And remember that the national forests of the Great Lakes states are constantly changing. Land acquisitions, wilderness and research natural area designations, local and Washington politics, heightened environmental awareness, growing public interest in using the outdoors and such unpredictable natural forces as tornados and floods all play a role.

NATIONAL FOREST
RECREATION POLICIES

Specific access and use policies vary from national forest to national forest, reflecting the special management needs of different ecosystems. One forest may require backcountry campers to tent at least 100 feet from a trail or waterway, while the minimum setback is 200 feet at another. There are sometimes variations within a single national forest; that's the case at Superior, where no permit is required for backcountry camping except within the popular Boundary Waters Canoe Area Wilderness.

The policies, rules and guidelines in this chapter generally apply throughout the national forests of the Great Lakes states, but check in advance if you're uncertain. After all, it's disappointing to drive hours towing your gas-powered boat to fish, only to discover on arrival that only electric motors or motorless boats are allowed on the lake you want to use.

Remember, weather and other realities of nature, politics or budgets can trigger rule changes, sometimes on short notice. Among them are bans on campfires due to high fire risk, designation of land as low-impact wilderness or research natural area, or higher camping fees. New campgrounds or trails may open and old ones may close. Trails may be rerouted. Even the size of each national forest is subject to change as the government acquires or exchanges land.

For a free map and color brochure of all national forests, entitled "A Guide to Your National Forests," write to U.S. Forest Service, Box 96090, 14th and Independence Ave. S.W., Washington, DC 20090-6090.

🚐 Camping

Developed campgrounds generally charge a daily fee. If there is no attendant or host, you place the money in a locked fee box near the campground entrance; the boxes are checked later by national forest staff.

Campgrounds usually operate on a first-come, first-served basis, with reservations recommended at least 14 days in advance. Many accept reservations by credit card, check or money order for individual and group sites through a computerized nationwide system. There are cancellation penalties. Call ☎ (800) 280-2267 or write to Biospherics Inc., Box 900, Crossroads Venture Center, 3 Commercial Drive, Cumberland, MD 21507. Some national forest campgrounds also take direct reservations.

Most developed sites have a paved, hard-packed dirt or gravel parking spur; fire ring or grill; and picnic table. Some sites are designated handicapped-accessible. A water pump or faucet will be in easy walking distance. Restrooms tend to be vault toilets and few campgrounds have shower facilities or sump pumps for trailers.

Primitive camping offers established but rustic sites with few, if any, amenities such as toilets or drinking water. Many sites will accommodate more than one family. There may be natural ruggedness but, at the same time, a peaceful and quiet wooded or waterfront setting. Boat accesses are unimproved. Large RVs and trailers are not recommended due to limited turning space; some primitive sites are inaccessible by RVers. Check on permit requirements; reservations may be available for a small fee, depending on the national forest and season.

Dispersed camping outside established recreation areas offers only limited amenities, if any. Some are relatively accessible by motor vehicle; others can be reached only by foot or by boat. There may be a fire ring and a cleared area to pitch your tent, but don't expect drinking water, toilets or picnic tables.

Backcountry camping is allowed almost everywhere in the

Along with campgrounds and designated camping areas, national forests allow backcountry camping. Setting up camp off-trail is allowed in most areas of a national forest.

national forests except in research natural areas or where otherwise posted. There are setback requirements - no-camping zones within a designated distance from a trail, lake, road or river. Open fires may be prohibited, so bring a camp stove. Permits are required in a few areas, and elsewhere you may be asked to sign in.

Good backcountry sites are often found on hills and ridges with natural drainage. As part of the leave-no-trace ethic, hide your campsite from view, stay as few nights as possible in one spot and don't dig a ditch or trench around your tent.

🏕 Golden Age Passports

Although there's no charge for entry to national forests, you may be eligible for a 50-percent discount on camping fees, whether the campground is operated by the government or a private concessionaire. The Golden Age Passport is a $10 lifetime entrance pass for people 62 and older. The Golden Access Passport is free for people who are blind or have disabilities.

In addition, both passports provide free admission to any national park, historic site, recreation area and wildlife refuge administered by the federal government. There's also a 50-percent discount on user fees for campgrounds, parking, boat launches and other facilities run by the National Park Service, Forest Service and U.S. Fish & Wildlife Service,

Passports are available in person at most federally operated recreation areas, including all Forest Service supervisor offices and most Forest Service district offices. Bring identification.

Day Use Areas

Normal hours for swimming beaches, picnic sites and other day use areas are 6 a.m. to 10 p.m. unless different times are posted. Most beaches do not have lifeguards.

Horses & Pets

Pets must be restrained or leashed in developed recreation sites. The only animals allowed in swimming areas are guide dogs.

To prevent environmental damage, keep horses on designated horse trails. Water them away from well heads. Don't hitch your horses to trees. Dismantle temporary hitches and scatter manure piles to aid decomposition and discourage flies. Stay on marked trails and be alert to conditions, especially after heavy rains when trails are slippery.

Hiking

In this book, all trail lengths are generally rounded up to the next mile and may not include spurs. Not all the listed trails are maintained; some are officially abandoned but remain open for use. Some trails, especially in wilderness areas, are unmarked.

Up-to-date trail maps are important, especially for backpackers planning multi-day trips. Markers may be missing; sections of trail may be temporarily impassable or closed due to weather, reconstruction or erosion, or the Forest Service may change a route for environmental reasons. Check about conditions at national forest headquarters, the visitor center or a district office.

 Skiing

One of the best features of the national forest system is access to thousands of miles of trails, active and abandoned logging trails and forest roads for cross-country skiing. Only a small percentage of them are groomed, so it's not always easy to tell at the trailhead how difficult the terrain will be. Follow arrows that show the proper direction for skiing. Keep dogs off the tracks, and avoid walking or snowshoeing on the tracks.

Off-road Vehicles

Tread Lightly. Each national forest has travel maps explaining the rules for snowmobiles, all-terrain vehicles and off-road motorcycles. Main inactive logging and high-clearance roads and trails outside wilderness areas are open to motorized use most of the year, subject to posted restrictions. Wildlife nesting areas, soft and wet trails and roads, and wildlife winter habitat areas may be closed part of the year. For more Tread Lightly information, call ☎ (800) 966-9900.

Wilderness areas are off-limits to all vehicles. So are meadows, new forests, steep hillsides, stream banks, lakeshores, wetlands and endangered wildlife habitat.

Fishing

State fishing laws, such as license requirements, limits and open seasons, are enforced. The Forest Service may impose additional restrictions for environmental, research, safety or other purposes. Respect private property owners whose land is scattered through or adjacent to the national forest. Get your fishing licenses from the state; they are not available at Forest Service offices.

You'll find a combination of ice, warm-water and cold-water fishing in the national forests of Michigan, Minnesota, New York, Pennsylvania and Wisconsin. Warm-water fishing predominates in the national forests of Illinois, Indiana, Ohio.

A growing number of national forest waters have barrier-free fishing piers. They are open to everybody and make ideal destinations to take young children fishing.

Bicycling

Mountain bikers should remember that forest roads and trails often have steep grades, corners and intersections, loose sand and gravel, and bumps and holes created by burrowing animals. Stay on trails, carry a map, always yield the right of way and be alert for hikers and horseback riders. Bikes are prohibited in wilderness areas. Outside the wildernesses, some trails are closed to mountain bikes, so check with a Forest Service office.

Boating & Canoeing

State and federal boating laws, including operating under the influence of alcohol and drugs, are enforced. Obey Forest Service restrictions on types of boats and motors allowed on various lakes and rivers, including those in designated wildernesses. Boaters should stay well away from swimmers and keep aware of their wake.

Outfitters

Need to rent a canoe, camping gear or horses? Want a guide for backcountry fishing, hunting or canoeing? Eager to challenge the fish or the shipwrecks of the Great Lakes? Local outfitters can provide those services, as well as helping plan your trip and providing transportation to upriver access points and from downriver take-outs. For information about canoe liveries, horse stables, charter boats, dive shops and guides, ask at the national forest supervisor's office or district office; or contact the local tourism or visitors bureau or chamber of commerce.

Barrier-Free Accessibility

The Forest Service is actively working to improve access to recreation sites for the handicapped. That effort is reflected in accessible campsites, fishing piers, interpretive trails, visitor centers and other facilities.

Historic Sites

Federal law prohibits disturbing or removing any objects from these sites, both on the land and underwater. Don't camp near them either.

Plant Collecting

Collecting plants has become so popular that permits are now required in some national forests to protect the plants from over collection. There is generally an exception for small amounts of forest products for personal use, such as pine cones, berries, mushrooms or rose hips. Permits specify what species can be gathered and what areas are open to collecting; some areas are closed to collecting for land management reasons. Endangered, threatened, sensitive, rare and unique plants are off-limits to collectors. For permit information, contact the forest supervisor's office or district office.

Among the volunteer programs national forests offer is "Adopt-A–Trail," where groups maintain and police a stretch of trail.

Environmental
And Activity Programs

A variety of organized programs are offered within the national forests of the Great Lakes states, allowing visitors to discover archaeological and anthropological history, trace wildlife, repair trails and help other visitors. Some are sponsored and operated by the U.S. Forest Service; others are possible due to partnerships with outside groups.

Environmental Protection

National Wild & Scenic Rivers: Hundreds of miles of waterways in the national forests have been designated by Congress as national wild and scenic rivers or placed under study for potential future designation. Many virtually pristine stretches of river would be at risk of overuse or development without such protection. Among them are portions of the Ontonagon River in Ottawa National Forest, the Tahquamegon River in Hiawatha National Forest, the Pine River in Manistee National Forest and the Au Sable River in Huron National Forest. Similar state programs also protect some rivers that cross the national forests.

Research National Area: Since 1927, the Forest Service has set aside more than 250 research national areas with unique ecosystems, some in partnership with other government agencies, the Nature Conservancy and the Natural Areas Association. Such areas are permanently protected to maintain biological diversity and foster education. Together, they form a national network representing North American ecosystems, habitats, biological communities, and hydrological and geological conditions and forma-

21

tions.

Human intervention at these natural areas is limited; natural conditions usually prevail, although some are managed with prescribed fires or fenced to keep out grazing animals. Supervised educational activities such as field trips for graduate students and special tours for horticultural organizations are allowed in some.

For more information, contact the Research Natural Area Coordinator, U.S. Forest Service, Box 96090, Washington, D.C. 20090-6090; ☎ (202) 205-1149.

National Natural Landmarks Program: Run by the National Park Service, this program has designated a variety of sites within the national forest system, including La Rue-Pine Hills Ecological Area in Shawnee National Forest; Keeley Creek Natural Area in Superior National Forest; Hearts Content Scenic Area in Allegheny National Forest; Bose Lake Hemlock Hardwoods in Nicolet National Forest; and Pine Point Natural Area in Chippewa National Forest. The program identifies, recognizes and protects nationally significant natural areas that are among the best examples of their type of biotic community or geologic features.

Plant-A-Tree Program: The Forest Service will select and plant 10 to 15 seedlings for a contribution of at least $10. Those trees are used for ecosystem management, including wildlife habitat, timber and recreation area development. For more information, contact a Forest Service office or the Plant-A-Tree Program, Box 96090, Washington, DC 20090-6090.

National Forest Heritage & Activities

Eyes On Wildlife: The Forest Service's Watchable Wildlife Program is intended to help visitors see wildlife as part of a larger ecosystem. The *Eyes on Wildlife* program includes outdoor classes, exhibits, guided tours and presentations. Participants use such facilities as viewing platforms, blinds and interpretive trails.

For more information, contact the individual national forest or contact the Eyes on Wildlife Program, Forest Service Eastern Region, 310 W. Wisconsin Ave., Room 500, Milwaukee, WI 53203;

☎ (414) 297-3693.

National Forest Scenic Byways: The number of national forest scenic byways in the Great Lakes states is growing, including Whitefish Bay in Hiawatha National Forest, Longhouse in Allegheny National Forest, Great Divide in Chequamegon National Forest and Black River in Ottawa National Forest. Across the country, the byway system now covers more than 5,000 miles in about three dozen states. These auto routes pass places of scenic beauty and natural or historic significance, mostly on national forest land.

Passport In Time Program: Volunteers assist in heritage projects on national forest land, including archaeological excavations, historic building restoration, archival research, site mapping and collecting oral histories. The program began in 1989 in Minnesota and has expanded to almost 100 individual projects across the country each summer and fall.

Participants in Passport in Time, or PIT for short, work a weekend or longer under the guidance of professional historians, archaeologists and other trained project supervisors. Enrollment is limited. Some projects seek specific qualifications such as excavation or carpentry experience or outdoor survival or historical research skills. However, most require no experience.

There's no registration or application fee for the program, and participants camp free at Forest Service campgrounds. You provide your own camping gear and are responsible for your own meals. In addition to work, some projects offer evening lectures and special tours of nearby sites.

Applicants are asked about their project preference, choice of dates and special interests and skills. For the latest newsletter, "PIT Traveler," with an application and list of scheduled projects, contact the Passport in Time Clearinghouse, CEHP Inc., Box 18364, Washington, D.C. 20036; ☎ (202) 293-0922.

Service Trips: The Sierra Club sponsors service - volunteer work - trips at national forests and other public lands. Participants rebuild trails, clean rivers, restore camping areas and archaeological sites, re-vegetate meadows, remove non-native plants and do other moderately strenuous work. No experience is necessary. About half your time is free for hiking, swimming, canoeing, photography, fishing, touring or other personal interests.

For information on upcoming national service trips, contact the Sierra Club Outing Department, 730 Polk Ave., San Francisco, CA 94109; ☎ (415) 776-2211. In addition, Sierra Club state chapters often sponsor shorter national forest service trips.

Members of the American Hiking Society, an advocacy group for non-motorized trail users, also do volunteer projects such as trail building and trail maintenance. For information, contact the society at Box 20164, Washington, DC 20041-2160; ☎ (703) 385-3252.

Campgrounds Hosts: Campgrounds in some national forests, such as Nicolet and Ottawa, rely on volunteer hosts who spend a few hours each day answering questions, providing information to visitors and doing light maintenance. In exchange, hosts receive free camping. A commitment for a minimum number of weeks is required.

Adopt-A-Forest & Adopt-A-Trail: Unfortunately, national forest land too often is used for illegal dumping and disposal of junked cars, broken appliances, construction debris, old tires, trash and even hazardous wastes. Trails and portages may fall into disrepair because of overuse or too little money for maintenance. At some national forests, organizations, businesses, schools, families and clubs "adopt" parcels of forest land or stretches of trail. Adopt-a-Forest volunteers periodically inspect and clean up "their" parcels and report litterers or vandals. For more information, contact the national forest supervisor's office.

More Volunteer Opportunities: Other full-time, part-time and seasonal volunteer opportunities are available as well. They include photography; planting trees and reseeding damaged areas; and answering phones, greeting visitors and answering mail at ranger stations and visitor centers.

Some jobs require a medical exam, which the government

pays for. You can volunteer as an individual or through youth, civic and environmental groups, schools, businesses and special interest clubs. Volunteers must be over 18 or have written permission from a parent or guardian. You can get an application from the volunteer coordinator of each national forest.

Civilian Conservation Corps Legacy: Another thing visitors can see - and appreciate - is the lasting legacy of the Civilian Conservation Corps; Franklin Delano Roosevelt's "tree army" of the Depression. Enrollees were paid $30 a month to work on reforestation, fire fighting, fish stocking, construction and erosion control. They built roads and bridges, fire towers and dams, recreational buildings and trails. For the volunteers, the CCC offered food and shelter, a job at a time of high unemployment and training for the future.

Most CCC camps are gone - torn down, destroyed by weather or swallowed up by the forest around them. A few have been preserved as historic sites, such as Camp Rabideau in Chippewa National Forest; some abandoned sites are commemorated by informational markers. However, other evidence of their activities remain, including pine plantations, picnic pavilions and beach shelters.

MINNESOTA

Superior National Forest
Chippewa National Forest

With its cold winter temperatures and abundance of snow, Superior National Forest is a cross country skier's paradise.

SUPERIOR

Box 338
Duluth, MN 55801
☎ **(218) 720-5324**

2,155,230 acres

When Superior National Forest was designated in 1909, the Duluth Herald predicted, "The new reserve is quite likely to be a permanent forest reserve, and by reason of its size and location, it will become in time one of the most important in the country." In truth, the largest national forest in the Great Lakes region is a place of superlatives, including the largest timber wolf stronghold in the lower 48 states, more than 1,400 miles of canoeing routes, 1,977 lakes, 40 endangered plant species and the Sawtooth Mountains, one of the oldest mountain ranges in North America.

Visitors looking for alternatives to canoeing among the aspen, white pine and paper birch can hike, ski, snowmobile or bike, try dog sledding or take advantage of the fall salmon run. Most visitors come in the spring, summer and fall, but many others are lured by the 100-plus inches of snow that winter brings. S u p e - rior National Forest is less famous under its own name than for its internationally renowned component, the Boundary Waters Canoe Area Wilderness. The vast preserve is the most popular wilderness in the United States and, as the Forest Service notes, "The popularity of BWCAW as a destination, along with the con-

troversy surrounding its establishment, management and use may
have brought significant publicity to Superior. "

What is now Superior was shaped by glaciers and became
home to a Paleo-Indian culture 10,000 to 20,000 years ago and
more recently to the Sioux and Chippewa. When a trickle of white
explorers first appeared in the 17th century, they encountered
Dakota Sioux occupying the area and living a migratory lifestyle
that involved hunting, trapping, fishing and harvesting wild rice.
Heated competition over the fur trade led to the arrival of the
Chippewa from the east along the shores of Lake Superior. They
in turn drove out the Sioux to the south and west.

European explorers, searching for beaver-rich country, are
credited for developing the fur trade and opening this region.
Radisson and Groseilliers explored the area as early as 1660, when
they loaded their canoes with pelts and returned to Montreal.
Jacques de Noyons arrived in 1688, and by 1689 trader Sieur du
Lhut had established operations along the north shore of Lake
Superior. He also established a post to the south and today the
city bears his name, Duluth. In the 1730s, Sieur de la Verendrye
and his sons, seeking the fabled Northwest Passage, established a
trade route between Lake Superior and Lake Winnipeg that passed
through Superior National Forest and would eventually evolve into
the present international boundary.

The English gained control of the area as a result of the French
and Indian War, which ended in 1763. The Americans took control
after the War of 1812; by 1860, loggers and miners had settled in
northern Minnesota. Following the construction of the first railroad in the area in 1884, widespread logging, attempts at gold
mining and wildfires took their toll on the area. The destructions
of a once-great forest alarmed Minnesota residents who pushed
for public management of the area, and in 1909 Superior National
Forest was established. At more than 2 million acres, Superior is
a vast forest, stretching from its border with Voyageurs National
Park, just 24 miles E of International Falls, to its border with
Ontario's Quetico Provincial Park to the N, to Lake Superior to

the E. The U.S. Forest Service headquarters is in Duluth, only 60 miles S of forest land.

 ## The Forest

Despite extensive logging at the turn of the century, Superior is almost completely forested. Native coniferous trees are jack pine, white pine and red pine, white and black spruce, balsam fir, northern white cedar and tamarack. Broadleaved trees include quaking aspen, paper birch, yellow birch, black ash, sugar maple and red maple. Within the forest, most notably the BWCAW, there are stands of pines that have never been harvested.

Common ground plants found in Superior are bunchberry, wintergreen, goldthread, twinflower and clintonia while shrubs include willow, chokecherry, pin cherry, alder and serviceberry. In bogs, you'll often encounter sphagnum moss as well as the carnivorous pitcher plant and sundew. The forest is also home to 30 native orchids, which prefer Superior's cool, moist woodlands. The most cherished orchid most visitors encounter is the showy lady's slipper, Minnesota's state flower.

Along with largest population of timber wolves living in the Lower 48, another 50 mammal species inhabit Superior. They include whitetail deer, moose and black bears. Smaller mammals that can be seen include beavers, muskrats, porcupines, red fox, red squirrel, otters, fishers and minks.

More than 200 species of migratory and resident birds are found in Superior. The favorite is the common loon, which is often seen and heard on many of the lakes. Just as impressive are bald eagles, ospreys and great blue herons. Other possible encounters include spruce, ruffed and sharp-tail grouse, pileated woodpeckers, various hawks and owls, mallards, mergansers and other waterfowl. A huge influx of wood warblers occurs each spring.

 ## Camping

Superior combines splendid backcountry and primitive camp-

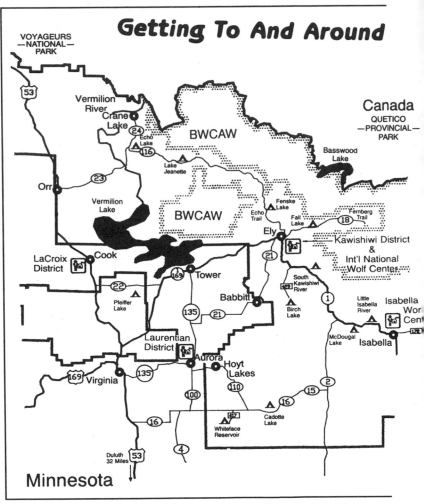

Getting To And Around

Minnesota

ing with more than two dozen developed campgrounds, some with only a handful of sites. Most are on the water, offering opportunities for fishing, boating, swimming or canoeing. Some feature interpretive programs, playgrounds, pavilions, nature trails and berry picking. Group camping is available at Echo Lake, Fenske Lake and Crescent Lake.

The developed campgrounds outside BWCAW and number

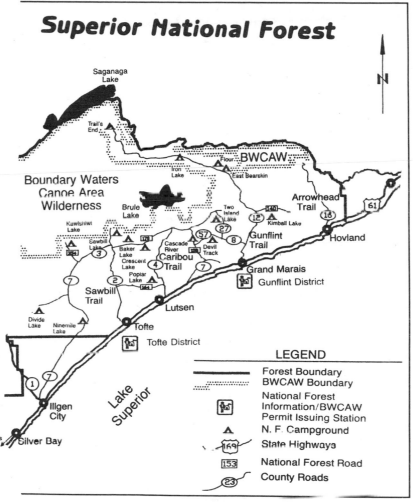

Superior National Forest

Saganaga Lake

Trail's End

Flour BWCAW

Iron Lake

East Bearskin

Boundary Waters Canoe Area Wilderness

Brule Lake

Arrowhead Trail

61

Kawishiwi Lake

Two Island Lake

Kimball Lake

18

Sawbill Lake

Cascade River

Devil Track

Gunflint Trail

Hovland

Baker Lake

Crescent Lake

Caribou Trail

Poplar Lake

Grand Marais

Gunflint District

Sawbill Trail

Lutsen

Divide Lake

Ninemile Lake

Tofte

Tofte District

LEGEND

▬▬▬	Forest Boundary
∴∴∴	BWCAW Boundary
🏠	National Forest Information/BWCAW Permit Issuing Station
▲	N. F. Campground
169	State Highways
153	National Forest Road
23	County Roads

Lake Superior

Illgen City

Duluth 42 Miles

Silver Bay

of sites are:

Gunflint Ranger District

Cascade River (4), 14 miles NW of Grand Marais on Forest Road 158;

DevilTrack Lake (16), 12 miles N of Grand Marais on County Road 8;

East Bearskin Lake (33), 28 miles NW of Grand Marais on

Forest Road 146;

Flour Lake (35), 30 miles NW of Grand Marais on Forest Road 147;

Iron Lake (7), 38 miles NW of Grand Marais on County Road 92;

Kimball Lake (10), 13 miles NE of Grand Marais on Forest Road 140;

Trail's End (32), 58 miles NW of Grand Marais on Gunflint Trail;

Two Island Lake (38), 15 miles NW of Grand Marais on County Road 27.

Kawishiwi Ranger District
Birch Lake (28), 14 miles S of Ely on Forest Road 429;
Fall Lake (66), 14 miles E of Ely on Forest Road 551;
Fenske Lake (15), 13 miles N of Ely on SH-16;
South Kawishiwi River (32), 12 miles SE of Ely on SH-1.

La Croix Ranger District
Lake Jeanette (12), 25 miles NE of Orr on Echo Trail;
Echo Lake (24), 6 miles N of Buyck on Forest Road 841.

Laurentian Ranger District
Cadotte Lake (27), 11 miles N of Brimson on Forest Road 778;
Pfeiffer Lake (16), 30 miles N of Virginia on Forest Road 256;
Whiteface Reservoir (53), 14 miles S of Hoyt Lakes on Forest Road 417.

Tofte Ranger District
Baker Lake (5), 23 miles N of Tofte on Forest Road 1272;
Crescent Lake (33), 27 miles NE of Tofte on Forest Road 165;
Divide Lake (3), 6 miles E of Tofte on Forest Road 172;
Kawishiwi Lake (5), 32 miles NW of Tofte on Forest Road 354;
Little Isabella River (11), 4 miles W of Isabella on SH-1;
McDougal Lake (21), 10 miles W of Isabella on Forest Road 106;

Ninemile Lake (24), 14 miles NW of Schroeder on County Road 7;

Poplar River (4), 18 miles NE of Tofte on Forest Road 164;

Sawbill Lake (50), 25 miles N of Tofte on County Road 2 (Sawbill Road);

Temperance River (9), 11 miles N of Tofte on SH-2.

Outside BWCAW, there are 265 backcountry sites, 226 of which are accessible only by water or trail.

For information on camping, see the BWCAW section.

 ## Trails

Given its sprawling size, Superior is literally a natural place for trails, ranging from short interpretive and casual walking trails to those more suitable for day-long and multiple-day activities. In addition, old logging roads and Forest Service roads are used for ATV riding, hiking, skiing, snowmobiling, mountain biking and snowshoeing. Trails are generally marked by signs, tree blazes or rock piles known as cairns; be aware that some spurs are unmarked and overgrown. Before setting out, check on permit and other requirements because some trails are within the BWCAW. Some trails cross lakes, so cross-country skiers should know surface conditions can be slushy in December and March, early and late in the season. Skiers also should be alert for windfallen trees. Here are some popular trails.

Kawaishiwi Ranger District

Angleworm Trail, 14 miles: In winter, this BWCAW trail crosses Spring Creek, runs up the center of Angleworm Lake and crosses Home, Gull, Mudhole, Thunder and Beartrap lakes. During hiking season, it skirts the lakes. High rock ridges allow scenic overlooks along this rugged trail. It can be hiked in a single day but is best done as an overnight trip. Pick-up the trailhead from Forest Road 116.

Bass Lake Trail, 6 miles: Also on Forest Road 116, N of Ely, this trail is highlighted by Dry Falls and scenic overlooks. The 3- to 5-hour hike is through an area shaped by glacial action as the trail skirts Bass Lake and passes near Dry and Low lakes.

Birch Lake Plantation Trail, *4 miles:* There are rolling hills along this relatively easy hiking and skiing trail through Birch Lake Plantation, a red pine research area. This was Superior's first pine plantation. Access is from County Road 623.

Coxey Pond Ski Trail, *12 miles:* The area has been logged several times, and much of the trail network follows old logging roads. It passes old pines known as "the Sentinels." The trail is accessed from North Arm Road (County Road 644) on Burntside Lake.

Hogback Lake Trail, *6 miles:* The ridgeback - or hogback - between Carp and Hogback lakes offers scenic views. There's access to seven lakes and the remains of an old railroad trestle bridge built in the 1930s, a logging canal and square posts that marked Civilian Conservation Corps work projects. There are four wilderness campsites along the trail. The trailhead is at Hogback Lake Picnic Area on Forest Road 172, E of Isabella.

Jasper Hills Trail, *18 miles:* These ski loops cross Rookie Pond, Tofte Lake, Moose Lake, Jasper Lake, Enchanted Lakes and Jasper Creek. Terrain includes cedar swamps, hills and marshes. To reach the trail, take County Road 18 to Tofte Lake.

Kane Lake Trail, *4 miles:* Hikers use this trail through a ruffed grouse management area forested with aspen and alder. There's also a beaver dam here. The trail is located 2 miles E of County Road 2 on Forest Road 107 (Kane Lake Road).

North Junction Trails, *8 miles:* This series of cross-country ski loops includes beaver territory, hilly uplands, a spruce swamp and a scenic area along high rock bluffs. The trailhead is on County Road 644 (North Arm Road), just W of County Road 116 (Echo Trail).

North Arm Trails, *26 miles:* The ski trails wind amid panoramas, 300-year-old pines and rolling hills. Follow North Arm Trail (County Road 644) to reach the trailhead.

Secret/Blackstone Trail, *5 miles:* There are steep hills along this route. A rock cliff at the end overlooks Ennis Lake, a popular rock rappelling spot. The trailhead is at Moon Lake on Moon Lake Road.

Slim Lake Ski Trail, *1 mile*: The route is fairly flat, with some rises and falls; it's part of the North Arm ski trail system. There are rocky bluffs near Slim Lake. The trailhead is at Burnside Lake on North Arm Road (County Road 644).

Snowbank Lake & Old Pines Trail System, *41 miles*: This trail system starts at the parking lot on the Fernberg Road W of Lake One landing and follows the S side of Snowbank and Parent Lake. At this point, the trail swings N between Parent and Disappointment Lakes to the NE corner of Snowbank Lake. The N side of Snowbank features high rock ridges for excellent views. The Old Pines segment leaves the Snowbank Trail just N of Becoosin Lake and passes a stand of virgin white pines more than 300 years old. It returns to Snowbank Trail near Boot Lake. Most of these trails and their loops lie in the BWCAW.

South Farm Ski Trail, *7 miles*: The trail crosses South Farm Lake and leads to the short Spruce-Muskeg Trail through a muskeg swamp. The trailhead is at Superior Forest Lodge on County Road 16, N of Ely off State Highway 169.

White Pine Interpretive Trail, *1 mile*: This self-guiding trail winds through majestic white pines, many 200 years old. White Pine is accessed from County Road 2, 25 miles SW of Isabella.

Laurentian Ranger District

Big Aspen Trail System, *20 miles*: This system, primarily designed for cross-country skiers but used by hikers and mountain bikers as well, passes through deer and grouse habitat along logging roads and old railroad grades from the Virginia And Rainy Lake Lumber Co. There are scenic overlooks of the Rice River Valley. The trailhead is at the end of County Road 405, just E of U.S. 53.

Big Lake Trail, *2 miles*: The trail passes wild rice-gathering spots and then follows boardwalks through a boggy stretch to provide access to Big Lake and Stone Lake. The trailhead is E of Hoyt Lakes on Forest Road 120.

Bird Lake Trails, 10 miles: This ski trail system crosses bogs, wooded hills and thick stands of black spruce. The trailhead is at the E end of Hoyt Lakes on County Road 110.

Giants Ridge Ski Area, 31 miles: World Cup races have taken place on this system of loop trails. There are chair lifts to the top of the ridge. Trailhead and parking areas are off County Road 416.

Lookout Mountain Ski Trails, 15 miles: There are scenic overlooks along this network of loop trails straddling the Laurentian Divide. The trailhead is N of Virginia on State Highway 53.

North Dark River Trail, 2 miles: It follows the shore of the Dark River through a 1930s pine plantation, then loops back along an old logging road. There are wildflowers and evidence of beaver activity along the trail, while from the vistas hikers can see the small valley the river carved. This trail begins from County Road 688.

South Dark River Trail, 1 mile: This trail passes through mixed pine and hardwood forests to scenic vistas of the Dark River. Terrain varies from flat to rolling hills. The trail starts on Forest Road 271.

Sturgeon River Trail System, 20 miles: A system of skiing and hiking trails pass through a variety of habitats, including mature pines and grassy openings. It also skirts high bluffs along the Sturgeon River for scenic views of the waterway. There are three trailheads N of Chisholm: on State Highway 73, on County Road 65 and on Forest Road 279.

La Croix Ranger District

Ashawa Ski Trail, 15 miles: These trails traverse a hilly area along Lake Vermilion and are accessed from County Road 24.

Astrid Lake Trails, 7 miles: The loops of this system provide access to small lakes, old-growth white and red pines, beaver ponds, a spruce bog, oak-covered ridges and large exposed glacial boulders. The first trailhead is at Lake Jeanette Campground on Echo Trail (County Road 116).

Big Moose Trail, 2 miles: The trail goes through rolling jackpine and red pine country and into BWCAW to reach Big Moose Lake,

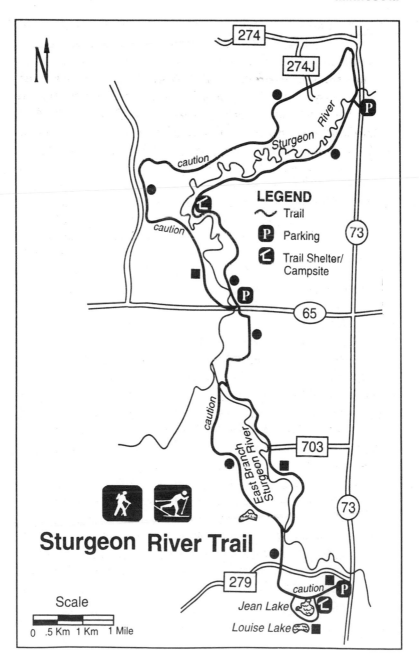

Sturgeon River Trail

LEGEND
~ Trail
P Parking
Trail Shelter/Campsite

Scale
0 .5 Km 1 Km 1 Mile

which features a backcountry campsite. Trailhead access is from Moose Loop Road (Forest Road 464).

Devil's Cascade Trail, 5 miles: This trail within BWCAW is wet and rugged at spots; beaver dams serve as bridges across some drainages. A feature of the trail is Devil's Cascade, a narrow gorge with cascading rapids at the outlet of Lower Pauness Lake. Plan on 10 hours for a round-trip hike on this point-to-point trail. The main trailhead is on Echo Trail (County Road 116), E of County Road 24.

Echo Lake Trail System, 12 miles: This hiking, skiing and biking trail system is part of a ruffed grouse habitat management area with aspen stands. Access is from Echo Trail (County Road 116).

Fire And Ice Interpretive Trail, 0.1 mile: The short trail, reached from Echo Trail (County Road 116) overlooks the site of the 1971 Little Indian Sioux fire. Signs explain how fire and glaciers have shaped the surrounding landscape. There's blueberry picking along the way.

Herriman Lake System, 14 miles: A combination of loops compose this system, about half of it within BWCAW. Along the way are the Echo River and Dovre, Knute, Herriman, Baylis and Little Vermilion lakes, as well as rock ledges and beaver ponds. The trail system begins off County Road 424 near Crane Lake.

Sioux-Hustler Trail, 49 miles: Most of this trail is within the BWCAW. There are a number of lakes, several canoe portages and beaver dams that hikers use to cross impoundments and flowages. Wilderness campsites are provided on Emerald, Range, Devils Cascade and Pageant lakes. Access the trail from Meander Lake Road (Forest Road 467).

Stuart Lake Trail, 8 miles: Also accessed from Echo Trail (County Road 116), Stuart Lake Trail starts in a grassy wildlife opening, crosses the Stuart River rapids and intersects two portages through gently rolling terrain. Wildlife viewing opportunities are excellent.

Vermilion Falls Interpretive Trail, 1 mile: This trail leads to an observation platform at the "Chute," where a constriction in the Vermilion River produces a waterfall. Nearby a wild rice bed grows in a small upriver area. The site is off Forest Road 491, W of County Road 24.

Vermilion Gorge Interpretive Trail, 2 miles: Expect to climb. In addition to signs about local history, the fur trade, logging and mineral prospecting, there's a good view of the Vermilion River flowing into Crane Lake. Part of the trail parallels the rugged granite cliffs and rock outcrops of Vermilion River Gorge. The trail is accessed from Crane Lake at the end of County Road 24.

Tofte Ranger District

Arrowhead Creek Trail, 5 miles: This trail along old logging roads offers assorted habitats - pine plantation, brushy lowland and mixed forest - that provide food and shelter for a variety of game, such as moose, ruffed grouse, woodcock and whitetail deer. The trailhead is on Forest Road 173, N of Kelly Landing.

Britton Peak Trail, 0.25 mile: This short trail leads through a maple and birch forest to the top of Britton Peak, providing a vista of Lake Superior, Carlton Peak, the Temperance River valley and surrounding hills. Take Sawbill Trail (County Road 2) to the trailhead.

Flathorn-Gegoka Ski Trail, 29 miles: This trail system includes a short run across Lake Gegoka. Other terrain includes hills, open spruce bogs and the flat shore of the Little Isabella River. Access is from Forest Road 177.

Leveaux National Recreation Trail, 4 miles: An easy loop with scenic overlooks, this trail crosses a flat grassy area where moose and deer are visible in the early morning, then starts climbing after crossing the Onion River. Leveaux Mountain tops off as a high rocky cliff and offers excellent views of Lake Superior and the Sawtooth Mountain Range. The trailhead is on Onion River Road (Forest Road 336).

North Shore Mountains Ski Trail, 97 miles: The trail runs through the Sawtooth Mountains, with widely divergent difficulty levels, elevation, terrain and scenery. There are several access points

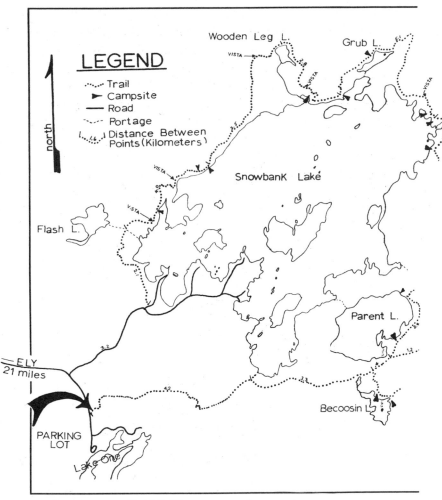

to the system off U.S. 61.

Oberg Mountain National Recreation Trail, *2 miles:* Sharing a trailhead with Leveaux National Recreation Trail on Onion River Road (Forest Road 336), Oberg is a series of switchbacks that climbs nearly 1,000 feet above Lake Superior. There are nine scenic overlooks along the way with spectacular panoramas from the ledges and rock cliffs at the top.

Pancore Lake Mountain Bike Trail, *25 miles:* Blueberry

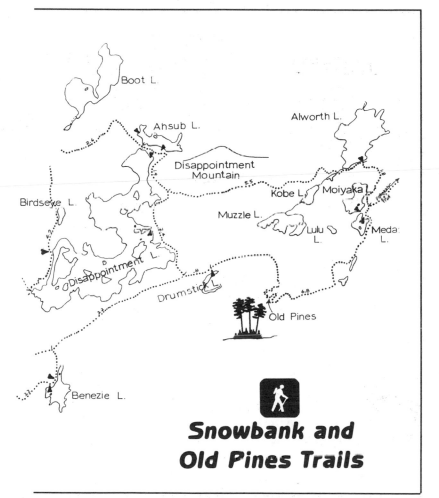

Snowbank and Old Pines Trails

patches are scattered along the loop. Part of the surface is graveled but other sections are rougher. Access is Forest Road 338.

Powwow Lake Trail, 55 miles: There are a number of lakes along the way: Superstition, Mirror with its cold spring, Path with its old-growth white pines, Rock of Ages with its outcrops, Lake 3 with its mossy black spruce groves, South Wilder, Pose, Horseshoe with its canoe portage, and North Wilder. The entire trail system lies in the BWCAW, and campsites are situated on the rocky outcrops of many of the lakes, roughly every 3 or 4 miles. The trail originates at the Forest Center Landing, N of Isabella on Forest Road 377.

Sugar Bush Ski Trail, 17 miles: There are sugar maples, birch-aspen forests and open vistas. The trail is used by mountain bikers from spring through fall. The trail is reached from Sawbill Trail (County Road 2).

Superior National Scenic Hiking Trail, 75 miles: Once complete, this trail will stretch almost 250 miles between Duluth and the Canadian border, including the Superior stretch. Along the way are log bridges and walkways, rock outcrops and challenging wilderness terrain, as well as moose, wolf, hawk and whitetail deer habitat.

Tomahawk Corridor Snowmobile Trail, 59 miles: Most of it follows forest and logging access roads, with sections along old railroad grades and ski trails, through gently rolling terrain and past lakes and streams. It combines with local Mitawan Lake Area offshoot trails. Access to this trail is along Forest Roads 172, 177 and 386.

Gunflint Ranger District

Border Route Trail, 45 miles: The highpoints of this trail is the moderately rugged terrain and the rock ledges and spectacular views of Mountain and Rose lakes. Most of it is within BWCAW. The trail extends from the Loon Lake landing on the Gunflint Trail to the public boat landing on Little John Lake at the end of Arrowhead Trail.

Caribou Rock-Split Pine Trail, 3 miles: Steep but scenic, this trail offers overlooks of Caribou Rock and West Bearskin, Moss, Duncan and Daniels lakes. There's a waterfall at the Stairway Portage. The trail begins at County Road 65.

Cascade River Trail, 2 miles: Some of the loveliest scenery along Lake Superior's North Shore is visible here as the Cascade River runs through a narrow gorge towards the nation's largest lake. Pick up the trail on the N side of the Cascade River on State Highway 61.

Cascade Loop Biking Trail, 17 miles: Located nearby is this system of gravel roads, cross-country ski trails and a little pavement that make up a hilly route along Lake Superior and over the Sawtooth Mountains. The trailhead is on County Road 41.

Eagle Mountain Trail, 9 miles: Eagle Mountain is Minnesota's highest point at 2,301 feet. The trail extends from Forest Road 153 N to the mountain, where there are spectacular views of Crow, Eagle, Shrike and Zoo lakes, to the NW. It ends in the Brule Lake Area. There are wilderness campsites along the route.

George Washington Memorial Pines Trail, 3 miles: Skiers and snowshoers enjoy this virtually flat trail. It is reached from the Gunflint Trail (County Road 12) and runs through a pine plantation that was established after a 1927 forest fire.

Greenwood Lake Trail, 25 miles: Most of this biking trail is a surface of hard gravel. It loops through remote spruce and pine forests, with picnicking and swimming available at Greenwood Lake. Forest Road 309 crosses the route twice.

Honeymoon Bluff Trail, 1 mile: Another short but steep trail, Honeymoon leads to bluffs overlooking Hungry Jack Lake and West Bearskin Lake. It was named in honor of John Mulligan, the first permanent Forest Service ranger in Cook County, who walked this trail on his honeymoon. Access is on Clearwater Road near the entrance of Flour Lake Campground.

Kimball Creek Trail, 8 miles: This rugged route parallels Kimball Creek, a brook trout stream. The first trailhead is on County Road 304.

Magnetic Rock Trail, 2 miles: The reward at the end of the walk is a building-sized magnetic rock, a glacial age memento; test it with your compass. The trail begins along the Gunflint Trail (County Road 12) and crosses a bog, Larch Creek and good spots to pick blueberries and high bush cranberries.

Pincushion Mountain Ski Trail, 15 miles: Hilly loops offer views of Lake Superior, Grand Marais harbor and the Devil Track River Valley. The trailhead is at the Sawtooth Mountain Overlook off the Gunflint Trail (County Road 12).

Pine Lake Loop Biking Trail, 20 miles: The route includes paved and gravel roads with long, gentle grades. It crosses the Cascade River twice. Access is from Fifth Street in Grand Marais.

South Lake Trail, 4 miles: Passing through stands of old-growth red and white pine and alongside a beaver pond, this trail provides access to Partridge and South lakes. The South Lake Trail intersects the Border Route Trail in the BWCAW. The trailhead is on Gunflint Trail (County Road 12) near Poplar Lake.

Sweetheart's Bluff Nature Trail, 1 mile: This short trail provides a view of the Grand Marais harbor and the Lake Superior shoreline. It begins from Eighth Avenue in Grand Marais.

Boating & Canoeing

If you don't bring your own boat or canoe, there are liveries and outfitters in the gateway communities. Boat and canoe rentals are also available at Fall Lake Campground, the largest developed campground in Superior, while canoe rentals are available at Sawbill Lake Campground.

Whiteface Reservoir in the Laurentian Ranger District is popular for boating because of its many bays and islands. Other well-known boating lakes in the Laurentian Ranger District include Big Rice, Twin, Pine, Long, Whitewater, Colby, Salo, Otto, Harris, Dark, Knuckey, Clear, Cadotte and Bassett; in the Gunflint Ranger District there are Saganaga, Round, Little John and Sea Gull; and in the Kawishiwi Ranger District is Agassa.

Although the BWCAW is the big draw for many canoeists, there are plenty of opportunities outside the restricted region to experience wilderness-like adventure and recreation.

BWCAW water entry points in the Tofte Ranger District include:

Bog Lake: No navigable rivers enter or leave this small, isolated lake just inside the BWCAW border. Primarily used as a day fishing spot, the lake is N of Isabella off Forest Road 377.

Hog Creek: The creek leads to Perent Lake, named for an early 20th-century trapper, and from there down the Perent River to Isabella Lake through an area known as moose country. The access site is S of Kawishiwi Lake Campground on Forest Road 354.

Isabella Lake: After paddling Isabella Lake, one route follows the Isabella River to its juncture with the Island River, then over the Rice Lake Rapids portage to Rice and Quadga lakes. Alternatives are to head toward Boga Lake and the Perent River, or to take Pow Wow Creek to Ferne Lake. The access site on Isabella Lake is N of Isabella at the end of Forest Road 377.

Island River Canoe Route: Island River, upstream of its intersection with the Isabella River, is a 10-mile route through an area that abounds with moose. Portions of the river extend into the BWCAW where the semi-wilderness route involves 10 short portages. The W end of the route is where Forest Road 377 crosses Island River, N of Isabella and the E end is where Forest Road 356 crosses it.

North Kelly: Follow the Little Isabella River to the slowly meandering Isabella River, which reaches Bald Eagle Lake. An access site on the Little Isabella is off Forest Road 386, E of State Highway 1.

Snake Creek: Take Forest Road 173 to paddle into the Snake River and Bald Eagle Lake. One portage from Bald Eagle Lake follows an old logging road and passes an abandoned logging camp. There are osprey and bald eagle nests around Gabbro and Bald Eagle lakes.

Here is a sampling of other canoeing opportunities:

Gunflint Ranger District

Twin Lake Loop, 4 *miles:* There are four short portages along the route, which includes West Twin, Tahus, Pine and East Twin lakes. The East-West Twin Lake boat launch is on Forest Road 152.

Kawishiwi Ranger District

Bass-High-Dry-Little Lakes Canoe Route, 3 *miles:* This is a primitive canoe route 7 miles N of Ely. Although not in the BWCAW, it's a good substitute. There are four portages on this route and developed campsites on Bass and High Lake. From Echo

Trail (County Road 116) head N on County Road 66 to reach parking and a portage sign to Bass Lake.

Birch Lake Canoe Route, 20 miles: This route features no portages and passes 16 developed campsites as well as two drive-in campgrounds on South Kawishiwi River and Birch Lake. The terrain varies from rocky ridges to rolling hills with rock outcroppings. Fishing is good for walleyes and northern pike. Begin at South Kawishiwi River Campground on State Highway 1 or Birch Lake Campground on Forest Road 429.

Fenske-Grassy-Low Circle Route, 20 miles: This loop is one of Superior's longest established canoe routes outside BWCAW. The complete loop has 10 portages but can be shortened by stopping at County Road 116 (Echo Trail). There are several access points to the loop from Ely, including Burntside Lake and Fenske Lake Campground.

Range Lake, 10 miles: A loop from Range Lake passes the site of an early 20th-century logging camp on Horse Lake. Fourtown and Mudro lakes are along the route. There is access from the Old Cloquet Road.

Stony River, 8 miles: This route combines rapids with slow-moving pools while passing through some rough but scenic country between Stony Lake and Birch Lake. Below the Birch Lake takeout it turns to white water - nicknamed the "Roaring Stony" - and is recommended for rafting rather than open canoes. Access is from State Highway 2 and Forest Road 424.

LaCroix Ranger District

Astrid Lake and Picket Creek, 22 miles: Small lakes and creeks, a number of portages, sandy beaches and beaver dams mark the route. The campgrounds at Lake Jeanette and Echo Lake serve as access points.

Little Indian Sioux River, 10 miles: The route lies in the BWCAW and includes a portage around the waterfall, Devil's Cascade. In addition to the river, you cross Upper Pauness and Lower Pauness lakes. You can access it where Echo Trail (County Road 116) crosses the river just E of Jeanette Lake Campground.

Superior National Forest includes the Boundary Waters Canoe Area Wilderness, one of the great canoe destinations in the country. The BWCAW consists of hundreds of lakes and a vast system of portages between them.

Vermilion River, 39 miles: The river, popular among voyageurs, flows from Lake Vermilion to Crane Lake, the southeast border of Voyageurs National Park. There are 12 portages as paddlers are not able to run all the rapids. Scenic Vermilion Falls is 25 feet high and Table Rock Falls is 20 feet high. There are seven access points off County Road 24 including Vermilion Dam at Lake Vermilion and at Buyck.

Laurentian Ranger District
Burntside Lake-Dead River-Twin Lakes Canoe Route, 11 miles: This ideal one-day paddle combines river and lake paddling and is highlighted by Burntside Lake which features more than 100 islands. There are two portages along the route and campsites on Twin Lakes and Burntside Lake. Access is from a public landing near the end of County Road 803, the portage to Everett Lake, which is adjacent to Echo Trail (County Road 116), or a public landing on North Arm Road (County Road 644).

St. Louis River, 12 miles: This stretch meanders through typical northern Minnesota terrain, with opportunities to see wildlife and wild rice beds along the way. There are some fast-moving rocky areas but five portages allow you to skip them during low water level. The river can be accessed at Norway Point Picnic Area off Forest Road 790, just S of Hoyt Lakes.

Tofte Ranger District
Baker Lake, 24 miles: The Temperance Lake Loop crosses the Laurentian Divide twice; several portages are steep and rocky. Features include an abandoned mine shaft, steep cliffs, 13 lakes and the Temperance River. Baker Lake is on Forest Road 165.

Brule Lake, 26 miles: The Brule Loop connects Homer, Whack, Vern, Pond and Juno lakes in the E end of the BWCAW. The connecting Winchell Loop includes paddling Brule, Lily, Mulligan, Grassy, Wanihigan, Winchell, Cliff, North Cone, Middle Cone and South Cone lakes. The route can be accessed from Homer Lake Forest Road 326.

Crescent Lake-Rice Lake Canoe Route, 5 miles: The route crosses bald eagle territory and white pine groves as it connects a

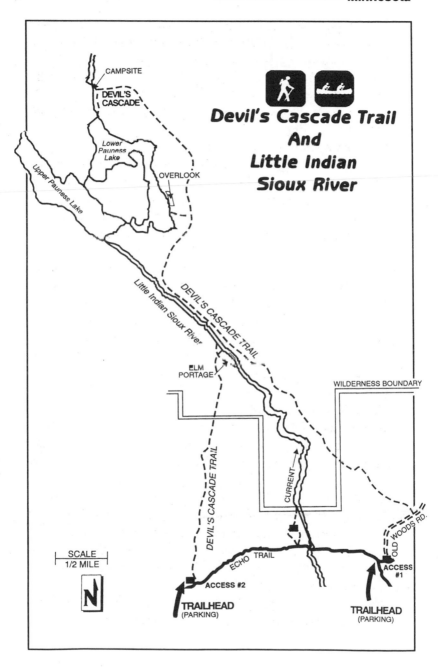

CAMPSITE

DEVIL'S
CASCADE

Lower
Pauness
Lake

OVERLOOK

Upper Pauness Lake

Devil's Cascade Trail
And
Little Indian
Sioux River

Little Indian Sioux River

DEVIL'S CASCADE TRAIL

ELM
PORTAGE

WILDERNESS BOUNDARY

DEVIL'S CASCADE TRAIL

CURRENT

OLD WOODS RD.

SCALE
1/2 MILE

N

ECHO TRAIL

ACCESS #2

ACCESS
#1

TRAILHEAD
(PARKING)

TRAILHEAD
(PARKING)

series of shallow lakes with short portages. There are two campsites on Crescent Lake and two on Rice Lake. The best access is at Crescent Lake Campground, N of Tofte.

Kawishiwi Lake, 21 miles: The Kawishiwi River and eight lakes compose the route. Native American pictographs are evident about midway on the N side of Fishdance Lake. Access is from Kawishiwi Lake Campground NE of Isabella.

Sawbill Lake

This lake is the starting and finishing point for several canoeing routes that extend into BWCAW. To reach Sawbill head to the N end of Sawbill Trail (County Road 2) from U.S. 61 near Tofte.

Here are the most popular:

Frost River Loop, 22 miles: The route includes 15 lakes, Ada Creek and Frost River. Frost River has a number of short portages and "liftover" sand bars, beaver dams and sunken logs.

Kelso Loop, 7 miles: It connects Sawbill, Alton, Kelso and Lujenida lakes with five level portages. Osprey and eagle are often seen here.

Lady Chain, 30 miles: Portages range from flat to hilly. It's nicknamed "Lady Chain" because several lakes were named for women, including Grace, Ella, Phoebe, Beth, Hazel and Polly.

Little Sage Loop, 45 miles: This rugged route goes through BWCAW, offering spectacular scenery and abundant wildlife in remote areas. Portages are required between most of the 15 lakes.

Louse River Loop, 36 miles: Beaver lodges are a frequent sight along the northern, less-traveled stretch. Along the way are 10 lakes and the Louse River.

Mesaba Loop, 25 miles: The well-used portages are level but become hilly and rocky in less-traveled areas. Most of the 14 lakes have scattered boulders and rock outcroppings along their shores; several hold abandoned beaver lodges.

Silver Island-Tee Lake-Windy Lake Canoe Route, 5 miles: Located outside of the BWCAW NE of Isabella, this route features excellent fishing with anglers casting for walleye and pike. There are two portages and campsites on all the lakes. Access is a portage from County Road 7 to Windy or Tee Lake.

Timber-Frear Loop, 9 miles: Seven level portages connect the lakes of this loop; Whitefish, Wigwam, Elbow, Timber, Frear and Lost lakes. The fishing is good and eagles are common in this area NE of Tofte. Whitefish Lake provides the best access and is reached from Forest Road 348.

 Fishing

Hundreds of lakes and thousands of miles of streams, often remote and pristine, create excellence and variety in fishing opportunities. Lake Superior lays claim to the densest and largest concentration of lake trout in the country as well as whitefish, coho, chinook, Atlantic and pink salmon. Other popular lake and stream species include walleye, northern pike, brown trout, brook trout, black crappie, largemouth and smallmouth bass, rock bass, perch, bluegill, muskellunge, splake and panfish. Ice fishing begins in late November or early December.

Information on Lake Superior charter fishing is available from the North Shore Charter Captains Association, Box 292, Duluth, MN 55801.

The Forest Service has built more than a dozen barrier-free fishing piers, many of them at campgrounds or picnic areas. Some piers, such as the one at Hogback Lake, do double duty as viewing stations for wildlife, including loon and osprey.

 Historical Attractions

Carlton Peak: An interpretive sign discusses Carlton Peak, one of the last remaining peaks of the ancient Sawtooth Mountains. It has resisted four major glacial periods and millions of years of erosion. It is a 2-mile round-trip hike from the Britton Peak trailhead on Sawhill Trail (County Road 2) near Tofte.

Fowl Lake Site: This site on a small wooded island on South Fowl Lake dates to the Copper Culture of 3000 to 1000 B.C. Artifacts from that prehistoric period have been excavated here. The site is listed on the National Register of Historic Places and located on the Minnesota\Ontario border N of Hovland.

Height of Land Portage: This was a major voyageur route between North and South lakes. It's on the Laurentian Divide, where streams to the N flow into Hudson Bay and streams to the

S flow into the Great Lakes. The faces of new voyageurs arriving at the portage were ritualistically slapped with a wet cedar bough; the men were required to promise never to kiss another voyageur's wife without the husband's permission. Located on Voyageurs Highway, the portage is another National Register of Historic Places site.

Longyear Drill Site: Here a steam-powered diamond-bit drill first searched for iron on the Mesabi Range. Although Edmund Longyear drilled almost 1,300 feet without success at this spot, his later explorations were successful. Access is by the short Physical Fitness Trail at Laurentian Divide Picnic Area off U.S. 53.

Wilderness Area

The name and reputation of Boundary Water Canoe Area Wilderness are enough to set many canoeists drooling in anticipation. The more than 1 million acres stretch nearly 150 miles along Canada's adjoining Quetico Provincial Park. Today's visitors, in the words of the Forest Service, can "canoe, portage and camp in the spirit of the French voyageurs of 200 years ago." Its official origin was the 1938 creation of the Superior Roadless Primitive Area. As the largest wilderness preserve E of the Rockies, it now attracts about 200,000 visitors a year or about a third of all visitors to Superior National Forest.

To protect its wilderness status, the Forest Service has adopted a number of restrictions and requirements for BWCAW users. Those rules are subject to change. Among the most important:

Permits: All overnight visitors between May 1 and Sept. 30 need a free wilderness travel permit; day-use and winter permits may also be required in the future. Permits are also required for most day users when motorized watercraft are used, where legally permitted. Reservations are recommended; however, district ranger offices and cooperating businesses such as local lodges and outfitters can issue walk-in overnight and day-use motor permits — if available — up to 24 hours before your desired entry.

Access: There are more than 80 designated entry points, some reachable only by boat or foot. Most are near Ely, Crane Lake, Tofte and Grand Marais, but there's also access from Tower and from the Arrowhead Trail, N of Hovland. Visitors must use their designated entry point on the permit date.

The 10 most heavily used entry points are: Moose Lake; Lake One; Sawbill Lake, Saganaga Lake; Fall Lake; Seagull Lake; Moose River/Portage River; Mudro Lake; Brule Lake; and Kawishiwi Lake. Quotas: To protect the physical resource and provide a quality wilderness experience, the Forest Service uses a Visitor Distribution Program. There are quotas for overnight use for each entry point. The 10 entry points whose quotas fill most often are: Mudro Lake; Seagull Lake; South Hegman Lake; Snowbank Lake; Bower Trout Lake; Little Gabbro Lake; Lizz Lake; Pine Lake; John Lake; and Snake River.

Camping: During the ice-free season, camping is allowed only at one of the 2,200 designated sites; there's an exception for certain remote, hard-to-reach areas within primitive management areas or along some trails, as specifically approved on the permit. Each site has a wilderness box latrine and steel fire grate. You cannot use the same campsite more than 14 consecutive days.

Travel: The BWCAW is generally off limits to mechanized travel, with or without motors, including bicycles. Motors are allowed on boats in about a dozen designated lakes; most of those lakes have 10 or 25-horsepower limits. There's even a minimum altitude requirement for aircraft flying over BWCAW.

Maps: There are few signs within its borders because of the wilderness designation; users should carry up-to-date maps.

Other Regulations: Party size and the number of watercraft per party are limited. Disposable, nonburnable metal or glass food and beverage containers are not allowed. Neither are metal detectors. BWCAW information is available at national forest headquarters and district ranger stations, but Forest Service offices cannot process reservations. Reservations are accepted each year

IN THE FOREST

Boundary Waters
Wilderness Thoughts

The vastness of the Boundary Waters Canoe Area Wilderness guarantees a vast array of experiences, emotions and reactions. Here's a sampling:

On winter ice:

There's a sense of incredible spaciousness. When it's cold, it's clear with expanses of snow on the lakes and blue sky. In early December, it sounds like whales as the ice thickens below you; you can almost call it alive because it continues to change.

Kim Marshall, Outward Bound instructor

On loon self-defense:

After cleaning out the tent, airing out the sleeping bags and packing up, we started across the lake toward the portage. We saw two adult loons in the bay to the right of the portage. As soon as we were within 100 yards, the loons began to act rather strangely. One of them would sort of dive bomb the other, skimming across the water and shrieking. Then the other loon would basically do the same thing. We thought it was rather bizarre behavior until we discovered a baby loon farther into the bay. The adults were just trying to get our attention away from the baby in case we were planning on hurting it. The adults kept on with the 'play acting' until they determined we were far enough away.

Lynn O'Kane, Voyageur North Canoe Outfitters

On portaging:

I carry the canoe up a forested ridge, brushing against ferns and brackens, stumbling over rocks in the premature twilight. At the other end of the portage, a tiny lake perches on a glacial shelf rimmed with birches. Water lilies, yellow with blossoms, float in its rippled shallows, their pads curling in the wind. I double back for the pack. A stream tumbles from the smaller lake into the bigger one, cutting inexorably away at the rock straining to contain it. Here, even the rock is on the move.

Paul Gruchow from "Travels in Canoe Country"
On wilderness:
This is a land set apart from the rest of the world, a special place reserved for people who are willing to explore it only by foot or in a canoe.

Robert Beymer from "Superior National Forest"
On spring fishing:
At this time of year the lake trout are very near the surface. Water temperatures shiver near 48 degrees, a temperature loved by lakers, and these deep denizens swim up to a surface world often denied them by heat. We eased two orange and gold minnow-imitating plugs out behind the canoe as we paddled down the shore. They throbbed 10 feet below the surface. Ecstasy, I thought. That's what this first fishing trip is. It is water gurgling down the side of your boat, the promise of warmth in the sun on your neck, the possibility you may actually catch a fish.... In camp, trout fillets curled crisply in a frying pan teased by yellow flames.

Michael Furtman, editor of Superior Experience
On the future:
Today, our generation is threatening to leave our mark on the canoe country. Regrettably, the signs we leave may tell a different story than the original pictographs. A story of `progress.' Of profit. And of a short-sightedness that promises future generations a very different canoe country than we've enjoyed for hundreds of years. Acid rain, an invidious by-product of our industrialized society, silently causes contamination of the fish. Developers on the edge of the BWCAW threaten to form a noose around the previous few acres of wilderness that are left. And, ironically, in our love of the BWCAW, we are recklessly creating the problem of overcrowding which destroys the very tranquility we seek.

Friends of the Boundary Waters Wilderness

by mail starting Jan. 15 or by phone starting Feb. 1. There's also a non-refundable reservation fee. Contact BWCAW Reservation Center, Box 450, Cumberland, MD 21501-0450; ☎ (800) 745-3399. Other important numbers: U.S. Customs, ☎ (218) 720-5201; U.S. Immigration, ☎ (218) 720-5207; Canadian Customs, ☎ (807) 274-3751; Canadian Immigration, ☎ (807) 274-3815; Quetico Provincial Park, Atikokan, Ont. POT 1CO, ☎ (807) 597-2735.

 # Natural Areas

Keeley Creek Natural Area, *1,280 acres:* Because this area in the Kawishiwi Ranger District has avoided fire for more than a century, it represents a major undisturbed landscape with black spruce forests, mature jackpine forests, bogs, rock outcroppings and open sedge meadows. There are ferns, mosses and lichens as well as a lake and two streams. It's on the National Natural Landmark roster.

Lac LaCroix Research National Area, *973 acres:* Located in the LaCroix Ranger District within the BWCAW, this National Natural Landmark is most accessible by water. It includes old-growth virgin forests of red pine, white pine and jackpine and has high granite cliffs.

Marble Lake Research Natural Area, *120 acres:* It hosts a variety of plants associated with northern hardwoods in the Tofte Ranger District.

Schroeder Research Natural Area, *360 acres:* The core of this natural area in the Laurentian Ranger District is covered with virgin northern hardwoods. The Lake Superior Trail passes through it.

 # More Things To See & Do

Berry picking: Blueberries, raspberries, strawberries, wild roses and pincherries are the most plentiful and grow in various locations within Superior. Good picking spots include gravel pits, long sloped sides of recently constructed roads, ditches along abandoned roads, burned-over areas and island lakes. Meander Lake and the Fire & Ice overlook are recommended blueberry spots; both are in the LaCroix Ranger District. Highbush and wild cranberries are also found in Superior, generally in sphagnum bogs, wet acidic soil, along streams and in low, cool, open woods or thickets. Choke cherries prefer well-drained soil in clearings, along open shores and roadsides, and in young woods. Thimbleberries grow in moist, partly sunny sites and rocky woods, especially near Lake Superior. However, Superior's red elderberries are poisonous.

Birding: About 200 species of birds have been identified in Superior, including bald eagles and ospreys, great blue herons and bittern, common snipes and terns. The Bonaparte's gull, rusty blackbird and Virginia rail are among the less common birds found here. The only known Wilson's warbler nesting spot in Minnesota was located within the national forest.

Devil Track Wildflower Sanctuary: A brochure and interpretive plaques along a short loop trail help visitors identify an assortment of wildflowers in the sanctuary, which is maintained by the Grand Marais Garden Club. It's on Gunflint Trail (County Road 12) 6 miles N of Grand Marais.

Dog sledding: Mushers generally take their dog teams on unplowed Forest Service roads, mountain bike trails and some snowmobile routes. Cross-country ski trails may also be suitable, but some are off-limits to mushing. There are about 30 miles of dog-sled routes near Trout Lake, while other recommended routes include Snow Beaver Snowmobile Trail, Thomas Lake Trail, Knife-Kekakebic Lakes Area and North Shore State Trail. Some outfitters offer dog-sled tour packages combining winter camping with driving the teams. Call the Minnesota Office of Tourism for a complete list of outfitters at ☎ (800) 657-3638 .

Fitness Trails: The Laurentian Divide Picnic Area off U.S. 53 in the Laurentian Ranger District includes the Lookout Mountain Physical Fitness Trail, a half-mile jogging path with 14 exercise stations. Longyear Physical Fitness Trail on County Road 110 is a quarter-mile long and leads to the site of the Mesaba Iron Range's first diamond drilling rig. Signs describe and illustrate the exercises.

International Wolf Center: The center is dedicated to research about and protection of wolves. Some activities, such as field trips and research, take place in Superior National Forest, home to an estimated 300-400 timber wolves. There's also a BWCAW permit station in the center. Contact the International Wolf Center, 1396 Hwy. 169, Ely, MN 55731; ☎ (800) ELY-WOLF.

John Beargrease Sled Dog Marathon: Mushers and viewers from around the world attend this rugged 500-mile race round-trip between Duluth and Grand Portage each January. It's named for John Beargrease, the son of a Chippewa chief whose mail route was the major communications source among lakeshore communities from 1887 to 1900. The event is actually a series of races of various lengths that all begin in Duluth's Ordean Stadium with 5,000 or more fans cheering on the mushers. Contact John Beargrease Marathon, Box 500, Duluth, MN 55801; ☎ (218) 722-7631.

Mountain biking: Bicycles are prohibited in BWCAW but there are plenty of alternatives on Superior's other trails and old logging roads. Hidden Valley Recreation Area in the Kawishiwi Ranger District has a hilly and wooded 12-mile network of loops for biking and skiing. King's Road, W of Gunflint and Loon lakes, is a 2-mile former logging road with steep grades and rolling hills that crosses prime moose country. Lima Mountain, NW of Grand Marais, offers 20 miles of gravel roads, connecting several lakes and crossing the Brule River.

There are networks of old forest roads suitable for biking in the McDougal Lake, SE of Ely; Nickel Lake, SE of Ely: and Fenske Lake areas, also N of Ely. Other suitable areas include Taconite Trail from Ely to Grand Rapids, 165 miles; Big Aspen Ski Area N of Virginia, 20 miles; Crane Lake Loops near the village of Crane Lake, 19 miles; Kawishiwi River Loop, SE of Ely, 26 miles; Forest Route 172 starting in Isabella, 14 miles; and Pine Lake Loop, W of

Grand Marais, 13 miles.

Naturalist programs: Naturalists trained or tutored by the Forest Service lead educational programs such as talks, escorted hikes and films. Programs are usually conducted at campgrounds, local resorts or other nearby facilities.

North Shore Discovery Tour: This auto route features natural and human historic sites. Each of the two loops is about 60 miles long and accessible from U.S. 61, the North Shore Drive National Scenic Byway, which runs from Schroeder to the national forest border SW of Grand Portage.

The Isabella Loop passes the remnants of a 1920 logging railroad trestle, the site of the once-bustling logging community of Sawbill Landing, and fields and foundations from the Wanless Farm that was abandoned more than a half-century ago. Another feature is the Laurentian Divide separating waters that flow N toward the Arctic and S toward the Atlantic. Hogback and Dumbbell lakes are along this loop.

The Tofte Loop with its winding, hilly glacial eskers passes melodramatically past a landmark named Heartbreak Hill, as well as the site of Pink Bridge, a segregated camp for African Americans in the Civilian Conservation Corps. The loop provides access to the North Shore Corridor Trail, Honeymoon Trail, Superior Hiking Trail, Moose Fence Ski Trail and Sugar Bush Ski Trail, among others.

The North Shore Drive National Scenic Byway, 58 miles: This route follows U.S. 61 along the Lake Superior shore from NE of Grand Marais to Shroeder. On one side is the lake; on the other, rocky inland hills of the Sawtooth Mountain range and Superior Hiking Trail. The road is Minnesota's busiest two-lane highway, but there are many places to pullover. Along the way are the trailhead and interpretative marker for 1,600-foot-high Carlton Peak, as well as vistas visible from Moose Mountain, Black Point and Red Cliff. Two lakeshore state parks are on the byway.

Magnificent as the view along the byway is, bicyclists should know that the road surface is rough. Writing in the New York

Times, Bruce Weber called it "the most disagreeable pavement I've encountered in nearly 3,000 miles of riding. For me, the choice was a dangerous one: Ride the actual roadway, bumpy in itself, or hope that bike and body could endure the harsh rattling of riding the cracked shoulder."

Passport in Time Program: Volunteers and archaeologists have tested the Misiano site, with its rich deposits of artifacts such as copper tools, stone arrow and spear points, pottery, animal bones and fire hearths. A Paleo-Indian encampment believed to date back 3,000 to 11,000 years ago was here. Artifacts and soil analysis indicate that dugout canoes may have been built between 8000 and 4000 B.C. The site is at McDougal Lake Campground in the Tofte Ranger District.

Picnicking and swimming: Picnic facilities and beaches are available at a number of campgrounds and other sites. There are picnic areas in the Laurentian Ranger District at Salo Lake, Laurentian Divide, Bassett Lake and White Pine; in the LaCroix Ranger District at Meander Lake and Norwegian Bay; and in the Tofte Ranger District at Hogback Lake, among others. Swimming and picnicking are allowed in the Laurentian Ranger District at Whiteface Reservoir and Lake Leander; and in the Tofte Ranger District at Flathorn Lake.

Pictographs: Nobody knows exactly why prehistoric people of the Canadian Shield painted pictures on rocks; theories include depiction of events, magic, religion and incantations to spark successful hunting. Some rock paintings, or pictographs, are visible on the E shore of King Williams Narrows, the N shore of Oyster Lake, the N shore of Fishdance Lake, the E shore of Lac LaCroix just N of Beatty Portage, the N shore of Island River, the cliffs between North Hegman and Trease lakes, and the W shore of Crooked Lake just above Curtain Falls. Others may be still undiscovered within the vastness of Superior. More than 1,200 historic and buried prehistoric sites have been inventoried.

Sightseeing: Here are some sightseeing spots:
Grand Marais Scenic Overlook: The city, its harbor and light-

The North Shore Drive National Scenic Byway takes motorists along the Lake Superior shoreline.

house piers are visible from this point, as is the Sawtooth Mountain skyline. On clear days, the far-from-scenic sight of smoke from a taconite plant 60 miles away in Silver Bay is visible. The overlook is off Gunflint Road (County Road 12).

Gunflint Lake Overlook: The view includes Gunflint Lake and Canada. The overlook in the Gunflint Ranger District is also a trailhead for a hiking and skiing trail and is reached from the Gunflint Trail (County Road 12).

Hovland Lookout: The area is among the most colorful in Superior, and many types of wildlife are seen here. It's on Hovland Tower Road in the Gunflint Ranger District.

Jackpine Mountain: There's a scenic drive to the top of this

1,655-foot bald knob, where a cement base is all that remains of a fire lookout tower. It also features the old site of a wolf den, a turkey vulture nest and scenic forest vistas. The mountain is accessed from Tomahawk Road (County Road 173) in the Kawishiwi Ranger District.

Jackpot Forest Fire Site: This 1,200-acre area has quickly regenerated since it was replanted in 1981, a year after the Jackpot Fire. This site is along County Road 2 in the Kawishiwi Ranger District.

Laurentian Divide Overlook: The overlook on the Gunflint Trail has views of Birch Lake and separates the Hudson Bay and Lake Superior watersheds. It's in the Gunflint Ranger District.

Pine Lake: This area, on Forest Road 332 in the Gunflint Ranger District, is popular for fall color touring with its large stands of maple, birch, aspen and spruce.

Spirit of the Land Hostel: An American Youth Hostel, this facility is on an island in Seagull Lake within the BWCAW. It's accessible only by boat and features environmental study groups and naturalist programs. Contact Spirit of the Land Hostel, 940 Gunflint Trail, Grand Marais MN 55604; ☎ (218) 388-2241.

Vermilion Community College: An award-winning environmental studies program offers wilderness seminars and field trips within Superior. Programs and activities include snowshoeing, cross-country skiing, dog sledding, research demonstrations and presentations on wolf, moose, deer and bear ecology, forest ecology, astronomy and other scientific topics. Contact Vermilion Community College, 1900 E. Camp St., Ely, MN 55731; ☎ (800) 657-3609 or (218) 365-7200.

Watchable wildlife: Wildlife viewing spots include forest openings and beaver ponds. Recommended areas include the Pelican and Vermilion rivers, Echo Trail, Moose Loop and Echo Lake. Dawn and dusk are the best observation times.

Wilderness Outings: Superior in general and the BWCAW in particular are popular locations for Outward Bound summer and winter expeditions for youths and adults. They feature canoeing, kayaking, backpacking, cross-country skiing, dog sledding and rock climbing. Contact Voyageur Outward Bound, 111 Third Ave. South, Suite 120, Minneapolis, MN 55401; ☎ (612) 338-0565 or (800) 328-2943. The Sierra Club also offers wilderness outings in the BWCAW. Contact Sierra Club, Outing Department, 730 Polk St., San Francisco, CA 94109; ☎ (415) 776-2211.

More than a dozen commercial outfitters offer guided canoeing, fishing, camping and dog-sledding trips. There are packages available that combine wilderness exploration with overnight stays at lodges. For more information, contact the travel bureaus in the gateway communities at the end of this chapter or call the Minnesota Office of Tourism at ☎ (800) 657-3638.

Wild rice gathering: Wild rice is actually the seed of an annual cereal grass that grows primarily in slow-moving streams and shallow lakes or bays. It's harvested in the fall by canoe. Only Minnesota residents can gather wild rice in Superior; a state permit is required.

Ranger Districts

Gunflint: P.O. Box 790, Grand Marais, MN 55604; ☎ (218) 387-1750.

Kawishiwi: 118 S. 4th Ave. East, Ely, MN 55731; ☎ (218) 365-7600.

LaCroix: P.O. Box 1085, Cook, MN 55723; ☎ (218) 666-5251.

Laurentian: 318 Forestry Rd., Aurora, MN 5570; ☎ (218) 229-3371.

Tofte: P.O. Box 2157, Tofte, MN 55615; ☎ (218) 663-7981.

Gateways

Cook: Cook Chamber of Commerce, P.O. Box 59, Cook, MN 55723; ☎ (218) 387-2524 or (800) 648-5897.

Crane Lake: Crane Lake Visitor & Tourism Bureau, 7238 Handberg Rd.; Crane Lake, MN 55725; ☎ (218) 993-2901 or (800) 362-7405.

Duluth: Duluth Convention & Visitors Bureau, 100 Lake Place Dr., Duluth, MN 55802; ☎ (218) 722-4011 or (800) 438-5884.

Ely: Ely Chamber of Commerce, 1660 E. Sheridan St., Ely, MN 55731; ☎ (218) 365-6123.

Grand Marais: Tip of the Arrowhead Assn., P.O. Box 1048, Grand Marais, MN 55604; ☎ (218) 387-2524 or (800) 622-4014.

Tofte: Lutsen-Tofte Tourism Assn., Box 2258, Tofte, MN 55615; ☎ (218) 663-7804.

Tower: Tower-Soudan Chamber of Commerce, Box 776, Tower, MN 55790; ☎ (218) 753-2301.

CHIPPEWA

Route 3, Box 244
Cass Lake, MN 56633
☎ (218) 335-8600

663,000 acres

Located near - and divided by - the headwaters of the Mississippi River, Chippewa National Forest encompasses more than 700 lakes. The largest of them are Leech Lake and Lake Winnibigoshish, nicknamed Winnie. There's even a lake on an island within a lake - Lake Windigo on Star Island in the middle of Cass Lake. There are an additional 920 miles of rivers and streams and 150,000 acres of wetlands in this terrain shaped by the last Ice Age glaciation 10,000 years ago.

Beaver dams here stretch as long as 2,000 feet. There are extensive trails, a variety of canoe routes and prime nesting territory for bald eagles.

In his book Wild Woodlands, Bill Thomas describes a grove of towering virgin pines in Chippewa's Lost Forty this way:

The understory was almost nonexistent. This, I decided, was cathedral country. Not all of the North Woods is cathedral country, or ever was. Even when the French voyageurs traveled well-worn trails through the woods and lakes country of western Ontario and Minnesota, much of the forest was stunted. Seldom, if ever, do we find trees, even the 400-year-old ones, rising to more than 100 feet. Foresters of the Pacific Northwest or of the awesome redwoods and sequoias of California would not be impressed. But for middle North America, these are behemoths.

This region was home to the Cree, Winnebego, Dakota (Sioux) and Anishinabe (Chippewa or Ojibway). Europeans came to map and locate the source of the Mississippi River, and then to seek furs, to log the northern woods and to settle.

Chippewa was called Minnesota National Forest in 1884 when it became the first national forest east of the Mississippi. In 1928, it was renamed for the Chippewa, or Anishinabe, tribe. The national forest shares a boundary with Leech Lake Indian Reservation.

 Camping

Chippewa has more than two dozen developed campgrounds. The improved campgrounds, number of sites and locations are:

Blackduck Ranger District

Noma Lake (14), 2 miles NW of Wirt on County Road 31;

Webster Lake (22), 7 miles S of Blackduck on Forest Road 2236.

Cass Lake Ranger District

Cass Lake (21), 4 miles E of Cass Lake on Forest Road 2171;

Chippewa (46), 4 miles E of Cass Lake on Forest Road 2171;

Knutson Dam (14), 6 miles E of Cass Lake on Forest Road 2171;

Norway Beach (55), 4 miles E of Cass Lake on Forest Road 2171;

South Pike Bay (21), 3 miles SE of Cass Lake on Forest Road 2137;

Wanaki (46), 4 miles E of Cass Lake on Forest Road 2171;

Winnie (42), 18 miles NE of Cass Lake on Forest Road 2168.

Deer River Ranger District

Deer Lake (48), 24 miles NW of Deer River on Forest Road 3153;

East Seelye Bay (13), 20 miles N of Deer River on Forest

Road 2198;

Mosomo Point *(23),* 19 miles N of Deer River on Forest Road 2190;

O-Ne-Gum-E *(46),* 18 miles NW of Deer River on State Highway 46;

Six Mile Lake *(11),* 16 miles W of Deer River on Forest Road 2127;

Tamarack Point *(35),* 13 miles N of Deer River on Forest Road 2163;

West Seelye Bay *(22),* 20 miles N of Deer River on Forest Road 2198;

Williams Narrows *(17),* 17 miles NW of Deer River on Forest Road 2157.

Marcell Ranger District

Clubhouse Lake *(48),* 6 miles NE of Marcell on Forest Road 3758;

North Star *(21),* 4 miles S of Marcell on State Highway 38.

Walker Ranger District:

Stony Point *(45),* 14 miles NE of Walker on County Road 13;

Mabel Lake *(22),* 26 miles E of Walker on State Highway 200.

More than 400 primitive sites are dispersed along trails and canoe routes. Star Island Campground is a primitive campground on the largest island in Cass Lake, within the Cass Lake Ranger District. Nushka on Cass Lake in Cass Lake Ranger District has group camping only.

 Trails

Hundreds of miles of trails are marked for hiking, cross-country skiing, mountain biking, snowmobiling, horseback riding and other activities. Interpretive trails are found at Cass Lake, Chippewa, Norway Beach and Wanaki campgrounds; hiking trails pass by a number of other campgrounds including Webster Lake, Deer Lake, East Seelye Bay, Mosomo Point, O-Ne-Gum-E and West Seelye Bay.

Snowmobile trails connect with 200 miles of snowmobile routes outside the national forest; some cut across multi-agency public or private lands. The longest snowmobile trails include Cut Foot Sioux, 33 miles; Heartland, 50 miles; Snoway One, 58 miles; Soo Line, 58 miles; Bowstring, 42 miles; Northland, 40 miles; Paul Bunyan, 33 miles; and Eagle Country, 24 miles.

Two long trails that traverse the national forest and intersect are the North Country National Scenic Trail and Heartland Trail.

Heartland Trail, 50 miles: This multiple-use state trail follows a railroad bed built in 1897 by the Park Rapids & Leech Lake Railway Co.; the train route was operated by the Great Northern Railway and then the Burlington Northern until the 1970s, when it was abandoned. The western edge of Chippewa's portion is midway between Akeley and Walker, and has an asphalt surface for bicycling. The Heartland Trail leaves the national forest N of Kabekona Bay.

North Country National Scenic Trail, 68 miles: It passes through Chippewa National Forest along a corridor that runs from 3 miles S of Walker to 7 miles SE of Remer.

Here are some other popular trails:

Blackduck Ranger District

Camp Rabideau Interpretive Trail, 1 mile: Markers explain the history of the last remaining Civilian Conservation Corps camp in the country. It passes Depression-era buildings, an old survey marker, a 1940 spruce plantation and Carls Lake. The trail is S of Blackduck on Highway 39, with the trailhead at Benjamin Lake.

Lost Forty Trail, 1 mile: This short interpretive loop goes through a grove of 100-foot red and white pines, 300-to-400 years old. It's named for an 1880s surveying mistake, which saved the grove near Coddington Lake from logging. It passes virgin trees, conifer seedlings, fire-scarred trunks, Moose Brook, wetlands and snags - dead trees that serve as homes for cavity-dwellers such as tree frogs and flying squirrels. You can reach the trail, which is NW of Wirt, from Forest Road 2240.

Meadow Lake, 10 miles: Hikers and skiers enjoy this trail,

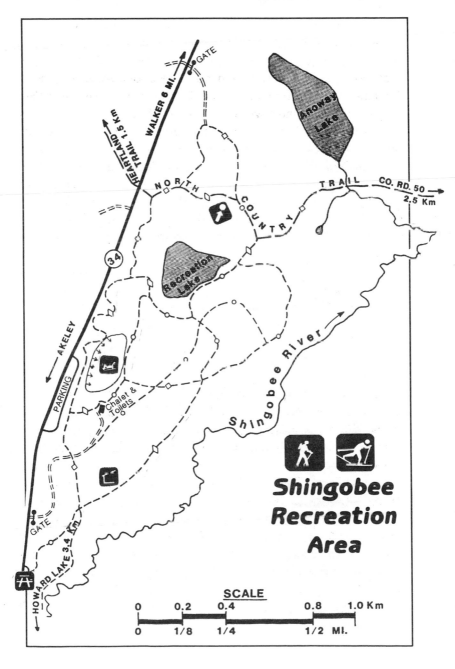

Snowway Lake

HEARTLAND TRAIL 1.5 Km

WALKER 6 MI.

GATE

NORTH COUNTRY TRAIL

CO. RD. 50
2.5 Km

34

AKELEY

PARKING

Recreation Lake

Chalet &
Toilets

Shingobee River

GATE

HOWARD LAKE 3.4 Km

Shingobee Recreation Area

SCALE

| 0 | 0.2 | 0.4 | | 0.8 | 1.0 Km |

| 0 | 1/8 | 1/4 | | 1/2 | MI. |

which passes both Meadow Lake and Turtle River. The trailhead is S of Tenstrike on Forest Road 2419.

Webster Lake Trail, *8 miles:* A walking and skiing trail near Anderson Lake, it passes an old beaver paddleway, a white spruce plantation planted in 1974, a beaver lodge and a bog walk. The trail is S of Blackduck at Webster Lake Campground.

Cass Lake Ranger District

Norway Beach Nature Trail, *2 miles:* This is a self-guided interpretive trail through stands of virgin red and white pines. The trailhead begins at the Norway Beach Visitor Center, E of Cass Lake at Norway Beach Campground.

Star Island Trail System, *6 miles:* This is a network of inter-connecting trails on Star Island, the largest island in Cass Lake. Parts of the system trace the shore of Lake Windigo, the island's interior lake. A number of marshes are along the way as the trail winds along deep woods and high banks. The trail is E of Cass Lake; the only access is by water or, in winter, over the ice.

Deer River Ranger District

Cut Foot Sioux Trail, *18 miles:* Running along the Continental Divide, this well-used trail takes mountain bikers and hikers through the scenic Farley Hills area. It runs N of Little Cut Foot Sioux and Cut Foot Sioux lakes.

Simpson Creek Trail, *13 miles:* The trail leads to viewing areas for bald eagle, loon and osprey. The terrain, logged in the early 20th century, is rolling; the trail goes along glacial eskers, through cedar swamps, and overlooks Cut Foot Sioux Lake. The trailhead is off State Highway 46, NW of Deer River.

Marcell Ranger District

East Lake Pine Trail, *1 mile:* This nature trail includes 200-year-old Norway pine, kettle topography caused by melting glacial ice, a variety of bird species and a hilltop vista overlooking East Lake. The trailhead is NE of Marcell on County Route 45.

Miller Trail, *8 miles:* This hiking and skiing trail leads to Miller Lake Geologic Area, where a lake sank in 1982 and again in 1993 when its outlet failed. There are other lakes along the route: Orange, Little Horn, Big Horn, Amen, Lucky, Hill and Little Bear. Reach it from State Highway 38, S of Marcell.

Walker Ranger District

*Lake Erin Trail, 1 mile:*This trail provides good opportunities for families to view lake and wetlands wildlife. There is access from Highway 371, S of Walker.

Shingobee Trail, 6 miles: This trail system cuts through the scenic hills of the Shingobee River Valley and provides access to the river and Recreation Lake. It's a popular and demanding cross-country ski area. Access is from County Road 34, S of Walker.

 ## Mountain Biking

There are 18 designated mountain bike routes in the national forest. They range from 4 to 35 miles in length and from easy to tough in difficulty level. Some routes have primitive or developed campsites, lakes, scenic views, picnic areas and wildlife viewing areas along the way. Among them are *Trout Lake Trail* (10 miles), SE of Marcell, which leads to the historic Joyce Estate, and *Webster Loop* (16 miles), SE of Blackduck, which leads to the self-guided Webster Lake Bog Interpretive Trail.

Popular bike routes include:

Wirt/Talmoon Biking Loop, 35 miles: Cross the Bigfork River several times on Chippewa's longest mountain bike route. The terrain is moderately difficult. The trailhead is at the Bigfork River boat access site at the intersection of County Road 14 and State Highway 6. There are rest areas in Talmoon, Spring Lake and Wirt.

Little Ruby Biking Loop, 10 miles: If you ride Little Ruby in the fall, you'll see brilliant foliage colors along the route, which passes several lakes including Trout, Cutaway, Burrows and Ruby. It follows Forest Roads 2143, 3855, 3850, 3756, 3510 and 3755, NE of Marcell.

Lost Forty Biking Loop, 27 miles: This moderately difficult route passes the old growth pines at Lost Forty. It runs along Forest Roads 2227, 2229, 2240 and County Roads 26 and 31.

The others are: *Rabideau Loop* (8 miles), S of Blackduck;

Kenogama Loop (13 miles), NE of Cass Lake; *Norway Beach Loops* (26 miles), E of Cass Lake; *Pike Bay/Lake Thirteen* (4-10 miles), E of Cass Lake; *Pigeon Lakes Loop* (22 miles), NW of Deer River; *Simpson Creek* (13 miles), NW of Deer River; *Clubhouse Loop* (5 miles), NE of Marcell; *Suomi Hills* (21 miles), NW of Grand Rapids; *Gadbolt Lake* (8 miles), SE of Walker; *Hanson Lake* (15 miles), SE of Walker; and *Stony Point* (9 miles), NE of Walker.

Boating & Canoeing

Hundreds of lakes provide immense opportunities for boating, with or without motors. Some have improved launches and ramps; others require boats to be carried in.

Many river routes through Chippewa were used by Native Americans who lived or camped along these rivers and lakes: first the Dakota (Sioux) and then the Chippewa (Anishinabe) who came into the area in the mid-1700s. Explorers followed some of these rivers searching for a Northwest Passage between the Mississippi and Hudson Bay. Fur traders, voyageurs, missionaries and government Indian agents used them for transportation; loggers later floated timber on them to reach mills downriver. Many canoeists enjoy the Mississippi River meadows between Lake Winnibigoshish and Cass Lake; a 55-mile canoe route on the Mississippi gives little hint of the river's eventual size to the S. The Mississippi and Cass Lake meet at Knutson Dam in the Cass Lake Ranger District. The 120-mile Chippewa Headwaters Loop is rated the most difficult in the national forest.

Here are other popular canoeing routes:

Blackduck Ranger District

Big Fork River: The first portion of this 165-mile route is within Chippewa. It starts at Dora Lake and passes wild rice beds, marshes and easy rapids.

Cass Lake Ranger District

Pike Bay Connection, *8 miles*: A traditional Native American route links Leech Lake and Pike Bay. In between are 10 Section, Moss, Twin, Little Twin, Little Moss and Portage lakes and Lake 13,

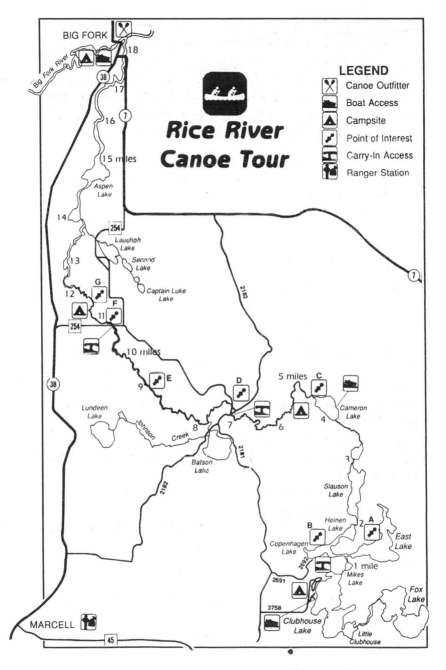

BIG FORK

Big Fork River

18

38

17

7

16

15 miles

Aspen Lake

14

254

Laughoh Lake

Second Lake

13

G

12

Captain Luke Lake

F

254

11

10 miles

38

9

E

Lundeen Lake

Johnson Creek

8

7

Batson Lake

2182

2181

Slauson Lake

5 miles

C

D

Cameron Lake

6

4

3

Heinen Lake

2

A

B

Copenhagen Lake

East Lake

2692

1 mile

Mikes Lake

2691

Fox Lake

3758

Clubhouse Lake

Little Clubhouse

MARCELL

45

Rice River Canoe Tour

LEGEND

Canoe Outfitter

Boat Access

Campsite

Point of Interest

Carry-In Access

Ranger Station

75

plus six portages.

Turtle River, 16 miles: The route begins at Lake Julia, enters Chippewa after leaving Turtle River Lake and flows through Big Rice and Kitchi lakes. It ends at Cass Lake on the Mississippi. Points of interest include the sites of a splash dam, a sawmill and a ford used by early settlers to cross the Turtle. Wild rice beds are also visible.

For side trips, try the North Branch of the Turtle River, 14 miles; Big Fork River, 165 miles; and Shingobee River, 2 miles.

Marcell Ranger District

Rice River, 18 miles: It heads N from Fox Lake through several other lakes to the junction of the Rice and Big Fork rivers. There are no portages. It passes an original growth grove called East Lake pines and the remains of Cameron Lake Sluice Dam. Log drives along the Rice River ended by 1925.

Walker Ranger District

Boy River, 23 miles: This historic route, also known as Inguadona Canoe Tour, follows the lower part of the Boy River drainage. It begins at Ten Mile Lake, enters Chippewa at Inguadona, flows through Boy Lake and ends at Boy Bay on Leech Lake. There are no portages and only one set of rapids. You can see signs of logging, such as the remains of an old splash dam below Boy River and stranded logs - called "dead heads" - that were lost during spring drives. Towards the N, the river bed widens into expanses of wild rice and meadow.

 Fishing

So far, 54 species of fish have been identified in Chippewa, where the Shingobee and Necktie rivers are state-designated trout streams. Northern pike, walleye, bass, bluegill, trout, muskie, crappie and panfish are among the most popular among anglers. Fisheries habitat improvement projects are underway. Check for special events at Chippewa during National Fishing Week in the spring.

Large lakes such as Leech, Winnibigoshish and Cass are major fishing destinations with plenty of challenges and trophy-size fish.

But smaller lakes are popular too. First River Lake is known for its spring walleye. Other smaller ones include Clear Lake for walleye and panfish; Noma Lake for bass, northern pike and panfish; Day Lake for muskie, bass and panfish; Six Mile Lake for walleye; Cut Foot Sioux and Little Cut Foot Sioux lakes for northern pike and walleye; Greeley Lake for rainbow trout; and Kitchi Lake for walleye, northern pike, muskie, black bass and panfish.

The 11 lakes in the Trout Lake Semi-primitive Non-motorized Area offer walk-in fishing opportunities for trout, northern pike, bass, splake and panfish.

Natural Areas

Battle Point Research Natural Area, 329 acres: On Lake Winnibigoshish in the Cass Lake Ranger District, this is an old growth, hardwood forest community at the northern edge of its range.

Gilfillan Natural Area, 114 acres: Located in Blackduck Ranger District, Gilfillan is one of several spots known for unusual plant life; it has abundant orchids in a white spruce seed production area. Others in the Blackduck Ranger District are *Webster Lake Bog* (18 acres) with its rare abundance of linear-leaved sundew plants; *Pennington Bog* (15 acres) which is known for its orchids and requires a state permit to visit; and *Elmwood Island* (43 acres) in Island Lake, which features a tract of virgin upland cedar. In the Marcell Ranger District, is *East Lake* (65 acres) with its mature red pines.

Pine Point Research Natural Area, 1,339 acres: Towering red and white pines 350 years old dominate this old growth tract. Most of the area is mature red pine, with stands of jack and white pine and nests for bald eagles and osprey. It's a National Natural Landmark because of its unique mix of vegetation, wildlife, and historic and archaeological features. The natural area is in the Walker Ranger District.

Stony Point Research Natural Area, 480 acres: This is an

Among the wildflowers most visitors want to see in Minnesota national forests are lady's slipper orchids. The showy lady's slipper is the state flower.

old growth hardwood forest in the Blackduck Ranger District along Lake Winnibigoshish.

Suomi Hills, 6,000 acres: Named for a small Finnish community north of Grave Lake, this area is restricted to semiprimitive, non-motorized foot travel. It has 21 miles of trails through rolling terrain, with a variety of lakes and an abundance of loons and beaver. In an unusual incident, Miller Lake catastrophically disappeared - sank - in April 1982 when its outlet failed, creating a 40-foot gully. A similar occurrence happened in 1993, enlarging the gully. It's designated as Miller Lake Geologic Area and is 11 miles SE of Marcell off State Highway 38.

Trout Lake Semi-primitive Non-motorized Area, 4,500 acres: There are primitive campsites and 26 miles of shoreline on 11 lakes, including pristine Trout Lake. This area of rolling hills was logged in the early 1900s and later became the site of Nopeming - the Joyce Estate - a private resort with a lodge, cabins and teahouse, now on the National Register of Historic Places. Trout Lake is N of Marcell and is reached via State Highway 38.

 ## Historic Attractions

Rabideau CCC Camp Site: Rabideau is the last of Minnesota's 25 Depression-era CCC camps still standing. Company 3749 began construction in 1936. The next year, Company 708 arrived, staying until 1941. CCC volunteers built a nearby ranger station and fire towers, conducted deer censuses and rescued lost hunters and berry pickers. Fifteen buildings remain, including the officers quarters, several barracks and classrooms, the hospital and administrative building. Gone, however, are the mess hall, Army headquarters, one barrack, latrine, garage and tool shed. A mile-long interpretive trail highlights the buildings and local history. The camp is on the National Register of Historic Places. It's in the Blackduck Ranger District, N of Penningon along Scenic Highway (County Road 39).

Old Cut Foot Sioux Ranger Station: The building is believed to be among the oldest ranger stations in the United States. It was constructed in 1904 and is on the National Register of Historic Places. This one-room structure was built on a traditional campsite at the end of an old portage. In the 1930s, it was converted into a museum of fur trade, Indian and logging artifacts. Artifacts found here range from 2,000-year-old clay pottery fragments and rock waste chips used in stone toolmaking to a ceramic insulator, tiny glass button and 1934 sewing pattern catalogue. The building has been renovated as an interpretive site NW of Deer River in the Deer River Ranger District.

Turtle Mound: To the Dakota, who built the mound with its sunken intaglio effigy, and the Chippewa, who later used it, this is a holy place, a setting to consult with the turtle oracle. Under an agreement with the Leech Lake Tribal Council, the Forest Service no longer interprets the site for visitors, but it's listed on the National Register of Historic Places. The mound is located in the Deer River Ranger District but visitors are discouraged.

Chippewa National Forest Headquarters: Built in 1935-1936 of notched and grooved native red pine logs from the Star Island and Lake 13 areas, this building was constructed in Finnish style by Finnish artisans and laborers from the CCC and Work Projects Administration. There's a 50-foot-high fireplace of split native glacial boulders. Sitting on the western edge of the national forest near Cass Lake and off Highway 37, it's on the National Register of Historic Sites.

📷 More Things To See & Do

Avenue of the Pines National Scenic Byway, 39 miles: Running along State Highway 46 near Deer River, this route goes through Cut Foot Sioux Experimental Forest, where pine management practices are evaluated, and passes the site of an old fire tower. The byway also goes by wetlands and lakes such as Round, Squaw, Cut Foot Sioux, Little Ball Club and Winnibigoshish. Nearby campgrounds include Williams Narrows, O-Ne-Gum-e and Winnie.

Birding: Bald eagles and about 240 other species have been

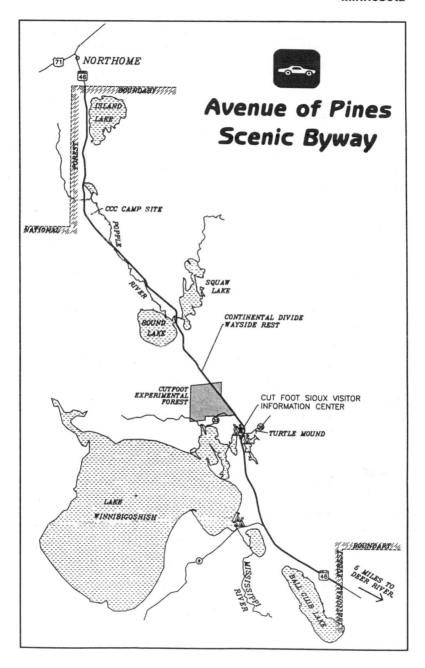

Avenue of Pines Scenic Byway

spotted in Chippewa's varied habitats of marshland, hardwood and conifer forest, lakes and open areas. Several are classified as sensitive or threatened, such as the common loon, double-crested cormorant, great blue heron and peregrine falcon. Chippewa has more than 150 pairs of osprey. Trumpeter swan restoration projects have been undertaken. The national forest also hosts a variety of waterfowl, owls, sandpipers, woodpeckers, cranes, king-birds, gulls, thrushes, vireos, warblers, blackbirds, sparrows and flycatchers.

Prime areas for birding expeditions include Leech Lake's Stony Point, Bear Island and Headquarters Bay, as well as Mud Goose Wildlife Area and dozens of impoundments.

Chippewa Adventure Auto Tour, 17 miles: This self-guided route begins near Marcell. At marked stops, visitors can see wetlands, an osprey nest, red pine, aspen, bogs, an eagle feeding site, wildflowers and a boardwalk that leads to Jack the Horse Lake.

Cut Foot Sioux Scenic Tour, 20 miles: This driving loop starts near the Cut Foot Sioux Visitor Center and offers opportunities to pick blueberries, fish for walleye and observe wildlife. Along

IN THE FOREST
Miller Lake
By Nancy Berlin

They say the roar was so loud that a cabin owner on nearby Amen Lake thought it was a tornado. True, it was a catastrophic event, but caused by water, not wind.

The wildlife and fish of Miller Lake had little warning. Under the stars in July 1993, the beaver dam on the east end of Miller Lake gave way. What resulted was amazing.

The 20-acre lake 12 miles from Marcell, or what was left of it, looked like someone pulled the plug. Water lilies coated the mucky perimeter. Perch and sucker minnows dried in the sun. Two days after the event, young toads were in exodus every-where. Wild water cut a gully 30 or 40 feet deep, washing away the way are lakes, ponds, an experimental forest, Pigeon River Dam and the Continental Divide Wayside Rest, where an interpretive sign explains how water flows S to the Gulf of Mexico or N to Hudson Bay.

Eagle Watching: Chippewa has the largest breeding population of bald eagles - more than 170 known pairs - in the United States outside Alaska. Viewing eagles with their 7-foot wingspans is popular; a boat lets you see them perched on dead or dying trees along the water or on islands. The locations of nesting sites are confidential to protect the eagles, but eagles are often associated with larger lakes such as Winnibigoshish, Leech, Cass and Bowstring. They also can be seen while canoeing on the Mississippi between Cass Lake and Lake Winnie, and along the Big Fork and Leech Lake rivers.

A few eagles winter over at Chippewa, but most return in late February or early March to nest. They lay their eggs in early April and remain until November or December, when the lakes freeze over. More than 1,000 eagles have been banded to help study their migratory patterns and survival.

---

trees, large rocks and tons and tons of sand.

Had humans dug this trench, some might look at it differently. But this was part of nature's hand. One of nature's ways of carving landscapes, designing vegetation and creating animal movements.

Ecologists tell us huge forest fires once roared across Chippewa National Forest every 30 or 40 years. We have all heard of 100-year floods and experienced a tornado or two. Yet we fight it. We build homes and cities in flood plains. Smokey Bear convinces us that fire doesn't belong here anymore, and we mourn the sight of trees toppled by wind.

A week after the washout, beavers patched their dam and the lake was up 2 of the 10 feet it lost. Miller Lake was healing. Are these disasters or amazing forces of the natural world that deserve our respect?

Fall Color Tour, *36 miles:* This route between Bigfork and Pughole Lake passes a 20-acre red pine plantation started in the 1930s, Suomi Hills Recreation Area, Clubhouse Lake Campground and the Rice River.

Great River Road: The Great River Road begins at Lake Itasca, the headwaters of the Mississippi, and follows the course of the river toward southern Minnesota and eventually to the Gulf of Mexico. Part of this scenic and historic route crosses Chippewa National Forest near Cass Lake and Lake Winnibigoshish.

Joyce Estate: In 1917, Chicago lumber baron David Joyce began construction of Nopeming - "place of rest" - on 4,500 acres, The distinctive Aridondack style architecture of Joyce Estatye is reflected in the dozens of buildings on the grounds. Now managed by the Forest Service, there's an interpretive trail and brochure. It's N of Marcell on State Highway 38.

Northwoods Scenic Byway, *22 miles:* Following part of Highway 38, the Northwoods Scenic Byway parallels the abandoned "Gut and Liver" railroad route - now a snowmobile trail - between Bigfork and Grand Rapids. It intersects the Laurentian Divide, which separates the flow of rivers toward Hudson Bay or the Gulf of Mexico. It also passes the Suomi Hills and Trout Lake semiprimitive, non-motorized areas and North Star Campground.

Norway Beach Visitor Center: Set amid spectacular red pines, the center offers interpretive programs and displays on such subjects as Native American heritage and the Civilian Conservation Corps. The center is on U.S. 2, E of Cass Lake in the Norway Beach Recreation Area.

Passport in Time Program: Volunteers have helped restore the bath house and several other significant buildings at the Joyce Estate on Trout Lake. The estate was a 31-building family summer retreat built by timber heir David Joyce between 1917-1937.

Scenic Highway, *28 miles:* This driving route crosses the Mississippi and CCC Camp Rabideau, Pennington Bog scientific natural area and Webster Lake Campground. It runs through forest, farmland and wetlands along County Roads 39 and 10.

Sledding: Shingobee Recreation Area carries the Chippewa word for cedar, spruce and balsam. The area features sliding hills, as well as cross-country ski trails and a warming chalet that's open on winter weekends. One of Minnesota's first downhill ski areas operated here from the 1930s until 1984.

Winnie Dam: Built in 1884, the dam is managed by the Army Corps of Engineers and is a good spot to watch eagles. It's on the E side of Lake Winnibigoshish and reached via State Highway 9.

Ranger Districts

Blackduck: HCR 3, P.O. Box 95, Blackduck, MN 56630; ☎(218) 835-4291.

Cass Lake: Route 3, P.O. Box 219, Cass Lake, MN 56633; ☎ (218) 335-2283.

Deer River: P.O. Box 308, Deer River, MN 56636; ☎ (218) 246-2123.

Marcell: HCR 1, P.O. Box 600, Marcell, MN 56657; ☎ (218) 832-3161.

Walker: HCR 73, P.O. Box 15, Walker MN 56484; ☎ (218) 547-1044

Gateways

Bemidji: Bemidji Visitor & Convention Bureau, P.O. Box 66, Bemidji, MN 56601; ☎ (800) 458-2223 or (218) 759-0164.

Cass Lake: Cass Lake Civic and Chamber Association, P.O. Box 548, Cass Lake, MN 56633; ☎ (800) 356-8615 or (218) 335-6723.

Grand Rapids: Grand Rapids Visitor & Convention Center, 1 N.W. 3rd St., Grand Rapids, MN 55744; ☎ (800) 472-6366 or (218) 326-9607.

Park Rapids: Park Rapids Visitor & Convention Bureau, P.O. Box 249, Park Rapids, MN 56470; ☎ (800) 247-0054 or (218) 732-4111.

Walker: Leech Lake Chamber of Commerce, P.O. Box1089, Walker, MN 56484; ☎ (800) 833-1118 or (218) 547-1313.

WISCONSIN

Chequamegon National Forest
Nicolet National Forest

The 600-mile Ice Age Trail, which passes through Chequamegon National Forest, is a route through glacial terrain that ranges from rocky slopes to gently rolling hills.

CHEQUAMEGON

1170 4th Ave. South
Park Falls, WI 54552
☎ (715) 762-2461

857,782 acres

The Ojibway called Lake Superior's Chequamegon (pronounced Sho-Wah-Ma-Gon) Bay the "place of shallow water." The landscape that is now national forest was formed by four glacial ages, creating hundreds of lakes and carving such rivers as the Flambeau, the Namekagon and the Chippewa. The forest itself blends pines, bogs, meadowlands and northern hardwoods that are home to hundreds of wildlife species. The terrain is gently rolling, but the forest also boasts St. Peter's Dome, the second-highest point in Wisconsin at 1,710 feet, and 70-foot-high Morgan Falls.

Native Americans, French voyageurs, religious missionaries and loggers used this land. Woodland Indians were here as long ago as 1,000 B.C. Timber prospectors arrived in the 1870s, followed by railroads in the 1880s; by 1924 the era of heaviest logging had ended. Chequamegon National Forest was established in 1933 and is now larger than Rhode Island.

While logging continues today, outdoor enthusiasts use hundreds of miles of trails and thousands of miles of forest roads, including stretches of the North Country National Scenic Trail and Ice Age National Scenic Trail. Historic and archaeological sites are scattered through the national forest, including battlefields and powwow sites. For motorists, there's the Great Divide National Forest Scenic Byway. There are more than 800 lakes, and more than 700 miles of rivers and streams.

 Camping

There are 25 developed waterfront campgrounds in Chequamegon National Forest. Group camping is available at Sailor Lake; Smith Rapids has been expanded to accommodate horseback riders. Here are the improved campsites, number of sites and locations:

Glidden Ranger District
Beaver Lake (10), 13 miles W of Mellen on Forest Road 198;
Day Lake (66), 1 mile N of Clam Lake on County Highway GG;
East Twin Lake (10), 5 miles NE of Clam Lake on Forest Road 190;
Mineral Lake (12), 10 miles W of Mellen on County Highway GG;
Lake Three (8), 12 miles W of Mellen on Forest Road 187;
Stockfarm Bridge (7), 11 miles SW of Glidden on Forest Road 164.

Hayward Ranger District
Black Lake (29), 35 miles E of Hayward on Forest Road 173;
Namekagon (34), 17 miles NE of Cable on Forest Road 209;
Moose Lake (15), 35 miles E of Hayward on Forest Road 1643.

Medford Ranger District:
Chippewa (90), 4 miles NW of Perkinstown on Forest Road 1417;
Eastwood (22), 23 miles NW of Medford on Forest Road 104;
Kathryn Lake (8), 20 miles NW of Medford on Forest Road 121;

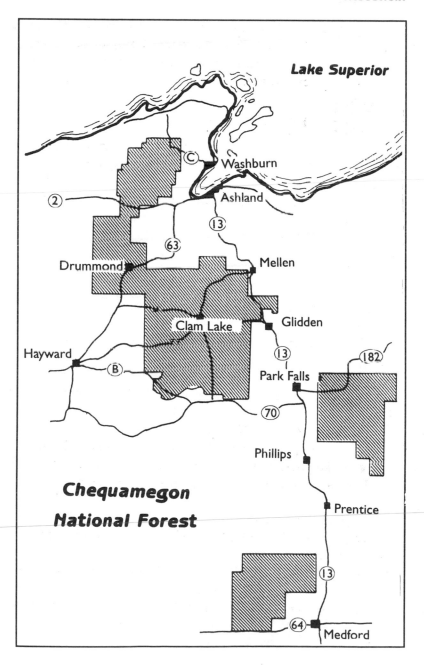

Lake Superior

C Washburn

② Ashland

⑬

⑥③ Mellen

Drummond

Clam Lake Glidden

Hayward ⑬ ⑱②

Ⓑ Park Falls

⑦⓪

Phillips

Chequamegon
National Forest

Prentice

⑬

⑥④ Medford

North Twin Lake (6), 19 miles NW of Medford on Forest Road 566;

Picnic Point (4), 23 miles NW of Medford on Forest Road 106;

Spearhead Point (27), 21 miles NW of Medford on Forest Road 106;

West Point (15), 22 miles NW of Medford on Forest Road 1563.

Park Falls Ranger District

Emily Lake (9), 4 miles W of Lac du Flambeau on Forest Road 1178;

Sailor Lake (18), 11 miles SE of Fifield on Forest Road 139;

Smith Rapids (13), 15 miles NE of Fifield on Forest Road 148;

Twin Lakes (17), 21 miles E of Park Falls on Forest Road 142;

Wabasso Lake (2), 1 mile W of Lac du Flambeau on Forest Road 514.

Washburn Ranger District

Birch Grove (16), 12 miles W of Washburn on Forest Road 435;

Perch Lake (16), 6 miles N of Drummond on Forest Highway 35;

Two Lakes (90), 5 miles SE of Drummond on Forest Road 214;

Wanoka Lake (20), 7 miles E of Iron River on Forest Road 234.

 ## Trails

Chequamegon has about 200 miles of developed trails for hiking, horse riding, cross-country skiing, snowmobiling and mountain biking, including segments of the North Country National Scenic Trail, Ice Age National Scenic Trail and Rock Lake National Recreation Trail. The Round Lake Semi-Primitive Non-Motorized Area in the Park Falls Ranger District is crisscrossed by 5 miles of foot and ski trails. Part of the Tri-County Recreational Corridor, developed along a former Burlington & Northern Railroad right-of-way, passes through Chequamegon.

Sixty miles of the North Country National Scenic Trail run through the national forest in the Glidden, Hayward and Washburn ranger districts. The western part combines wetlands and uplands, while the more rugged eastern section passes scenic overlooks and rock outcroppings. It crosses the Porcupine and Rainbow Lake Wilderness Area. Other points of interest include Lake Owen, Swedish Settlement, a number of campgrounds and a panoramic view of the Marengo River Valley. There are trailheads on County Highway A, S of Iron River; State Highway 63, N of Hayward; State Highway 63, S of Ashland; Forest Road 390, W of Mellen; County Highway D, S of Grand View; Forest Road 187, W of Mellen; Forest Road 213, SE of Drummond; and Forest Road 392, N of Drummond.

Interpretive trails are located at the Day Lake, Lake Namekagon, Black Lake, Birch Grove, Eastwood and Two Lakes campgrounds.

The Chequamegon Area Mountain Bike Association is working with the Forest Service to identify, mark and promote a network of suitable trails for mountain biking. And the Washburn Ranger District has worked with Bayfield County and the Wisconsin Department of Natural Resources to develop an ATV trail system in the Washburn-Iron River area.

During the winter, more than 300 miles of trail are groomed for snowmobiling; they interconnect with county and state trail systems. Another 1,000 miles of unplowed forest roads are also open to snowmobilers.

Here are some popular trails:
Glidden Ranger District
Day Lake Campground Interpretive Trail, 1 *mile:* A short campground trail, it features tree and plant interpretation. The trailhead is N of Clam Lake on County Highway GG.
Dead Horse Run Motorcycle & ATV Trail, 70 *miles:* This

challenging trail is named for a 1910 incident in which a team of horses hauling a load of saw logs fell through the ice and was lost. Parts of the trail connect the Great Divide Snowmobile Trail and Tuscobia State Trail. The main parking area is at the site of former Civilian Conservation Corps Camp Loretta, on County Highway GG, N of Loretta.

Morgan Falls-St. Peter's Dome Trail, *2 miles:* This trail leads to Morgan Falls, a 70-foot waterfall on the South Fork of Morgan Creek, and to the granite summit of St. Peter's Dome, which provides a view of Lake Superior 20 miles away. An old red granite quarry is 850 feet down the trail from St. Peter's Dome. Foliage colors are dramatic during the fall. The trailhead is on Forest Road 199.

Hayward Ranger District

Black Lake Interpretive Trail, *4 miles:* It features logging history - starting with the white pine era of 1880-1900, moving to the hemlock-hardwoods era of 1909-1924, and ending with selective cutting under the Forest Service. Stops include a white spruce plantation, the site of a pine-era logging camp and abandoned Stout Spur of Edward Hines Lumber Co.'s railroad. The trail is S of Clam Lake on Forest Road 173.

Namekagon Nature Trail, *1 mile:* This interpretive trail features tree and plant species in the hardwood-hemlock forest. The terrain is gently rolling and includes wildlife openings and wetlands. Numbered posts correspond with a free trail booklet that covers such topics as habitats, the importance of trees, animal adaptations for protection from weather and predators, specialized plants and geological features. The parking area is on Forest Road 209 near Namekagon Campground.

Medford Ranger District

Chippewa Lobe Interpretive Loop Trail, *7 miles:* The trail describes glaciation and its visible effects in one of Wisconsin's six glacial ice lobes. It adjoins the Ice Age National Scenic Trail, NW of Medford. The nearest parking area is on Forest Road 108.

Ice Age National Scenic Trail, *42 miles:* It crosses

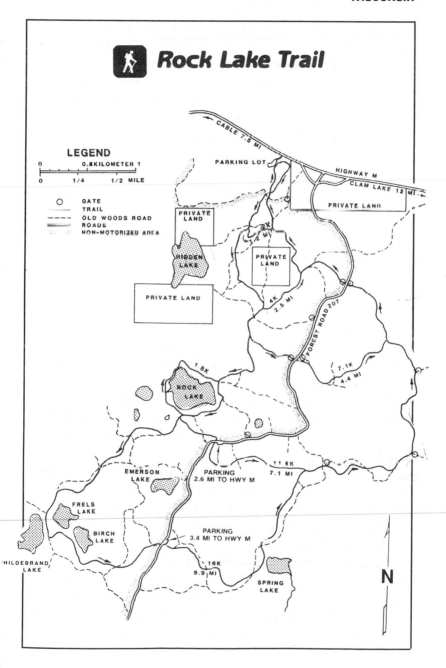

Chequamegon on its 600-mile route across the state between the St. Croix River on the W and Lake Michigan on the E. The trail follows the end moraines of the most recent glacial ice sheet, which retreated an estimated 10,000-12,000 years ago. The trail passes through glacial terrain characterized by kettleholes, drumlins, eskers, bogs, marshes, lakes and other Ice Age legacies. The trail is W of Medford. The eastern trailhead within the national forest is on Forest Road 101 near the Mondeaux Flowage Recreation Area; the western trailhead is on Highway 64.

Mondeaux Interpretive Trail, 1 mile: Located at the Mondeaux Flowage Recreation Area, this easy trail highlights local topographic features and plant species. Reach it on Forest Road 106, NW of Medford.

Perkinstown Motorized Trail, 22 miles: This ATV and motorcycle trail crosses forest trails and a winter sports area near Kathryn Lake and Chippewa campgrounds and Chequamegon Waters Flowage. The trailhead is W of Medford on Highway 64.

Park Falls Ranger District

Flambeau Trail, 60 miles: The trail name comes from the French word for "flaming torch" because early Indians here used torches to spear fish at night. This ATV and motorcycle trail passes through ruffed grouse habitat, Hay Creek Flowage, the South Fork of the Flambeau River, Camp Nine Springs vista, Round Lake Logging Dam, Riley Lake Wildlife Area, Spur Lake esker and Fifield Fire Tower. Although the trail was designed for motorized use, mountain bikers and horseback riders also use it. Access spots include Sailor Lake Campground, Round Lake boat launch and Highway 182.

Popple Creek & Wilson Flowage Wildlife Viewing Trail, 1 mile: From this short trail, visitors can see wetland and upland wildlife, including migratory waterfowl in the spring, ospreys and eagles in the summer, and coyotes, fishers and snowshoe hares in the winter. The trail is SE of Fifield on Forest Road 137.

Smith Rapids Saddle Trail, 19 miles: Scenic vistas combine with gently rolling terrain along this northwoods trail near the

South Fork of the Flambeau River. It connects with the Flambeau Multiple-Use Trail System. Access is at Smith Rapids Campground, which accommodates horses, and at the Round Lake boat launch.

Washburn Ranger District

Birch Grove Interpretive Trail, 1 mile: This easy walking trail features plants and animals of northern Wisconsin. It's W of Washburn on Forest Road 435.

Iron River Trail, 18 miles: This is a tough ATV trail - sandy, winding and with limited visibility - partly along an abandoned railroad grade. It runs just S of Moquah Barrens Wildlife Area. Access is from Forest Road 242, Forest Road 245 and Long Lake boat landing W of Washburn.

Lenawee ATV Trail, 16 miles: Old Baldy Lookout near the W end of the trail offers a panoramic view of Lake Superior, Minnesota, Canada and Wisconsin. There's a sandy surface most of the way along this winding trail. The trailhead is on Forest Road 246, NW of Washburn.

Pigeon Lake Interpretive Trail, 2 miles: Interpretive signs identify plants and signs of animals. It's W of Drummond on Forest Road 228.

Valhalla ATV Trail, 16 miles: Viewpoints along the loop trail include the Sun Bowl and the peak of Old Valhalla Ski Hill. The surface is loose sand and the terrain heavily forested. Access is on County Road C, NW of Washburn.

 # Cross Country Skiing

The national forest has many trails designed for Nordic skiing as well as being the site of the Birkebeiner Cross-Country Ski Race, the largest citizen's race in North America. Nicknamed the "Birkie," the event is held each February over the hilly terrain between Cable and Hayward. It's been called the "Boston Marathon" of cross-country competition. For information, contact Birkebeiner, Box 911, Hawyard, WI 54843; ☎ (800) 872-2753 or (715) 634-5025.

Popular Nordic trails in the national forest are:

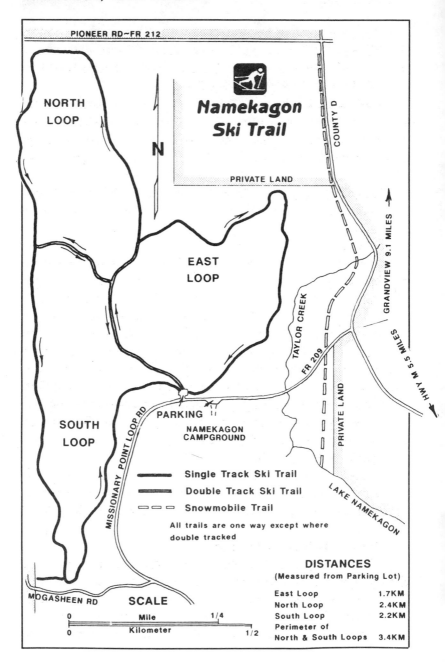

PIONEER RD~FR 212

Namekagon Ski Trail

NORTH LOOP

PRIVATE LAND

COUNTY D

N

EAST LOOP

GRANDVIEW 9.1 MILES →

TAYLOR CREEK

FR 209

HWY M 5.5 MILES

PARKING

MISSIONARY POINT LOOP RD.

NAMEKAGON CAMPGROUND

SOUTH LOOP

PRIVATE LAND

—————— Single Track Ski Trail

══════ Double Track Ski Trail

╍ ╍ ╍ Snowmobile Trail

All trails are one way except where double tracked

LAKE NAMEKAGON

MOGASHEEN RD

SCALE

0   Mile   1/4

0   Kilometer   1/2

DISTANCES
(Measured from Parking Lot)

East Loop	1.7KM
North Loop	2.4KM
South Loop	2.2KM
Perimeter of North & South Loops	3.4KM

Glidden Ranger District

Penokee Mountain Ski Trail, *7 miles*: There are three loops that connect with the North Country National Scenic Trail. It is W of Mellen on County Highway GG.

Viekko Ski Trail, *4 miles*: The name means "brotherhood" in Finnish. The trail winds through the towering hardwood forests of the Morgan Creek Valley, with scenic overlooks, outcroppings and dramatic views of St. Peter's Dome. Park on Forest Road 187.

West Torch River Ski Trail, *7 miles*: This system of interconnecting ski trails near the West Torch River is SE of Clam Lake on County Highway GG.

Hayward Ranger District

Namekagon Ski Trail, *5 miles*: Three loops comprise this cross-country trail near Namekagon Campground. The terrain offers gentle hills. Reach it on Forest Road 209, S of Grandview.

Rock Lake National Recreation Trail, *14 miles*: This was designed principally for cross-country skiing but is popular with mountain bikers as well. There are maple, oak, paper birch, aspen and scattered stands of white pine in glaciated, rolling terrain. The trail has a system of loops of varying lengths. Much of it parallels rough but less hilly old logging roads that are open to hiking, biking and skiing. A snowmobile trail crosses Rock Lake Trail at four points. The trailhead is E of Cable on Highway M.

Medford Ranger District

Sitzmark Ski Trail, *10 miles*: Loops range from under a mile to 2.5 miles on this network, which passes the Perkinstown Winter Sports Area. The trailhead is on Forest Road 119, NW of Medford.

Park Falls Ranger District

Newman Springs Ski Trail, *7 miles*: A series of loops pass through glaciated terrain, with lowland marshes and upland ridges. Trees include red pine, lowland conifers, northern hardwoods and white birch. The trailhead is E of Park Falls on Highway 182.

Wintergreen Ski & Hiking Trail, *11 miles*: This one includes rolling terrain with upland ridges and lowland marshes, as well as scenic vistas overlooking bogs and ponds. The loops go through red pine plantations, young aspen stands and other habitats. The trailhead is E of Fifield on Highway 70.

Washburn Ranger District

Teuton Ski Trail, 5 miles: There are three interconnecting loops near Mt. Valhalla Winter Sports Area. The trailhead is NW of Washburn on County Highway C.

Valkyrie Ski Trail, 11 miles: This trail system near the Mt. Valhalla Winter Sports Area, has four interconnecting loops. The trailhead is NW of Washburn on County Highway C, adjacent to the Teutron Ski Trails. One of the highlights of this trail is the scenic overlook on Loop C known as the Sunbowl.

 Mountain Biking

The Chequamegon Area Mountain Bike Association maintains six trail clusters, totaling more than 200 miles, crossing more than 1,600 square miles of national forest and other public land. The association also stages the Chequamegon Fat Tire Festival. Using the Birkebeiner's cross-country ski route, mountain bikers each September participate in the largest off-road bike race in the United States. It takes place in the Hayward Ranger District.

For information on the event or trail maps, contact the Chequamegon Area Mountain Bike Association, Box 141, Cable, WI 54821; ☎ (800) 533-7454 or (715) 798-3833.

In the Washburn District, riders will find the Drummond System of four interconnecting loops.

In the Hayward District, the Rock Lake Trail Cluster offers six interconnecting loops. The Washburn District is also the site of the Grandview Firehouse 50 Bike Race. The annual event, which calls itself the "oldest citizen's bike race in the Midwest," begins and ends in Grandview and follows a 50-mile course through the national forest. For information, contact the Cable Area Chamber of Commerce, Box 217, Cable, WI 54821; ☎ (800) 533-7454 or (715) 798-3833.

Hundreds of miles of mountain biking trails exist in and around Chequamegon National Forest.

Boating & Canoeing

Chequamegon includes 632 miles of rivers and streams such as the Chippewa, Namekagon, Yellow, Jump, Bad and Flambeau rivers. Parts of these rivers were historic canoe routes for the fur traders, Native Americans, missionaries and explorers. The Namekagon is a National Wild and Scenic River. There are Class II rapids on both the Namekagon and South Fork of the Flambeau. The upper reaches of the rivers are often shallow from mid-summer through fall, so expect to portage around low-water stretches.

The national forest has 411 lakes greater than 10 acres in size, for a combined 30,937 acres. In addition to 33 Forest Service boat landings, state and local agencies maintain launch sites on some lakes. The small size and relatively shallow depths of many lakes means larger boats are not accommodated.

Here are some suggested canoe routes:

East Fork of the Chippewa River, 20 *miles*: This is a scenic route between Gates Lake and Blaisdell Lake in the Glidden Ranger District and is known for both its scenery and its musky, walleye, bass and panfish. Stockfarm Bridge Campground is along the way. The first put-in is SE of Gates Lake on Forest Road 1285.

South Fork of the Flambeau River, 12 *miles*: Start at Round Lake Dam or the landing between Round and Pike lakes, E of Park Falls. End the route at Cedar Rapids, a fast-water stretch, with a take-out at Forest Road 149. In between are Fishtrap Rapids, the Depression-era Little Bull Dam, Riley Creek Dam, Smith Rapids and Natural Dam. The route is in the Park Falls Ranger District.

St. Croix River, 1 *mile*: The total route runs 107 miles from Namekagon Dam to Riverside. Portages are required at Pacwawong Flowage Dam, Phipps Flowage Dam and Hayward Dam. There are some small rapids. The starting point is Namekagon Dam landing, E of Cable in the Hayward Ranger District.

 Fishing

Some of Wisconsin's best musky fishing is found in

Chequamegon. In addition to muskellunge, favorite fish species include northern pike, walleye, largemouth and smallmouth bass, rock bass, brook and brown trout, rainbow trout, black crappies, bluegills, yellow perch, pumpkinseed, minnows and bullheads.

In the Glidden Ranger District, anglers can choose from among more warm-water streams such as Spider Creek, the West Fork of the Chippewa River and the East Fork of the Chippewa; dozens of lakes including Upper Clam, Day Lake Flowage, Blaisdell and Lake Three; and more than two dozen trout streams such as the Brunsweiler River, Bad River and Morgan Creek. In the Medford Ranger District, North Twin, South Twin and Kathryn Lake, Chequamegon Waters and the Yellow River are favored for large-mouth bass, while brook trout are featured in Mink Creek and smallmouth bass in the Jump River. Good fishing waters of the Hayward Ranger District range from huge Chippewa Flowage (15,300 acres), with its abundant walleye, to small lakes such as Coffee Lake (54 acres), with plentiful northern pike.

Multiple species are found at various Park Falls Ranger District waters such as Blockhouse, Miles and Pike lakes and the South Fork of the Flambeau River.

Each year, the community of Hayward hosts a Fishing Has No Boundaries celebration on the Chippewa Flowage.

Wilderness Areas

Porcupine Lake Wilderness, 4,292 acres: The terrain has rolling hills, flat uplands, bogs and six lakes at least 5 acres in size, including Porcupine Lake, the largest. There are smaller ponds as well, including Eighteen Mile Spring Pond, West Davis Lake, Lake Lizzie and Coburn Lake. Sugar maple, red maple and yellow birch cover about half the wilderness, with the rest marked by red oak, hemlock, balsam, spruce, cedar, aspen and tamarack. The North Country National Scenic Trail cuts through the wilderness. It's located in the Hayward Ranger District. There's access from Forest Road 213, Forest Road 214 and County Highway D.

Rainbow Lake Wilderness, 6,583 acres: This wilderness area

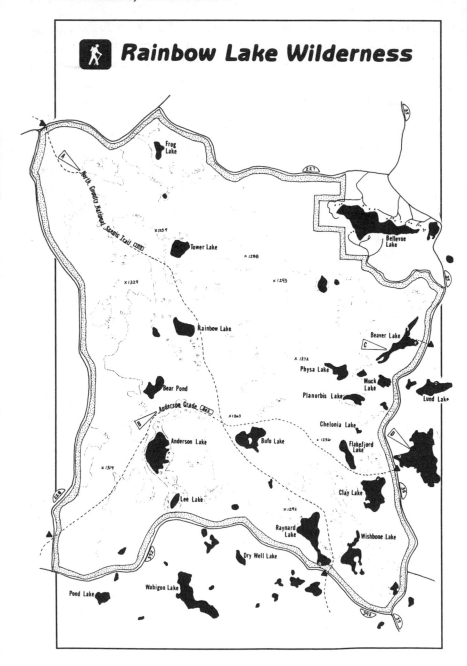

🚶 *Rainbow Lake Wilderness*

in the Washburn Ranger District contains 16 lakes and nine ponds for fishing, canoeing and wildlife viewing. Wildflowers include trillium, water lilies, violets, marigolds and hepatica; the forest mixes northern hardwoods and conifers such as maple, balsam, basswood, oak, aspen, pine and paper birch. It's crossed by the North Country National Scenic Trail and Anderson Grade, a trail that was used during lumbering days to transport logs on rail cars to sawmills. Points of interest include Perch Lake Campground and Beaver Lake, popular for watching and photographing wildlife. The wilderness is N of Drummond, with access on Forest Road 228, Forest Road 392 and Forest Highway 35.

 ## Natural Areas

Lake Namekagon is the headwaters of the Namekagon River, part of the St. Croix National Scenic Riverway. As a result, the first mile of the river is under National Park Service protection.

Moquah Barrens Research Natural Area, 110 acres: An outstanding example of jack pine-scrub oak barrens or savannas, this area is a National Natural Landmark. There are ice-block depressions as well as sand blowouts. The barrens were produced naturally by glacial action and plant colonization. They were affected by intensive logging in the late 1800s and early 1900s with the removal of mature pine and forest fires that followed.

Morgan Falls: Named for a silver miner of the 1800s, this is a 70-foot waterfall in the Glidden Ranger District. Park on Forest Road 199, hike to the falls, then continue on the same trail for another mile to the summit of St. Peter's Dome. The falls are also accessible in the winter with snowshoes.

 ## Historic Attractions

Mondeaux Dam Day Use Area: This unusual example of Depression-era architecture was developed by Forest Service engineers and architects specifically for recreational use. It was built and landscaped by Civilian Conservation Corps enrollees and local workers under the Work Projects Administration between

IN THE FOREST

The Relentless Timber Harvest

The North Woods logging industry first flourished in the mid-1800s, a time when Wisconsin's population increased tenfold. With this dramatic growth came a need for expanding the sources of lumber. Railroads had not yet penetrated northern Wisconsin. Instead, rivers became the highways for transporting logs to mills. Timber was cut and hauled to a port along the river, upstream of strategically placed driving dams.

The most perilous, yet colorful, aspect of the logging era was the river drive. It began with the spring thaw. Dam gates were cranked open and a giant wall of water flushed the logs downstream to the next dam. Nimble-footed river men controlled the flow of water and the movement of the logs on their journey to mills in central Wisconsin.

Relentless cutting, however, exhausted the North Woods pineries by the end of the 19th century. But the focus on pine trees had left the expansive forests of sugar maple and other hardwoods virtually untouched.

To reach deeper into the forests, lumber companies turned to the railroads by the 1880s. They cut through the interior, and once again northern Wisconsin's logging industry boomed.

The hardwoods were loaded on flatcars and transported to distant mills. Cutting continued at a brisk pace until the late 1920s, when diminishing supplies and the Great Depression slowed the industry, then brought it to a halt.

The sweeping timber harvests left the land barren. Land could be purchased at little cost, and thoughts turned to farming. On occasion, would-be farmers purchased land unseen and no doubt experienced a foreboding sight when they first viewed their new home.

The Rust-Owen Reservoir, a historic site in Chequamegon National Forest, was essential to the lumber mill in the town of Drummond. One spark of fire from the mill could easily have been the end of the entire town.

The soil was generally sandy, sometimes swampy and always littered with stumps. The arduous task of clearing the land met with limited success while the brevity of the growing season and the distance to major metropolitan markets made prosperity unlikely, if not impossible.

By the 1920s, most of those who had attempted farming had given up all hope of success. Those few who remained and survived the perils expanded into the livestock and dairy industries. But most left farming for logging-related work. Trees proved to be a more profitable crop.

- By U.S. Forest Service

1936-1938. Three buildings survive: the Bath and Club House, caretaker's dwelling and garage. Those buildings, a dam and the surrounding 6 acres constitute an historic district listed on the National Register of Historic Places. It is in the Medford Ranger District.

Round Lake Log Driving Dam: On the South Fork of the Flambeau River, this earthen dam and timber structure represents the region's logging legacy and the tradition of spring log drives. Built by Joseph Viles about 1878, the dam created Round Lake. During winter lumbering season, pine logs were hauled to the frozen lake. Then, when the river melted, the dam gates were cranked open so log drivers could guide the logs through; they floated southward to sawmills on the Mississippi and Chippewa rivers. The dam is in the Park Falls Ranger District.

The dam was rehabilitated in the 1920s-1930s and a preservation effort is underway. It's on the National Register of Historic Places. For more information, write to Friends of the Round Lake Logging Dam, Price County Historical Society, Old Town Hall Museum, Fifield, WI 54524.

Rust-Owen Reservoir: In the days when pine ruled, the Rust-Owen Co. developed a town called Drummond for its workers. There were rental houses, mills, stables, a blacksmith shop, boarding house and general store. A silo-shaped reservoir of native field-stone was built on a hilltop across Lake Drummond to provide water to the mills; a steam-powered sprinkler system used water from the reservoir to extinguish two major fires in town.

Timber resources became depleted, and the mill sawed its last log in 1930. The company sold most of its land to the federal government. Most of the buildings have disappeared, but the reservoir still stands. It's N of Cable on Forest Highway 35 near the town of Drummond in the Washburn Ranger District.

More Things To Do & See

Berry picking: Strawberries, high and low bush cranberries, blackberries, blueberries, serviceberries and raspberries grow wild in the national forest.

Birding: Among more than 250 types of birds sighted here are common loons, osprey, sharp-shinned hawks, merlins, sandhill cranes, killdeer, great horned and snowy owls, bald eagles, American woodcock, solitary sandpipers, Canada and snow geese, tundra swans, great blue herons, great egrets, mourning doves, double-crested cormorant, mallards, loggerhead shrikes and ruby-throated hummingbirds.

Great Divide Scenic Byway, 29 miles: South of the Penokee Range lies a ridge called the Great Divide; water flows S to the Mississippi River and N to Lake Superior. The byway runs along Route 77 between Hayward and Glidden, with opportunities to stop at the sites of several Depression-era Civilian Conservation Corps camps.

A local writer, Joe A. Moran, described the 19th-century tote road between Glidden and Clam Lake as a "seven-hour ordeal of lurching jolts through quagmire and the devil knows what, over hogbacks for a score of miles."

The route is, of course, now paved. There are wayside exhibits at the Clam Lake and Ghost Creek CCC camps. The byway provides access to prime fishing lakes, boat launches and Day Lake Campground.

Passport in Time Program: Projects have been undertaken at several of the hundreds of cultural resource sites identified within Chequamegon. Among them are archaeological investigations of the Flambeau-Springstead sites, where the remains of prehistoric campsites and an historic farmstead have been found along the South Fork of the Flambeau River.

At Star Lake, excavations have taken place at what is thought to be the lakeshore site of an Indian village of 1000-1400 A.D.

Penokee Overlook: Viewing platforms and interpretive wayside exhibits atop a bluff help visitors appreciate the panorama of the ancient volcanic Penokee Range and the Great Divide. It's on County Highway GG, W of Mellen in the Glidden Ranger District.

Picnicking & swimming: Favorite picnic spots with beaches include Day Lake in the Glidden Ranger District; Namekagon Campground Day Use Area in the Hayward Ranger District; Newman Lake Day Use Area in the Park Falls Ranger District; Mondeaux Flowage Recreation Area in the Medford Ranger District; and Lake Owen Day Use Area in the Washburn Ranger District.

Smith Rapids Covered Bridge: This span across the South Fork of the Flambeau River was built in 1991, the first covered bridge of its type built in Wisconsin in more than a century. The design is known as Town Lattice Truss and combines the 19th-century look with 20th-century technology. It replaces a three-span girder bridge with timber-plank deck that had been built in 1955. You'll find it at Smith Rapids Campground in the Park Falls Ranger District.

St. Peter's Dome: At 1,600 feet elevation, the red granite summit of St. Peter's Dome, part of the Penokee Range, provides a view of Lake Superior 20 miles away. Although a Civil War captain mined silver here, most other 19th-century miners found lots of red granite but, alas, no silver. Before World War I, however, the only U.S. deposit of a mineral named black gabbro was found here and proved valuable for building stone and monuments. There's a steep hike to the summit, Wisconsin's second-highest point. The dome is W of Mellen on Forest Road 199 in the Glidden Ranger District.

Swedish Settlement: Immigrants from Sweden started farming the area in the 1880s, but the soil proved marginal for agriculture. There's a three-hour, 5-mile self-guided tour that features the remains of three historic immigrant settlement sites in the Marengo River Valley: Green Mountain School, Calvin Beyzanson Homestead and Gust Welin Homestead. The settlement is SE of Grandview in the Hayward Ranger District in between Forest Road 198 (Wisco Road,) Forest Road 202 (Old Grade Road) and Forest Road 383.

Wildlife Viewing Areas: There are a variety of wildlife viewing areas with auto tour routes, brochures and interpretive way-side exhibits. They're at Chequamegon Waters Flowage, Popple Creek and Wilson Flowage, Day Lake, Lynch Creek and Moquah Pine Barrens. Nesting platforms and wood duck boxes attract bald eagles, ospreys, loons and wood ducks.

At Popple Creek and Wilson Flowage on Forest Road 137 in the Park Falls Ranger District, a short walking trail provides wild-life viewing opportunities. The 269-acre Wilson Flowage is a shal-low slough formed by glacial action and, with impoundments, at-tracts waterfowl such as tundra swans, Canada geese, loons, snow geese, goldeneyes, hooded mergansers and ring-necked ducks. A colony of yellow-headed blackbirds, which are uncommon in north-ern Wisconsin, nest here, as do osprey and eagles.

The Lynch Creek Waterfowl Management Area offers wet-land vistas and two trails: one with a viewing platform, the other through red pine forests. Eagles, otters, beavers, great blue her-ons and kingfishers are among the local wildlife. It's on Forest Road 662, SE of Cable in the Hayward Ranger District.

 Ranger Districts

Glidden: Box 126, Glidden, WI 54527; ☎ (715) 264-2511.

Hayward: Route 10, Box 508, Hayward, WI 54843; ☎ (715) 634-4821.

Medford: 850 North 8th, Highway 13, Medford, WI 54451; ☎ (715) 748-4875.

Park Falls: 1170 4th Ave. S., Park Falls, WI 54552; ☎ (715) 762-2461.

Washburn: P.O. Box 578, Washburn, WI 54891; ☎ (715) 373-2667.

 Gateways

Ashland: Ashland Area Chamber of Commerce, 320 4th Ave. West, Ashland, WI 54806; ☎ (715) 682-2500

Bayfield: Bayfield Chamber of Commerce, 42 S. Broad St.,

Bayfield, WI 54814; ☎ (715) 779-3335

Cable: Cable Area Chamber of Commerce, Box 217, Cable, WI 54821; ☎ (800) 533-7454 or (715) 798-3833.

Glidden: Glidden Area Chamber of Commerce, Glidden, WI 54527; ☎ (715) 264-4851.

Hayward: Hayward Lakes Resort Association, Box 1055, Hayward, WI 54843; ☎ (800) 826-3474 or (715) 634-4801.

Medford: Taylor County Tourism Council, 224 2nd St. South, Medford, WI 54451; ☎ (715) 748-3327

Minocqua: Greater Minocqua Chamber of Commerce, Box 1006, Minocqua, WI 54548; ☎ (715) 356-5266.

Park Falls: Park Falls Chamber of Commerce, 4th Ave. South, Park Falls, WI 54552; ☎ (715) 762-2703.

Phillips: Phillips Chamber of Commerce, 104 Lake Ave. South, Phillips, WI 54555; ☎ (715) 339-2278.

Washburn: Washburn Chamber of Commerce, 119 Washington Ave., Washburn, WI 54891; ☎ (715) 373-5017.

NICOLET

68 S. Stevens St.   661,290 acres
Rhinelander, WI 54501
☎ (715) 362-1300

Parts of Nicolet National Forest have changed little since 1634, when French explorer Jean Nicolet arrived in what is now northeast Wisconsin in an unsuccessful search for the Northwest Passage. Then and now, this is a land of more than a thousand lakes and more than a thousand miles of streams, of rugged terrain, of wilderness, of wild rivers and of wildlife.

Known as the "Cradle of Rivers" because it contains the headwaters of the Pine, Wolf, Oconto, Peshtigo, Wisconsin and Popple rivers, Nicolet is a favorite destination for canoeists, hikers and other outdoor enthusiasts. Lac Vieux Desert is Nicolet's largest lake and straddles the Michigan-Wisconsin border. Congress designated Nicolet as a national forest in 1933, five years after the state of Wisconsin began initiatives to restore fire and logging damage to the woods.

 ## Camping

Most developed campgrounds have boat landings. Some are adjacent to major trails, such as Anvil National Recreation Trail, or interpretive trails. It's even possible to hike between some campgrounds; such opportunities include a 3-mile trail connecting

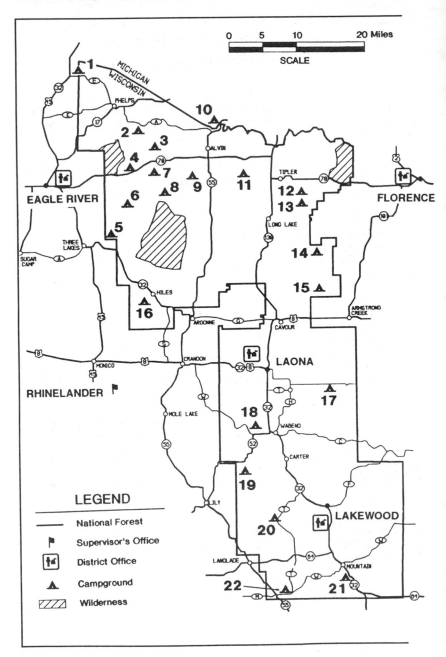

Nicolet National Forest Campgrounds

Map No.	Developed Campgrounds	Number of Sites	Group Sites	Picnic Areas	Boat Ramp	Swim Area	Hiking Trail	Boat Motor Limit
	EAGLE RIVER DISTRICT							
1	Lac Vieux Desert	31		*	*	*		
2	Spectacle Lake	34		*	*	*	*	
3	Kentuck Lake	31			*		*	
4	Anvil Lake	18		*	*	*	*	
5	Laurel Lake	12		*				
6	Sevenmile Lake	27		*	*	*	*	
7	Franklin Lake	77		*	*	*	*	
8	Luna-White Deer Lake	37		*	*	*	*	N.M.
9	Windsor Dam	8						
	FLORENCE DISTRICT							
10	Brule River	11			C.I.			
11	Stevens Lake	6		*				
12	Chipmunk Rapids	6			C.I.		*	
13	Lost Lake	27		*	*	*	*	N.M.
14	Morgan Lake	18	1	*	*	*		E.O.
	LAONA DISTRICT							
15	Laura Lake	41		*	*	*	*	E.O.
16	Pine Lake	12		*	*	*		
17	Bear Lake	27		*	*	*		
18	Richardson Lake	26		*	*	*		
19	Ada Lake	19		*	*	*		E.O.
	LAKEWOOD DISTRICT							
20	Boot Lake	34		*	*	*		
21	Bagley Rapids	30						
22	Boulder Lake	89	10	*	*	*		

E.O. - Electric Motor Only   C.I. - Carry In Only
N.M. - No Motors

Kentuck Lake and Spectacle Lake campgrounds and a 6-mile trail between Franklin Lake and Anvil Lake campgrounds. The developed campgrounds, number of sites and locations are:

Eagle River Ranger District
Anvil Lake (18), 10 miles E of Eagle River on Highway 70;
Franklin Lake (77), 16 miles E of Eagle River on Forest Road 2181;
Kentuck Lake (31), 17 miles NE of Eagle River on Forest Road 2176;
Lac Vieux Desert (31), 7 miles NE of Phelps on Forest Road 2205;
Laurel Lake (12), 7 miles NE of Three Lakes on Campground Road;
Luna-White Deer Lake (37), 21 miles E of Eagle River on Forest Road 2188;
Sevenmile Lake (27), 15 miles SE of Eagle River on Forest Road 2435;
Spectacle Lake (34), 16 miles NE of Eagle River on Forest Road 2572;
Windsor Dam (8), 25 miles E of Eagle River on Forest Road 2174.

Florence Ranger District
Brule River (11), 4 miles N of Alvin on Highway 55;
Chipmunk Rapids (6), 18 miles SW of Florence on Forest Road 2156;
Lost Lake (27), 10 miles SE of Florence on Forest Road 2156;
Morgan Lake (18), 11 miles SE of Long Lake on Forest Road 2161;
Stevens Lake (6), 16 miles SW of Iron River, Mich., on Forest Road 2424.

Lakewood Ranger District
Bagley Rapids (30), 12 miles SE of Lakewood on Forest Road 2111;
Boot Lake (34), 6 miles SW of Townsend on Highway T;
Boulder Lake (89), 19 miles S of Townsend on Forest Road

Nicolet National Forest features 22 campgrounds in four ranger districts that range in size from as large as 89 sites (Boulder Lake) to as small as six sites (Chipmunk Rapids and Stevens Lake).

2116.

Laona Ranger District
Ada Lake (19), 10 miles SW of Wabeno on Forest Road 2620;
Bear Lake (27), 10 miles SE of Laona on Forest Road 3770:
Laura Lake (41), 18 miles NE of Laona on Forest Road 2163;
Pine Lake (12), 14 miles NW of Crandon on Forest Road 2185;
Richardson Lake (26), 4 miles W of Wabeno on Forest Road 2880.

There are walk-in camping areas with five sites each at Perch Lake in the Florence Ranger District; Lauterman Lake in the Florence Ranger District; and Fanny Lake in the Lakewood Ranger District.

 ## Trails

Designated trails total hundreds of miles in length, including a variety of short nature and interpretive trails. The abandoned Chicago-Northwestern Railroad grade, which crosses Nicolet National Forest for 22 miles, is a county-designated hiking and snowmobile trail. Other popular trails, by ranger district, are:

Eagle River Ranger District
Anvil National Recreation Trail, 12 miles: Interconnecting trails, a Depression project of the CCC, are located between Anvil Lake and Upper Ninemile Lake in an area closed to motor vehicles. The trail passes Upper Ninemile Lake, Echo Lake and Ninemile Creek. Terrain varies from mostly level to a hilly stretch ominously named Devil's Run. Loops include Narrow Gauge, Butternut, Ash, Pat Shay and Meadow. The trail is E of Eagle River, with parking across Highway 70 from Anvil Lake Campground.

Franklin Nature Trail, 1 mile: This interpretive trail crosses Franklin-Butternut Creek and passes under a natural arch to Hemlock Cathedral's evergreen canopy. Along the way are sugar maples, bogs, Buttermilk Lake, tamarack swamp, raspberry and elderberry plants, ferns, an esker ridge and trees downed in a 1985 windstorm. The loops begins and ends at Franklin Lake Campground, E storm. The loops begins and ends at Franklin Lake Campground, E of Eagle River on Forest Road 2181.

Giant Pine Trail, 2 *miles:* This scenic loop in Headwaters Wilderness cuts through spruce swamps, hemlock ridges and, of course, giant pines 30 to 48 inches in diameter. Reach the trail from Forest Road 2414, N of Hiles.

Hidden Lakes Trail, 13 miles: The trail crosses glacial terrain, passing such geological features as a glacier-formed esker, kettle ponds and bogs. Along the way are Two Dutchmen, McKinley and Three John lakes. The trail begins at Franklin Lake Campground; it intersects Luna-White Deer Trail.

Luna-White Deer Trail, 4 *miles:* This one circles White Deer Lake, with its white sand beach, and Luna Lake; both are small, deep and clear, with a campground between them. The trail is SE of Eagle River on Forest Road 2188.

Sam Campbell Memorial Trail, 2 *miles:* An interpretive trail traverses natural forest and tree plantations. The trail is named in memory of nature writer, lecturer, philosopher and photographer Sam Campbell, known as the "philosopher of the forest." Hardwoods, red pine, balsam, cedar and spruce grow along the route. The trail is NE of Three Lakes, with parking on Old Military Road.

Sevenmile Lake Walking Trail, 2 *miles:* This trail is on a high bluff. It passes two ponds, red pine and blueberry patches. There's a boardwalk through a wetlands area. It's near Sevenmile Lake Campground, SE of Eagle River on Forest Road 2435.

Spectacle Lake-Kentuck Lake Trail, 3 miles: This gentle trail through hardwood forest connects two campgrounds E of Eagle River. Access is from Spectacle Lake Campground on Forest Road 2572 and Kentuck Lake Campground on Forest Road 2176.

Florence Ranger District

Lauterman National Recreation Trail, 9 miles: Built by the Youth Conservation Corps for mountain biking, hiking and skiing, this trail runs between Lauterman Lake and the Pine River, passing Little Porcupine Lake and Mud Lake. A 1-mile spur connects it to the Perch Lake walk-in campground. The trail is the scene of the popular annual Chili Ski-In for cross-country skiers. Located W of Florence, the trailhead is at Chipmunk Rapids Campground on Forest Road 2156.

Lakewood Ranger District

Boulder Lake Trail, 2 miles: This self-guided nature trail passes deer trails, primitive bog vegetation, woodpecker-marked tree trunks, and huge boulders that are legacies of the last Ice Age glacier that receded 10,000 years ago. Signs describe types of trees, groundhog holes, forest products and how a tree grows. The trail is near Boulder Lake Campground, S of Townsend on Forest Road 2116.

Jones Spring Trails, 11 miles: Skiing and hiking loop trails have been developed in the 2,000-acre Jones Spring Non-motorized Area. There are walk-in campsites at Fanny Lake. The trails also pass Lower Jones Lake and Jones Spring Impoundment. The Jones Spring Area is SW of Townsend, with parking on Forest Roads 2938, 2122, 2336 and 2283.

Lakewood Trail, 14 miles: Hikers, mountain bikers and skiers use this trail, which often follows old logging roads as it passes or crosses McCaslin Brook, Sullivan Springs, Bullfrog Lake and Snowfalls Creek. Parking is available on Old 32 Road, Smyth Road and Sullivan Springs Road.

Laona Ranger District

Catwillow Creek Trail, 12 miles: Named for a local stream, this trail crosses the Catwillow Wildlife Management Area and is used for hiking and snowmobiling. There are bogs, marshes, abandoned railroad grades and wildlife water holes along the route. The trail is NE of Laona, with access from Forest Road 2131.

Dendro-Eco Nature Trail, 1 mile: The dual themes of this self-guided trail near the Peshtigo River are dendrology - tree and shrub identification - and ecology. Interpretive signs describe various trees, wildflowers and shrubs, including linden, quaking aspen, maidenhair fern, yellow birch, white spruce, black cherry, witches broom, balsam and jack in the pulpit. Other signs explain holes in the trees, the role of fallen logs, bog plants and tree reproduction.

The trailhead is NE of Laona on Forest Road 2131.

Ed's Lake National Recreation Trail, 6 miles: The trail near Ed's Lake is used by skiers, mountain bikers and hikers. It consists of three loops of rolling terrain with an Adirondack-style shelter overlooking Ed's Lake. The trailhead is on County Highway W between Wabeno and Crandon, near Roberts Lake.

Michigan Rapids Trail, 2 miles: The main feature is Michigan Rapids on the Peshtigo River near Burnt Bridge, along the Peshtigo River Canoe Trail. Hikers can see a porcupine den tree, rock formations, islands and the junction of Armstrong Creek and the Peshtigo. The trail is E of Laona.

Boating & Canoeing

Boats and canoes are common sights at Nicolet, which boasts more than 1,200 lakes and 1,100 miles of trout streams. Lac Vieux Desert is the national forest's biggest lake, as well as the headwaters of the Wisconsin River; the first 2 miles of the Wisconsin flow in Nicolet. For boaters, Wheeler Lake has two Forest Service-owned islands for picnicking and camping.

There are significant seasonal changes on the rivers, so difficulty levels and river conditions vary. April through mid-June are most popular for river canoeing and kayaking. The Wolf and Peshtigo have a reputation for some of the Midwest's best whitewater canoeing. Popular canoe routes are, by ranger district:

Florence Ranger District:

Brule River, *30 miles:* Forest shorelines and marshes offer excellent scenery along the route. A number of streams feed into the river, which features former dam sites, eddies and the appropriately named Two Foot Falls. Access sites include Brule River Campground N of Alvin, Highway 139 on the Wisconsin-Michigan border and Forest Road 2150 (Rainbow Trail).

Pine River, *24 miles:* This state-designated wild river passes the ruins of a sawmill, remnants of a logging dam, frequent wildlife sightings and an old Civilian Conservation Corps camp. There's a

Anglers turn to a canoe and flyrods to fish for bluegills. Nicolet National Forest offers a wide range of opportunities for both fishing and canoeing.

intersections and a shallow rock garden. Portaging is necessary at several spots, including waterfalls. The first access site is on Highway 55. Among others is Chipmunk Rapids Campground, SW of Florence. About 7 miles beyond the forest border, the takeout spot is at Goodman Grade.

Popple River, 16 *miles:* Scenery is wild and undeveloped. Portaging around one set of rapids is recommended. There also are submerged rocks, a rock garden, excellent trout fishing and the remnants of a logging dam. Access points include the Highway 139 Bridge and bridges along Forest Road 2398 and Forest Road 2159.

Lakewood Ranger District
Oconto River, North Branch, 10 *miles:* In part this river is narrow and extremely fast with challenging rapids, but elsewhere it alternates riffles and quiet water as it meanders through pasture land and thickets. Scouting is recommended at several spots, including the Old Krammer dam site and by the Chicago and Northwestern Railroad Bridge. The first access point is Tar Dam Road Bridge, S of Lakewood. The route ends at Chute Pond, less than 2 miles below Bagley Rapids Campground.

Wolf River, 22 *miles:* The Wolf offers a series of rapids, sometimes with large waves. There are boulder beds, ledges and other challenges. One place, Gilmore's Mistake Rapids, was reportedly named for a lumber company scout who mistakenly advised his bosses that the river was too constricted at this spot to transport logs downstream to the mills, a competing company then acquired timber rights to the land upstream, used dynamite to enlarge the passage and reaped a fortune. The annual University of Wisconsin Hoofer's canoe and kayak slalom takes place at Hanson's Rip. Access spots include Hollister, Dierck's Landing, Langlade and the Highway 55 wayside near Markton.

Laona Ranger District
Peshtigo River, 23 *miles:* Although this area was heavily logged in the early 1900s, little development is evident along this forested stretch. There are rapids, an old mill dam site, an old pine

ested stretch. There are rapids, an old mill dam site, an old pine logging dam. oxbows, haystacks, chutes, a boulder field and fallen trees in the channel at spots. Some rapids require intricate maneuvering, and portages around waterfalls are mandatory. You can access the route within Nicolet National Forest at the former Big Joe Campground, CCC Bridge at Ovitz Creek, Burnt Bridge on Forest 2134 and Burton Wells Bridge on Forest Road 2136.

 ## Fishing

Fishing in Nicolet's streams and lakes features trout and panfish, including largemouth and smallmouth bass, brook trout, brown trout and rainbow trout, yellow perch, walleye, bluegill, giant muskellunge and black crappie. Pumpkinseed, northern pike, rock bass and bullhead are also found here.

Although trout are found on dozens of cold-water streams, creeks and rivers, those rated Class 1 include the Popple River, Armstrong, Rock, Spencer, Stoney, Little Popple, Knowles, Indian, Johnson, Gruman, Camp 8, Camp 20, Bills, Battle, the Oconto River and its branches, Pat, Shadow, Snowfalls, Temple, Thunder River, Waupee, Beaver, Blackjack, Brule River, Deerskin River, Jones, Muskrat, Wildcat, Chipmunk, Biller, Lily Pad, Montagne, Woods and Rock.

Lac Vieux Desert, the largest lake in the national forest, offers walleye, muskellunge, northern pike, three types of bass, crappie, yellow perch and pumpkinseed. Other big lakes with a variety of species include Halsey, Butternut, Franklin, Big Fork, Big Sand, Kentuck, North Twin, Archibald, Pine, Wabikon and Hiles Millpond.

 ## Wilderness Areas

Blackjack Springs Wilderness, *5,800 acres:* Within its borders are Blackjack Creek, Goldigger Creek, Whispering Lake and the springs that give this wilderness its name. It's in the Eagle River Ranger District. For access, the wilderness is bordered on two sides by Forest Road 2178 and Highway 70, E of Eagle River.

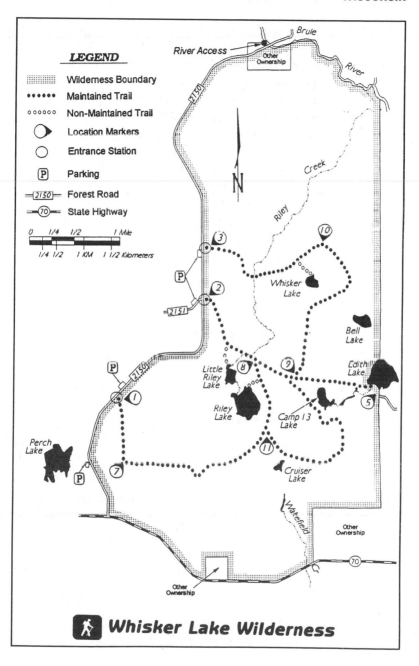

LEGEND

- Wilderness Boundary
- Maintained Trail
- Non-Maintained Trail
- Location Markers
- Entrance Station
- P Parking
- 2150 Forest Road
- 70 State Highway

0   1/4 1/2   1 Mile
1/4 1/2   1 KM   1 1/2 Kilometers

Brule
River Access
Other Ownership
River
Creek
Riley
N
3
10
Whisker Lake
P
2
2151
Bell Lake
P
2150
Little Riley Lake
8
9
Edith Lake
5
Riley Lake
Camp 13 Lake
Perch Lake
P
1
7
11
Cruiser Lake
Wakefield
Other Ownership
70
Other Ownership

🚶 Whisker Lake Wilderness

Headwaters Wilderness, 20,000 acres: Although this area was formerly managed for multiple uses, its upland ridges and lowlands proved to be natural barriers to resource development. The wilderness is made up of three units: Shelp Lake, Kimball Creek and Headwaters of the Pine; it adjoins the Argonne Experimental Forest. The terrain is generally flat and marked by hardwood ridges and muskeg, forested swamp and bog lowlands. Some of Nicolet's oldest and largest trees are found in Giant Pine Grove and near Shelp Lake, both of which are Wisconsin State Research Natural Areas. The wilderness is SE of Eagle River in the Eagle River Ranger District. Forest Roads 2176, 2177, 2174 and 2183 make up part of its borders; Forest Roads 2414 and 2182 cut through it.

Whisker Lake Wilderness, 7,500 acres: This tract in the Florence Ranger District is named for the "Chin Whiskers," large pines along the Whisker Lake shoreline that escaped harvest and early 20th century wildfires. The wilderness encompasses Wakefield Creek and Bell, Edith, Camp 13, Riley, Cruiser and Little Riley lakes. It is W of Florence and borders Michigan's Upper Peninsula. There's canoe access from the Brule River and parking on Forest Road 2150.

 # Natural Areas

Archibald Lake, 100 acres: Acquired through the Nature Conservancy, this area contains one of northeastern Wisconsin's finest stands of old growth timber. Located on the NW shore of Archibald Lake in the Lakewood Ranger District, it has bald eagle habitat; raptor nests and a great blue heron rookery are nearby. Access is from Forest Road 2121.

Bose Lake Hemlock Hardwoods, 29 acres: Although relatively small, this piece of the Eagle River Ranger District is the best remaining virgin stand of mature northern hemlock in Wisconsin, with no evidence of any logging. The central part of the site, between McKinley and Bose lakes, has undisturbed basswood, yellow birch and sugar maple, which have been saved from fire by

Among the intriguing habitats found within the national forest are bogs that feature insect-eating pitcher plants. Hikers can explore a bog from the Franklin Nature Trail.

a large black spruce swamp. It's a National Natural Landmark, as well as part of the state natural area system. Forest Road 2176 provides access.

Historic Attractions

Holt and Balcom Logging Camp No. 1: Decades of time and northern Wisconsin weather have been unkind to the abandoned logging camps of the 19th century; little is left except foundations, debris and legends. However, the Holt and Balcom Logging Camp on McCaslin Brook has been rehabilitated and is believed to be the last of its type in the region. The building was made of white pine logs harvested and peeled on the site; it has bunkhouse and cook-house areas, and a massive cast iron stove. Gone are other buildings including a blacksmith shop, horse barn and warehouse. The camp is on Holts Ranch Road, E of Lakewood in the Lakewood Ranger District.

Military Road: Now part of Heritage Drive Scenic Byway in the Eagle River Ranger District, this road was built between 1864 and 1870 to connect Fort Howard on Green Bay and Fort Wilkins on Lake Superior. It followed an Indian trail to the copper mines of Michigan's Upper Peninsula and was later used by settlers, fur traders and cattle drovers. When the federal government proposed it as a route for soldiers and military supplies, the aim was to have a back-up in case the water route between Michigan and Wisconsin was cut off. However, it never was used for military purposes.

Franklin Lake Campground: This campground was built by the Civilian Conservation Corps, Works Progress Administration and Forest Service and is listed on the National Register of Historic Places. The buildings were made of logs and fieldstones. Surviving buildings include the shelter and bathhouse built into a hillside slope, caretaker's dwelling, well and pump house and several comfort stations. Their rustic style was inspired by the 19th-century resort architecture of Adirondack Mountain resorts. The campground is E of Eagle River on Forest Road 2181 in the Eagle

River Ranger District.

Treaty Tree: In 1840, Chippewa Chief Ca-sha-o-sha and Capt. T. J. Cram approved a treaty allowing Cram, his companions and future surveyors to pass through Chippewa territory. The remains of a tamarack near the headwaters of the Brule River mark the treaty spot where Cram gave the Chippewa tobacco and other gifts. The site is NW of Alvin in the Eagle River Ranger District.

Rosen Dam Site: A flush dam was built here in the 1880s so loggers could store water to float their logs to sawmills downstream. The dam no longer stands, but a symmetrical pattern of hewn timbers and rock rubble remains visible at the bottom of Brule Creek. The site is on Forest Road 2200 (Rosen Dam Road) in the Eagle River Ranger District.

Thunder Lake Narrow Gauge Railroad Site: An historic marker tells about the railroad that operated here from 1919 to 1941, transporting harvested logs to the mills. An estimated 250 million board feet of pulpwood, logs, posts and pilings passed this point during that period. A remnant of a railroad bed and grade can still be seen. The marker is on Forest Road 2182, SE of Eagle River in the Headwaters Wilderness Area.

Fisher Reintroduction Marker: A marker commemorates the successful 1963 reintroduction of the fisher, a fur-bearing member of the weasel family, into Nicolet National Forest by the Forest Service and state conservation departments of Wisconsin, Minnesota and New York. The sign is on Forest Road 2178, E of Three Lakes in the Eagle River Ranger District.

More Things To Do & See

Birding: From bald eagles to loons to great blue herons to songbirds, Nicolet is home to hundreds of bird species, from the breathtaking to the familiar. Red-tailed hawks, red-shouldered hawks and northern goshawks are found here, along with a huge variety of owls, waterfowl, sandpipers, blackbirds, warblers and woodpeckers. Walking along the mile-long Halley Creek Bird Trail, it's possible to spot a variety of birds including osprey, wood

IN THE FOREST
Passport In Time
At Pat Shay Lake

By Kim Potaracke

During cold, windy and damp weather, this crew of amateur archaeologists steadily troweled in their excavation units as the rains pitter-pattered against the tarps over them. Intrepid visitors in galoshes and rain slickers were treated to the sight of a crew of busy bees.

We found evidence of human habitation and recovered a few stone tools, including scrapers, wedges and a projectile point. Quartz and chert flakes indicate a tool manufacturing site. We found small flattened fragments of copper, as well as a copper awl and a bead. In five of our nine test excavation units, we found pieces of broken pottery, some decorated with cord impressions, some with interior brush marks and others with a plain surface, all bound with grit. Based on artifacts found to date, Indians probably occupied the site for the last 2,000 years. Radiocarbon-dated charcoal samples will give us more specific occupation dates, and soil samples will help us reconstruct the environment.

While Pat Shay Lake has been harvested for wild rice, the explosion in the beaver population over the past few decades caused the water levels to rise, destroying the rice. Recent reseeding efforts seem to be working. The lake was probably used as a harvesting and processing area in earlier times. The many depressions may have served as ricing or jigging pits to facilitate husk removal after the rice had been parched. Soil samples will tell us if our hypothesis is accurate.

pewees, red-breasted nuthatches, sparrows, vireos, ovenbirds, pine warblers, finches and tree swallows.

Franklin Lake Interpretive Center: Exhibits explain the geological history of northern Wisconsin and the peoples who have lived in the area. The center is housed in a building erected by the Civilian Conservation Corps from glacial stones in 1937. It is on Forest Road 2181, E of Eagle River at Franklin Lake Campground.

Heritage Drive Scenic Byway, 15 miles: The byway follows a traditional Native American route and the 19th-century Military Road between the Keweenaw Peninsula on Lake Superior and Green Bay on Lake Michigan. It runs near two wilderness areas, Headwaters and Blackjack Springs, with developed camping at nearby Sevenmile Lake. Visitors can see jack pine stands planted during the Depression by the CCC, the giant trees of Hemlock Haven and the site of a 1986 forest fire. The Eagle River Ranger District route is made up of Forest Road 2178 (known as Military Road) and Forest Road 2181.

Chili Ski-In: This is an annual event for cross-country skiers, from novice to expert, along the Lauterman National Recreation Trail. For more information, contact Florence Resource Center, HC1, Box 83, Florence, WI 54121; ☎ (715) 528-5377.

General MacArthur White Pine: In 1945, this tree was determined to be the largest white pine then known in the United States. An estimated 400-plus years old and 148 feet tall at the time, it was named in honor of World War II Gen. Douglas MacArthur. The tree is NE of Hiles on Forest Road 2167 in the Eagle River Ranger District.

Laona Hostel: This American Youth Hostel facility in the Laona Ranger District offers inexpensive dormitory sleeping rooms, kitchen facilities and group activities including cross-country skiing, rafting and biking. For more information, contact Laona Hostel, 5397 Beech St., Laona, WI 54541; ☎ (715) 674-2615.

Lakewood Auto Tour, 65 miles: Sites along the Lakewood Ranger District route include Cathedral Pines with its great blue heron nests, Jones Spring Non-motorized Area, Oconto River seed

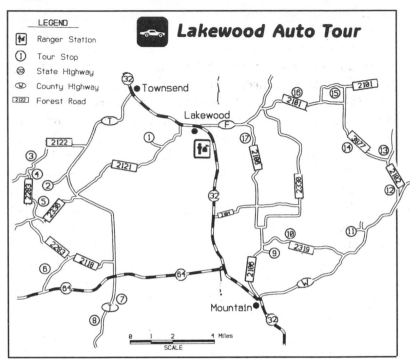

orchard, 1934 Mountain fire tower and Waupee Flowage, where bald eagles feed and osprey nest. Among the other stops are pine plantation, jack pine clearcut, Holt & Balcom logging camp, McCaslin Brook Ruffed Grouse and Woodcock Management Area and Forbes Spring, which forms the headwaters of Forbes Creek.

Last Ditch Slalom Race: This canoe and kayak slalom race is held each fall at the aptly named Gilmore's Mistake Rapids on the Wolf River. For more information, contact Green Bay Paddlers United, c/o 724 Cross Road, Sobieski, WI 54171; ☎ (414) 822-5876.

Naturalist Programs: Summer nature programs and classes are offered at Franklin Lake Campground in the Eagle River Ranger District. Typical topics deal with wildlife, such as eagles, wolves, wildflowers, bats, birds of prey and snakes. Winter and spring programs such as tracking workshops, snowshoe hikes and bird walks also are available.

Nicolet Wheel-A-Way: This annual bicycle tour through the national forest features three loops of 30, 41 and 52 miles for both road bikes and mountain bikes. The route follows winding, scenic roads and leads through Headwaters Wilderness in the Eagle River Ranger District. The September event begins and ends at Three Lakes Recreation Park. Helmets are required. For information, contact Three Lakes Information Bureau, Box 268, Three Lakes, WI 54562; ☎ (800) 972-6103 or (715) 546-3344.

Passport in Time Program: PIT participants have worked on an archaeological study of the Violet Road Site on the Oconto River. The site is believed to represent a Woodland Tradition food processing and hunting encampment from the first few hundred years A.D. Violet Road's logging era legacy is also under study.

At a second PIT site, Pat Shay Lake, pottery shards and broken stone tools from about the first 1,000 years A.D. have been found. Historic properties open houses also are held.

Picnicking & Swimming: In addition to picnic and swimming facilities open to non-campers at many campgrounds, beaches and picnicking are available at the Bass Lake and Green Lake recreation sites. Both have boat access and fishing.

Self-Guided Natural History Auto Tour, 80 miles: The route between Eagle River and Three Lakes passes the headwaters of the Wisconsin River, 1938 Military Hill fire tower, Rosen Dam site, Military Road, Franklin Lake nature trail, Headwaters Wilderness and Thunder Lake Narrow Gauge Railroad marker in the Eagle River Ranger District. The tour crosses the Eastern Continental Divide, where waters flow E toward the St. Lawrence Seaway and W toward the Mississippi.

Ranger Districts

Eagle River: Box 1809, Eagle River, WI 54521; ☎ (715) 479-2827.

Florence: HC 1, Box 83, Florence, WI 54121; ☎ (715) 528-4464.

Lakewood: 15085 Hwy. 32, Lakewood, WI 54138; ☎ (715) 276-6333.

Laona: Rt. 1, Box 11-B, Laona, WI 54138; ☎ (715) 674-4481.

Gateways

Crandon: Crandon Chamber of Commerce, 300 S. Lake Ave., Crandon, WI 54520; ☎ (715) 478-3450.

Eagle River: Eagle River Chamber of Commerce, 130 S. Railroad, Eagle River, WI 54521; ☎ (715) 479-8575.

Florence: Florence Chamber of Commerce, 501 Lake Ave., Florence, WI 54121; ☎ (715) 528-3201.

Lakewood: Lakewood Chamber of Commerce, Box 87, Lakewood, WI 54138; ☎ (715) 276-6500.

Rhinelander: Rhinelander Chamber of Commerce, City Hall, Rhinelander, WI 54501; ☎ (715) 362-7464.

Three Lakes: Three Lakes Information Bureau, Box 268, Three Lakes, WI 54562; ☎ (800) 972-6103 or (715) 546-3344.

ILLINOIS

Shawnee National Forest

Among the popular species anglers target in the lakes and rivers of Shawnee National Forest are largemouth bass.

SHAWNEE

901 S. Commercial St.   265,300 acres
Harrisburg, IL 62946
☎ (618) 253-7114 or (800) 699-6637

Illinois' only national forest is a land of caves and woods, rock formations and scenic vistas, water and wildflowers, and trails and campgrounds set in the 300-million-year-old Shawnee Hills. Although the names of the Mississippi and Ohio rivers are well-known, other waters carry such unfamiliar but intriguing names as Big Muddy River, Big Grande Pierre Creek, Lake of Egypt and Devils Kitchen Lake.

The sandstone formations and bluffs of Garden of the Gods, one of seven wilderness areas, are a major natural attraction. Human history also shaped Shawnee: prehistoric and Native American settlements; iron production before, during and after the Civil War; river pirates; mining of zinc, lead, fluorspar and clay; George Rogers Clark's expedition; and Civilian Conservation Corps camps. The Trail of Tears - the federal government's forced relocation march of the Cherokee to western reservations in 1838 - passed through here.

Shawnee was designated a national forest in 1939. The government acquired most of the land within its borders before World War II, during difficult economic times in southern Illinois.

137

Camping

Shawnee has more than 400 sites at a variety of developed camping areas. Nature trails are located at several, including Pharaoh, Tower Rock and Camp Cadiz. The improved campgrounds, number of sites and their locations are, by ranger district:

Elizabethtown Ranger District

Camp Cadiz (11), 4 miles E of Karbers Ridge on County Road 7;

Pharaoh (12), 4 miles NW of Karbers Ridge on Karbers Ridge Blacktop (Forest Highway 17) in Garden of the Gods Recreation Area;

Pine Ridge (76), 4 miles E of Karbers Ridge on Karbers Ridge Blacktop (Forest Highway 17) in Pounds Hollow Recreation Area;

Tower Rock (24), 4 miles NE of Elizabethtown on Forest Road 575.

Jonesboro Ranger District

Grapevine Trail (6), 5 miles SE of McClure on Grapevine Trail Road;

Pine Hills (12), 2 miles NE of Wolf Lake on Forest Road 236.

Murphysboro Ranger District

Johnson Creek (75), 14 miles NW of Murphysboro on Route 151;

Turkey Bayou (17), 15 miles SW of Murphysboro on Forest Road 786.

Vienna Ranger District

Buck Ridge (41), 6 miles SW of Creal Springs on Forest Road 871 in Lake of Egypt Recreation Area;

Oak Point (74), 21 miles S of Mitchellsville on Route 145 in Lake Glendale Recreation Area;

Red Bud (21), 8 miles NW of Eddyville on Forest Road 848 in Bell Springs Recreation Area;

Teal Pond (10), 6 miles NW of Eddyville on Forest Road 447 in Bell Springs Recreation Area.

Group camping is available at Bailey Place Campground, in the Vienna Ranger District, 21 miles S of Mitchellsville on Route 145 in Lake Glendale Recreation Area.

 ## Trails

There are more than 1,250 miles of dirt, paved, gravel and grass trails and roads within Shawnee, all used by hikers and most open to horseback riders. Some are also open to mountain bikes and motorized off-road vehicles.

The River-to-River Trail is the longest in the national forest and traverses ranger district borders. This popular horseback riding trail joins the Mississippi and Ohio rivers between Battery Rock and Grand Tower. Eighty of its 140 miles go through the national forest. It passes through Shawnee and state land near Garden of the Gods, Lusk Creek Canyon, Ferne Clyffe, Cedar Lake and Giant City.

Other popular trails are:

Elizabethtown Ranger District

Beaver Trail, 7 miles: The trail connects Camp Cadiz with Rim Rock National Recreation Trail. The access site is E of Karbers Ridge on County Road 7.

Cave Hill Trail, 3 miles: A loop trail, it starts within the boundary of the Saline County Conservation Area and enters Shawnee National Forest. The trailhead is NW of Glen O. Jones Lake on Forest Road 1450.

Garden of the Gods Observation Trail, 1 mile: A flagstone walk offers views of the sandstone bluffs. Access is NW of Karbers Ridge on Forest Road 114.

Garden of the Gods Trail System, 8 miles: This network of interconnecting trails lies within Garden of the Gods Wilderness. The trails provide access to a number of imposing stone formations, including Camel Rock, Shelter Rock, Anvil Rock, Noah's Ark, Big H, Mushroom Rock and Indian Point. The trail system is accessible from Garden of the Gods Recreation Area, NW of Karbers Ridge on Forest Road 114.

**Rim Rock
Recreation Area**

High Knob, 5 miles: This network of small interconnecting loops is accessible from the High Knob Observation Area. The trailhead is N of Karbers Ridge on Forest Road 114.

One Horse Gap Trail System, 10 miles: These trails wind through narrow rock outcroppings and pass unusual rock formations. One Horse Gap Lake provides a peaceful backdrop to the trail experience. Pick it up NW of Elizabethtown on Forest Road 126.

Rim Rock National Recreation Trail, 1 mile: The trail winds through a cedar plantation and hardwood forest, passing the remains of an Indian wall and along the Rim Rock escarpment. A stairway along the trail leads to Ox-Lot Cave, where 19th-century loggers built a fence to keep their horses and oxen in; the animals were watered from a natural spring. It's at Pounds Hollow Recreation Area, S of Harrisburg on Karbers Ridge Blacktop (Forest Highway 17).

Jonesboro Ranger District

Inspiration Point Forest Trail, 1 mile: It follows narrow, dry ridges along exposed limestone bluffs to deep, cool valleys. Inspiration Point provides a vista of the Missouri Ozarks, LaRue Scenic Area and Mississippi Valley farmlands. Inspiration point offers one of the best views in southern Illinois. Access is N of Jonesboro along Pine Hills Scenic Drive (Forest Road 236).

Murphysboro Ranger District

Cedar Lake Trail, 8 miles: It runs along the W half of Cedar Lake and loops around Little Cedar Lake. The trailhead is S of Murphysboro; follow the hiking signs from Route 127.

Green Tree Reservoir Interpretive Trail, 1 mile: This nature trail crosses through part of Green Tree Reservoir, circles a pond and has an elevated boardwalk. The trailhead is SW of Murphysboro on Forest Road 786.

Kinkaid Lake Trail, 20 miles: The trail winds around the SW part of Kinkaid Lake, NW of Murphysboro, and passes numerous wildlife openings and Buttermilk Hill beach along the way. Access is available from Highway 151 Trailhead, Buttermilk Hill Trailhead, Buttermilk Hill beach and State Trailhead.

Little Grand Canyon National Recreation Trail, 4 miles: The loop provides views of Oakwood Bottoms, the Big Muddy River and the canyon nicknamed "Hanging Gardens of Egypt." The trailhead is SW of Murphysboro on Forest Highway 25.

Pomona Natural Bridge Trail, 1 mile: This short trail leads to Pomona Natural Bridge, a natural formation that stretches 25 feet high and 90 feet wide. It's S of Murphysboro, with parking on Forest Road 750.

Vienna Ranger District

Bell Smith Springs, 8 miles: This system of interconnected trails is in a scenic and ecologically diverse natural area. You'll see wild cactus, natural springs and sandstone bluffs. The trailhead is SW of Harrisburg on Forest Road 848.

Burden Falls Trail, *1 mile*: A short trail begins at Burden Falls, a waterfall, and winds its way into the Burden Falls Wilderness. The trailhead is on Forest Road 402, SW of Harrisburg.

Millstone Bluff Trail, *1 mile*: This interpretive trail highlights the area's prehistoric heritage. Along the way are prehistoric Native American petroglyphs, a stone wall, cemetery and remains of a village. The trailhead is on Forest Road 532, NE of Vienna.

Signal Point Trail, *3 miles*: It starts in Lake Glendale Recreation Area and loops below and above the bluff line. Reach it along Highway 145, S of Harrisburg.

 # Boating & Canoeing

Although there are 150 miles of streams in the national forest, river canoeing opportunities are limited. Portions of the Big Muddy River, Hutchins Creek, Bay Creek, Big Creek, Big Grand Pierre Creek and Lusk Creek are under study for possible inclusion in the National Wild and Scenic Rivers program. Boating opportunities range from small ponds to lakes more than 2,000 acres large. Boat rentals are available at Pounds Hollow Lake in Pounds Hollow Recreation Area and at Lake Glendale Beach in the Lake Glendale Recreation Area.

Here are two canoe routes:

Murphysboro Ranger District

Big Muddy River, *15 miles*: This appropriately named river meanders without rapids through farm and forest country, passing the Little Grand Canyon and LaRue-Pine Hills natural areas SW of Murphysboro. It's seasonally changeable, but the water is of poor quality. The Big Muddy boat launch is on Forest Road 786, E of the Oakwood Bottoms Interpretive Site.

Vienna Ranger District

Lusk Creek, *20 miles*: The lower reaches of this river, NW of Golconda, are seasonally changeable because of backwater from the Smithland Dam. However, it can become a bit dangerous in the spring. Expect frequent obstacles such as fences and log jams. Canoe access points are at Rose Ford on Forest Road 425, Manson Ford at the end of Forest Road 420, and along Forest Road 488.

 ## Fishing

Largemouth, striped, hybrid striped and Kentucky spotted bass, rainbow trout, channel and flathead catfish, bluegill, white and yellow bass, redear sunfish and crappie are found in Shawnee's lakes and streams. So are walleyed pike, bullhead, grass pickerel, sunfish and sauger.

If you fish the national forest's three biggest lakes, you'll find largemouth bass, sunfish, channel catfish, trout, muskie and walleye in Kinkaid Lake; largemouth bass, crappie, channel catfish, bullheads, bluegill and redear sunfish in Cedar Lake; and largemouth bass, crappie, sunfish and channel catfish in Lake of Egypt. Other fishing spots with good public access include Dutchman Lake for largemouth bass, bluegill, redear sunfish, crappie, carp, bullhead and channel catfish; Lake Glendale for bluegill, largemouth bass, channel catfish, redear sunfish and crappie; Little Cache #1 for largemouth bass, channel catfish, sunfish and crappie; One Horse Gap Lake for largemouth and smallmouth bass, sunfish and channel catfish; and Pounds Hollow for catfish, bluegill and largemouth bass.

 ## Wilderness Areas

Bald Knob, *5,918 acres:* This wilderness contains rugged terrain with narrow ridgetops, steep slopes and narrow creek bottoms. Remains of small farms and abandoned homesteads are visible here, as well as old logging trails. It's in the Jonesboro Ranger District, SW of Carbondale. Access is on County Road 31.

Bay Creek, *2,866 acres:* Separated by a gravel road from Burden Falls Wilderness, it has moderately steep topography and canyon-like sandstone valleys. It's in the Vienna Ranger District, NW of Eddyville, with access on Forest Road 402.

Burden Falls, *3,683 acres:* This area is home to crayfish and sandstone-walled valleys; the sandstone is colored by iron oxide deposits that form swirls of brown and red. The wilderness adjoins Bay Creek Wilderness and is NW of Eddyville along Forest Road 402 in the Vienna Ranger District.

Clear Springs, 4,730 acres: This wilderness area SW of Carbondale has steep slopes and evidence of former homesteads. Abandoned roads and logging trails wind through the ravines and ridgetops. It's in the Murphysboro Ranger District with access on Forest Road 236.

Garden of the Gods, 3,293 acres: Glacial melt formed what botanist Robert H. Mohlenbrock describes as a "fairyland of rock formations" with such names as Monkey-face Rock, Big H and Mushroom Rock. Weathering and erosion produced cliffs, overhanging rock shelters and caves. The only type of wild cactus found in southern Illinois, prickly pear, grows here. Farkleberry is the predominant shrub and blackjack oak, post oak and red cedar are the predominant trees.

The adjoining Garden of the Gods Recreation Area has camping, picnic grounds and several other formations, such as Anvil Rock and Camel Rock. It's in the Elizabethtown Ranger District, NW of Karbers Ridge on Karbers Ridge Blacktop (Forest Highway 17).

Lusk Creek, 4,466 acres: Rugged topography with numerous sandstone outcroppings and boulders characterize this wilderness area. The 730-acre Lusk Creek Canyon National Natural Landmark lies within its borders; it contains a winding gorge-like valley with vertical sandstone bluffs and steep slopes. It's along County Highway 126, S of Harrisburg in the Vienna Ranger District.

Panther Den, 685 acres: Steep canyon walls were carved by creeks draining northward into Devil's Kitchen Lake. French's shooting star is among the wildflowers found here. Adjoining the wilderness is the U.S. Fish and Wildlife Service's Crab Orchard Wilderness. It's in the Murphysboro Ranger District, SE of Carbondale. Access is on Forest Road 749.

Ripple Hollow, 3,711 acres: This area has been conditionally

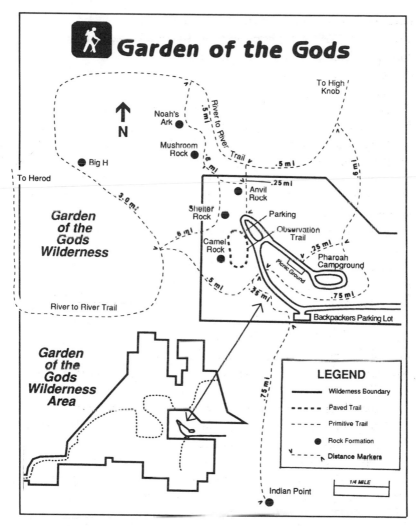

Garden of the Gods

recommended for wilderness study, subject to Forest Service acquisition of privately owned mineral rights. It's on Forest Road 290, S of Jonesboro in the Jonesboro Ranger District.

In addition, *Eagle Creek* (722 acres) adjacent to Garden of the Gods Wilderness, and *East Fork* (1,962 acres) adjacent to Lusk Creek Wilderness, are special management areas that are treated as wilderness except for mineral exploration and mining; depending on whether or not economically significant deposits of fluorspar are found, both areas will become wildernesses by 2010. Eagle Creek is in the Elizabethtown Ranger District, NW of Karbers Ridge; East Fork is in the Vienna Ranger District, S of Harrisburg.

Natural Areas

Atwood Ridge Research Natural Area, 955 acres: Dry upland forest with rock chestnut oak, which is a threatened species in Illinois, characterize this environmentally significant area. It contains a deeply dissected system of narrow ridges as well as deep valleys and major bluff outcroppings that overlook the scenic Mississippi River lowlands. Although a few prairie openings remain, most are under a natural form of invasion by sassafras, dogwoods and redbud. The natural area is SW of Jonesboro in the Jonesboro Ranger District.

Barker Bluff Research Natural Area, 60 acres: It holds the last remnant of what was once the largest continuous limestone glade system in the state. However, some scattered, undisturbed glades are left, with such plants as little bluestem, tall dropseed, drooping coneflower, flowering spurge, American agave and white prairie clover. It's in the Elizabethtown Ranger District, NE of Cave-In-Rock.

Bell Smith Springs, 1,260 acres: A now-dry stream carved a 30-foot-high natural bridge here, in an area of natural springs, sandstone bluffs, and canyons forested in oaks, beech, tulip poplars and hickories. There are prickly pear - the only type of wild cactus in southern Illinois - and alluringly named plants such as goat's rue, wild petunia, rushfoil, flower-of-an-hour, pinweed, Saint Johnswort, purple oxalis, Quaker-ladies, six-weeks fescue and Saint Andrew's cross. A National Natural Landmark, Bell Smith Springs contains the largest natural red cedar stand in southern Illinois. It's SW of Harrisburg in the Vienna Ranger District.

Burke Branch Research Natural Area, 300 acres: Burke

Branch and two of its small tributaries cut through this designated botanical area in the Vienna Ranger District S of Golconda. There are steep, rocky slopes with dry upland forest and dry mesic forest. Some of the best-known remnants of mesic barrens in Illinois lie along the Burke Branch flood plain.

Cave Hill Research Natural Area, 465 acres: Cave Hill, a sandstone-capped mountain with underlying limestone outcroppings near its base, towers over the Saline River lowlands and slope forest. An extensive but vandalized maze cave has several miles of passages under a single ridge; it's called Equality Cave or Cave Hill Cave. A relatively undisturbed dry upland forest includes post oak, black hickory, pignut hickory and black oak. The research area is in the Elizabethtown Ranger District, N of Herod.

Cave Valley/Cedar Creek, 1,700 acres: This non-game bird management area protects the endangered Swainson's warbler and other species. Dense bottomland hardwood forest and ridges with pine, oak and hickory are havens for breeding songbirds. It's S of Murphysboro in the Murphysboro Ranger District.

Dennison Hollow Research Natural Area, 205 acres: This Elizabethtown Ranger District site contains a high quality upland forest with rock chestnut oaks, an Illinois-threatened species. There is a shale glade rare for the Shawnee Hills and relatively undisturbed sandstone cliffs. The research area is N of Herod.

Grantsburg Swamp, 751 acres: Within this swamp are trees as varied as pumpkin ash, tupelo gum and swamp cottonwood while turkey vultures and black vultures can be seen roosting atop low sandstone cliffs. Poisonous water moccasins, copperheads and cottonmouths also live here.

And, as Robert H. Mohlenbrock notes in Natural History magazine, "From mid-April to the first frost in October, mosquitoes are an ever-present nuisance, particularly at dawn, dusk and on cloudy days. Twelve of the 60 species of mosquitoes recorded in Illinois have been found in Grantsburg Swamp."

The area is S of Simpson in the Vienna Ranger District.

LaRue-Pine Hills/Otter Pond Research Natural Area,

The Garden of the Gods Wilderness Area in Shawnee National Forest (Southern Illinois Tourism Council photo).

2,811 acres: This National Natural Landmark has more plant species than any comparable Midwest site. It includes 11 forest cover types, eight high-quality natural communities and 1,300 types of flowering plants, including pink azaleas, bird's-foot violet, swamp iris and Boott's goldenrod. Cliffs of Bailey limestone are found here, as are heavily forested coves and more than three dozen threatened or endangered plant and animal species. Migratory birds along the Mississippi Flyway use it, too. Clear springs from the base of limestone cliffs are home to the blind Ozark spring cave fish and feed LaRue Swamp, the remains of an ancient oxbow of the Big Muddy River. Within the research natural area, 2,000 acres are a designated ecological area. It is in the Jonesboro Ranger

District, NW of Wolf Lake.

Little Grand Canyon Area, *1,372 acres:* A National Natural Landmark dubbed the "Hanging Gardens of Egypt," it boasts a variety of ecosystems including hill prairies, wetland oak-hickory forests and bottomlands of the Big Muddy River and Cedar Creek. The sandstone box canyon with its vertical overhanging walls is a mile long, reaches 600 feet in width and is a haven for snakes. It's in the Murphysboro Ranger District, SW of Murphysboro.

Lusk Creek Canyon, *730 acres:* This gorge-like, winding valley has sandstone bluffs and steep slopes, with a maple-beech-tulip poplar forest along the stream terraces and a hickory-oak forest on the slopes. Fish, plants and insects are diverse; 10 plant species are endangered or threatened. A registered National Natural Landmark within the Lusk Creek Wilderness, it's in the Vienna Ranger District, S of Harrisburg.

Oakwood Bottoms Greentree Reservoir, *3,400 acres:* This is the only green tree reservoir in Illinois. Parts of this oak forest flood from October to February, providing shelter and food for uplands animals and for migrating and wintering waterfowl, especially mallards and wood ducks. It's SW of Murphysboro in the Murphysboro Ranger District.

Ozark Hill Prairies Research Natural Area, *535 acres:* Located in the Jonesboro Ranger District SW of Jonesboro, the site is marked by a diversity of habitats and rugged terrain. Small, undisturbed loess hill prairies dominated by Indian grass and little bluestem are interspersed with dry forest. It portrays a representative forest and prairie ecosystem of the Ozark Hills.

Panther Hollow Botanical Area, *180 acres:* Panther Hollow and Buckhart Hollow are sandstone canyons formed by major tributaries of Cane Creek. Overall, its sandstone cliffs and glade, dry upland forest and dry mesic ravine forest communities are typical of the Greater Shawnee Hills. Four endangered or threatened plant species are found in Panther Hollow, within the Elizabethtown Ranger District, NE of Cave-In-Rock.

Simpson Township Barrens, *65 acres:* More than 200 plant

IN THE FOREST
Little Grand Canyon
and Johnson Creek

Narrow, winding roads sided with Queen Anne's lace and orange day lilies lead to Little Grand Canyon, where a 3.6-mile hiking trail winds its way into one of Shawnee National Forest's hidden treasures. On route to the trailhead, the rolling farmlands outside Murphysboro give no hint of the different world that lies ahead.

I arrived on a humid midday, the temperature in the mid-90s, with tree-filtered sunlight dappling the steep trail. Although a butterfly darted 5 feet ahead of me, it was a medley of sounds rather than sights that initially grabbed my attention - the jackhammering of an unseen woodpecker, the croaking of frogs and the buzzing of an iridescent green fly that followed me down the path.

The 1,023-acre Little Grand Canyon is a designated National Natural Landmark with habitats that range from hill prairies and wetlands to oak-hickory forests and the bottomlands of the Big Muddy River and Cedar Creek. However, you needn't be a biologist or geologist to enjoy what's been called the "Hanging Gardens of Egypt." Simply explore the setting: the looming cliffs of Swallow Rock and Chalk Bluff, fallen trees, a meandering nearly-dry stream bed and a brilliant red male cardinal perched trailside. The area's well-known for its snakes, but I didn't spot any.

Suddenly I stopped as I first glimpsed the erosion-carved box canyon from above. *Danger High Cliffs!*, a wooden sign at the overlook cautioned. *Please stay on the trail.* I did.

I crossed paths with only a handful of other hikers — a pair of women with daypacks, then a father with two children and an adventuresome German shepherd that disappeared into the

woods, forcing its owner to set out in chase.

The hike over, I rested at the small trailhead picnic area, enjoying the black-eyed susans and the shade.

Then for a change of pace, I headed for Johnson Creek Recreation Area south of Ava. If Little Grand Canyon represents serenity, Johnson Creek represents activity. Dozens of power boats were on Kinkaid Lake, with others waiting their turn at the public launch. A few anglers, undaunted by the afternoon heat, fished for bass, muskie and walleye.

Kids and adults swam at the beach, played along a sandy strip of land or watched the boats and the swimmers from the grass. Other folks grilled their lunches by the picnic tables under the pines.

Developed campsites at Johnson Creek are relatively private, not directly across from each other; some sites are earmarked for horseback riders. Campers seeking more solitude can cross an arched wooden footbridge over Johnson Creek and hike into campsites.

Smokey Bear Lake, a small pond actually, adds a nice touch to the Johnson Creek Recreation Area's campground. You can fish for bluegills, channel catfish and largemouth bass.

For company, there's the sound of crickets.

species have been found in a prairie-like environment that's promoted by selective trimming of trees and controlled burning. Among them are Mead's sedge, bird's-foot violet, butterfly milkweed, purple coneflower, showy rudbeckia, prairie rosinweeds, sunflowers, evening primrose and the endangered Enslen's blackberry. It is part of the Vienna Ranger District, NE of Vienna.

Stoneface Research Natural Area, 176 acres: The area is marked by high sandstone bluffs, including Old Stone Face sandstone formation, a popular hikers' destination. Rock-laden intermittent streams run through the ravines, and blackened scars on gnarled hickories and oaks testify that fire once was prevalent here. It's N of Herod in the Elizabethtown Ranger District.

Whoopie Cat Mountain Research Natural Area, 17 acres: High-quality limestone glades, the Illinois-endangered coral-root orchid and a rare orange coneflower grow in this research area. Some long-lived survivors from the original forest have been identified, including a chinquapin oak more than 400 years old and a post oak more than 575 years old. It's in the Elizabethtown Ranger District, N of Elizabethtown.

Historic Attractions

Camp Cadiz: Remnants of a Depression-era Civilian Conservation Corps camp can be seen at what is now an 11-site campground in the Elizabethtown Ranger District. It's E of Karbers Ridge on County Road 7.

DAR Monument: Bronze plaques on a stone monument commemorate the 1920s cooperation between the Daughters of the American Revolution and the Forest Service. Together, they participated in a shortleaf pine and black locust reforestation project.

Illinois Iron Furnace: Illinois' first charcoal-fired iron furnace operated here from 1839-1883, producing pig iron for U.S. Navy use. It was rebuilt and restored in 1967. There's a half-mile trail and an interpretive display at the site on Forest Road 141, NW of Elizabethtown in the Elizabethtown Ranger District.

Millstone Bluff: The interpretive trail at this National Register of Historic Places site focuses on the region's Native American heritage. There are petroglyphs, a cemetery, a stone wall and other evidence of a Mississippian settlement. The site is on Forest Road 532, NE of Vienna in the Vienna Ranger District.

Great Salt Springs: For hundreds of years, prehistoric Native Americans and early American entrepreneurs made salt at this spot on the Saline River. Reach it along Forest Road 108, W of Shawneetown in the Elizabethtown Ranger District.

More Things To Do & See

Bicycling: U.S. Bike Route 76 Trail between Carbondale and Cave-in-Rock State Park cuts through the heart of Shawnee, past rivers, parks, lakes and historic sites. Two popular long-distance road bike routes pass through the forest: Big River Rendezvous Trail and Cairo Bicycle Trail.

A number of forest roads and trails are suitable for mountain biking, including Whoopie Cat, One Horse Gap, High Knob and Harris Creek in the Elizabethtown Ranger District; Trigg Tower and Burke Branch in the Vienna Ranger District; Opossum Trot, Horse Creek and Harris Creek in the Jonesboro Ranger District; and Kinkaid Lake and Little Grand Canyon in the Murphysboro Ranger District. Some roads near natural areas are closed to bicycling.

Birding: More than 237 species of birds have been spotted in Shawnee, some of them endangered. Among the birds found here are red-throated and common loons; snowy and great egrets; green and great blue herons; turkey and black vultures; red-tailed and Cooper's hawks; least and upland sandpipers; mourning and rock doves; screech and barred owls; yellow-bellied and great crested flycatchers; Carolina and short-billed marsh wrens; warbling and red-eyed vireos; Tennessee and yellow warblers; and Swainson's and hermit thrushes.

Horseback riding: Horses are allowed on all hiking routes unless posted otherwise. They can be watered at creeks, springs and wildlife ponds found along the trails and unpaved forest roads.

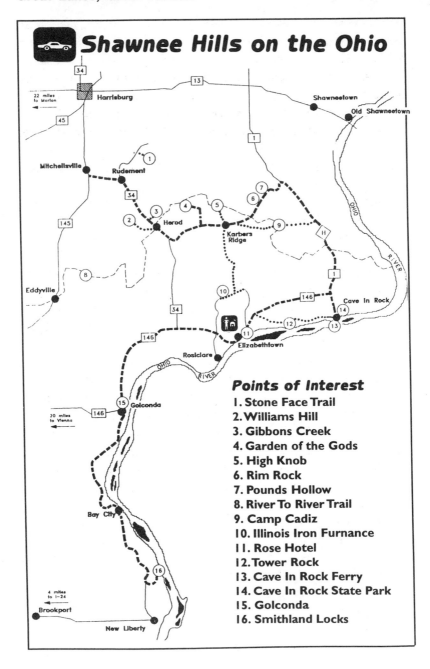

Shawnee Hills on the Ohio

Points of Interest

1. Stone Face Trail
2. Williams Hill
3. Gibbons Creek
4. Garden of the Gods
5. High Knob
6. Rim Rock
7. Pounds Hollow
8. River To River Trail
9. Camp Cadiz
10. Illinois Iron Furnace
11. Rose Hotel
12. Tower Rock
13. Cave In Rock Ferry
14. Cave In Rock State Park
15. Golconda
16. Smithland Locks

154

Horses are not allowed in developed recreation areas such as beaches and picnic areas; camping for horseback riders is available at Camp Cadiz and Johnson Creek campgrounds in the national forest and in state, municipal and private facilities outside Shawnee's borders.

Oakwoods Bottom Interpretive Site: Interpretive signs describe the wetlands' natural history at this prime waterfowl site. There are picnic facilities, a wheelchair-accessible circular boardwalk and fishing platforms. It's SW of Murphysboro on Forest Road 786 in the Murphysboro Ranger District.

Mushroom Gathering: Black morels, yellow morels and grey (or white) morels are generally gathered during a two-week season in early to mid-April. They are most often found near ash trees and dying elms.

Observation Points: Seven scenic observation points are accessible from Pine Hills Scenic Drive (Forest Road 236), NW of Jonesboro in the Jonesboro Ranger District. They are McGee Hill, Crooked Tree Trail, Pine Ridge, Saddle Hill, Government Rock, Old Trail Point and Inspiration Point.

Passport in Time Program: Excavations have taken place at a 1,200-year-old Late Woodland stone fort. A wall of earth and rock extending more than 6 feet deep and built on a "stone pavement" of a plate-like rock setting was found here. Other Middle (300 B.C. to 400 A.D.) and Late (400-900 A.D.). Woodland artifacts have been discovered near the habitation area.

At Dillow's Ridge, another PIT site, volunteers have helped excavate house remains from a Mississippian village and chert tool workshop occupied about 900-1,400 A.D.

Picnicking and swimming: There are 27 designated picnic areas in the national forest. In addition to those located at campgrounds, they include Iron Furnace, Lakeview and Indian Wall in the Elizabethtown Ranger District; Allen's Flat, Lincoln Memorial, McGee Hill, McCann Spring and Winters Pond in the Jonesboro Ranger District; and Buttermilk Hill, Hickory Ridge and Pomona Natural Bridge in the Murphysboro Ranger District. There are beaches at John Creek, Pounds Hollow Lake and Lake Glendale Beach, and at Buttermilk Hill, which can be reached only by boat or a 3-mile trail.

Pine Hills Scenic Drive, 7 miles: This auto route along Forest Highway 236 passes McCann Spring, Inspiration Point Trail, Old Trail Point, Government Rock, Twin Bridge, Saddle Hill, McGee Hill and Allen's Flat. It's N of Pine Hills Campground and E of the LaRue Scenic Area in the Jonesboro Ranger District.

Rock Climbing: The abundance of cliffs and hills make Shawnee a natural place for rock climbing, but freehand climbing and rappelling with ropes are discouraged. The sandstone is slippery when icy or wet; brittleness makes climbing dangerous in the western part of the national forest. Climbing is also discouraged at Garden of the Gods, Bell Smith Springs, Rim Rock, LaRue Pine Hills Ecological Area, Cedar Bluff Natural Area and Drapers Bluff Natural Area.

Shawnee Hills on the Ohio National Scenic Byway, 70 *miles:* Historic and natural features along this winding, three-county route include the Army Corps of Engineers' Smithland Locks and Dam, Karbers Ridge, Gibbons Creek Barrens, Garden of the Gods Recreation Area and Wilderness, the restored Illinois Iron Furnace and Pounds Hollow Recreation Area. There's also access to the River-to-River and Rim Rock trails, plus scenic vistas from Williams Hill, High Knob and Tower Rock. The byway follows Highways 1, 34 and 146 and County Roads 13, 9 and 1.

🚹 Ranger Districts

Elizabethtown: RR 2, P.O. Box 4, Elizabethtown, IL 62931; ☎ (618) 287-2201.

Jonesboro: 521 N. Main, Jonesboro, IL 62952; ☎ (618) 833-8576.

Murphysboro: P.O. Box 787, Murphysboro, IL 62966; ☎(618) 687-1731.

Vienna: Route 1, P.O. Box 288B, Vienna, IL 62995; ☎ (618) 658-2111.

Gateways

Carbondale: Carbondale Convention & Tourism Bureau, 1245 E. Main St., Carbondale, IL 62901; ☎ (618) 529-4451 or (800) 526-1500.

Marion: Williamson County Tourism Bureau, New Route 13, Marion, IL 62959; ☎ (618) 997-3690 or (800) 433-7399.

Harrisburg: Harrisburg Chamber of Commerce, 325 E. Poplar, Harrisburg, IL 62946; ☎ (618) 252-4192.

Mt. Vernon: Mt. Vernon Convention & Visitors Bureau, Box 2580, Mt. Vernon, IL 62864; ☎ (618) 242-3151 or (800) 252-5464.

Ullin: Southernmost Tourism Bureau, P.O. Box 278 Ullin, IL 62992; ☎ (618) 845-3777 or (800) 248-4373.

Whittington/Benton: Southern Illinois Tourism Council, RR 1, Box 40, Whittington, IL 62897; ☎ (618) 629-2506 or (800) 342-3100.

INDIANA

Hoosier National Forest

Hickory Ridge Fire Tower was the last active tower in Hooiser National Forest, used until the 1970s.

HOOSIER

811 Constitution Ave.   **193,036 acres**
Bedford IN 47421
☎ **(812) 275-5987**

Indiana's only national forest borders the Ohio River in a region known for its caves, scenic vistas, steep terrain and the state's largest reservoir, Lake Monroe.

The first human occupants of what is now southern Indiana were bands of hunters and gatherers who arrived about 12,000 years ago. Native American villages were eventually established here, and crops such as beans, squash and corn were grown along the fertile river bottoms and terraces. European settlements began in the early 1800s, mostly along the Ohio River, other rivers and streams. Heavy lumbering started in the mid-19th century and continued through 1910, leaving residual stands of trees with little market value. Farming followed with only mixed success and by 1930, most of what would become Hoosier National Forest contained small farms, pastures and wood lots.

Congress established the national forest in 1935 with overfarmed, eroded and tax-delinquent tracts willingly sold by their owners. The Civilian Conservation Corps soon began to reforest the hillsides and control major erosion problems. Hickory Ridge Fire Tower and other landmarks are legacies of the CCC's Depression endeavors.

Camping

The forest's largest developed campground is at Hardin Ridge Recreation Area, with about 200 sites. The most popular recreation area in Hoosier, Hardin Ridge also features a visitor center with evening programs, a boat launch on Lake Monroe and a sheltered sandy beach for campers and day users. Hoosier has several horse campgrounds, although non-riders are also welcome at these facilities: German Ridge, Hickory Ridge, Shirley Creek and Youngs Creek.

Improved campgrounds, their sites and locations are:
Brownstown Ranger District
Blackwell Horse Camp (100), 13 miles SE of Bloomington on Tower Ridge Road;
Hardin Ridge (201), 18 miles NE of Bedford on Chapel Hill Road;
Hickory Ridge (20), 2 miles N of Norman on County Road;
Shirley Creek (30), 6 miles S of Huron on County Road 775 W.
Tell City Ranger District
German Ridge (20), 10 miles E of Cannelton on County Road 3;
Lake Celina (63), 3 miles S of I-64 on Highway 37 South;
Saddle Lake (25), 12 miles NE of Tell City on Highway 37;
Springs Valley (13), 13 miles S of Paoli on County Road 375S;
Tipsaw Lake (41), 7 miles S of I-64 on Highway 37;
Youngs Creek (20), 6 miles S of Paoli on County Road 50 W.
There is also primitive camping at Buzzard Roost, 10 miles S of Sulphur on Alton/Magnet Road. It's in the Brownstown Ranger District.

 Trails

The longest trails in Hoosier National Forest are marked for horseback use; visitors also find hiking trails, as well as a variety of mountain biking routes along county roads. Several campgrounds offer trail access, including Hardin Ridge, German Ridge, Lake Celina, Saddle Lake, Tipsaw and Springs Valley. Here are some popular routes:

Brownstown Ranger District

Axsom Branch Loop Trail, 7 miles: This loop trail starts and ends at Grubb Ridge and heads into Axsom Branch Valley. It passes Terril Cemetery and Hickory Ridge Fire Tower and provides scenic views of Lake Monroe. It's in the Charles C. Deam Wilderness, with the trailhead at the tower on Tower Ridge Road.

Cope Hollow Trail, 9 miles: This is a loop trail for horses and hikers, winding into Tanyard Branch, along Cope Hollow Ridge and across Dennis Murphy Hollow. The trailhead is at Blackwell Horse Camp, SE of Bloomington.

Grubb Ridge Trail, 11 miles: A hiking and horse trail, it drops into Saddle Creek and climbs onto Grubb Ridge. The loop starts and ends at Blackwell Horse Camp, SE of Bloomington.

Sycamore Branch Hiking Trail, 8 miles: A loop trail in the Charles C. Deam Wilderness, it descends a series of switchbacks into Sycamore Branch, which is lined with maple, pine and sycamore. Much of it follows ridge tops through hardwood forests. The trailhead is at Hickory Ridge Fire Tower on Tower Ridge Road.

Tell City Ranger District

Buffalo Trace Trail, 6 miles: Part of the trail near French Lick Creek follows a "trace" - or salt lick - used by buffalo herds. Along the route are Tucker Lake, abandoned fields, pine plantations and a dam. Alan McPherson, author of *Nature Walks In Southern Indiana,* calls this "a quiet beauty spot" and "one of the finest day hikes in the Hoosier National Forest for its length, moderate difficulty, maintenance and scenery." Also known as Springs Valley Trail, Buffalo Trace Trail is in Springs Valley Recreation Area, S of Paoli.

Celina Interpretive Trail, 1 mile: This self-guided history and natural history trail passes the abandoned Celina village stagecoach stop and post office, Native American shelter rocks and a cemetery. It begins at Lake Celina Campground.

Hemlock Cavern Trail, 1 mile: This loop trail is in Hemlock Cliffs area, S of Mifflin. It passes shallow caves, boulders and rock shelters.

Lakeside Trail, 3 miles: As the trail circles Saddle Lake, it passes the Theis Creek inlet and cove, a beach and a dam; the dam area is a favored picnic spot. Saddle Lake Campground provides access.

Mogan Ridge Trail, 21 miles: A tough backcountry trail, it passes wildlife ponds, ridges and natural areas. At about 6,000 acres in size, Mogan Ridge is one of the biggest, solid blocks of land owned by Hoosier National Forest; the area is home to deer and wild turkey. To reach the trailhead, take Old State Route 37 to a marked gravel road that leads to Mogan Ridge Road.

Two Lakes Loop Trail, 12 miles: It circles Indian Lake and Lake Celina, with panoramic views of both. There are wooded ridges, draws and shoreline, as well as blooming dogwood and redbud. Connectors make it possible to take shorter hikes with access from Indian Lake Road. Two Lakes Loop Trail is a national recreation trail. The main trailhead is near Celina Lake Campground.

 # Horseback Riding

Hooiser National Forest features a number of horse trails and other facilities for equestrian facilities including Blackwell Horse Camp in Brownstown Ranger District. Here are the most popular horse trails:

Brownstown Ranger District

Hickory Ridge Horse Trail, 20 miles: Riders pass more than a dozen ponds along the route. Camping is available along the route. The trailhead is at Hickory Ridge Campground, N of Norman;

Shirley Creek Horse Trail, 16 miles: Riders often camp along this trail, which passes several ponds and traverses a variety of terrains in some of southern Indiana's most scenic wooded hills. It cuts through Hoosier's Lost River unit, which includes such entic-

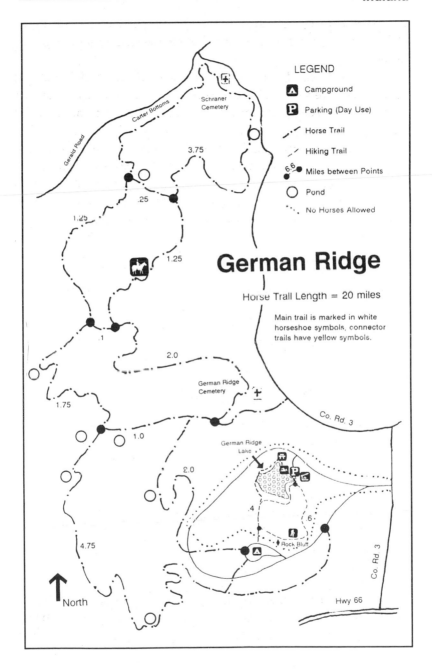

LEGEND

🅰 Campground

🅿 Parking (Day Use)

Horse Trail

Hiking Trail

6.6 Miles between Points

○ Pond

No Horses Allowed

German Ridge

Horse Trail Length = 20 miles

Main trail is marked in white
horseshoe symbols, connector
trails have yellow symbols.

Gerald Road

Carter Bottoms

Schraner Cemetery

3.75

.25

1.25

1.25

2.0

.1

1.75

German Ridge Cemetery

Co. Rd. 3

1.0

2.0

German Ridge Lake

.4

.6

4.75

Rock Bluff

Co. Rd. 3

Hwy 66

North

ingly named spots as Box Canyon, Tar Springs, Fuzzy Hole and Trout Lily Valley. The trailhead is at Shirley Creek Campground, S of Huron.

Tell City Ranger District

German Ridge Horse Trail, 20 miles: Horseback riders enjoy a series of loops with access at German Ridge Campground, the first recreation area in Hoosier National Forest. It passes several ponds and two cemeteries;

Youngs Creek Horse Trail, 10 miles: This rugged trail winds through forested hills and by ponds, overlooks and rock outcroppings. Nearby is Initial Point, used in 1795 as the "point of beginning of the Indiana Public Land Survey." The trailhead is S of Paoli and W of Highway 37.

 ## Boating

Boat launches are available at Indian, Celina, Tipsaw and Saddle lakes, all of which allow only electric motors. Mano Point in the Tell Ranger District offers the national forest's only boating access to the Ohio River; it's N of Derby, off State Route 66.

Lake Monroe, created by an Army Corps of Engineers dam, is Indiana's largest reservoir and a major boating and fishing destination. The national forest boat launch at Hardin Ridge Recreation Area offers access to Lake Monroe. The lake also has boat ramps at eight state-run recreation sites.

 ## Fishing

For fishing, try for striped and white bass, crappie, sunfish, bluegill, redear sunfish, sauger and channel catfish. Annual bass tournaments are held on the Ohio River and Lake Monroe.

 ## Natural Areas

Boone Creek Barrens Natural Area, 900 acres: This natural area contains such rare plants as Maryland butterfly pea, Canada lily and waxy-leafed aster. The area includes several grassy openings, known as barrens, within rugged, forested hills. The area is E of Oriole on Alton Road in the Tell City Ranger District.

Browning Hill, 300 acres: Located at the E end of Lake Monroe in the Brownstown Ranger District, this area has twisting hollows, steep wooded hills and narrow ridges. The Nature Conservancy describes it as "some of the roughest, most inaccessible land" in the national forest, and there are no trails or signs. Browning Hill itself is one of the highest points in Hoosier. The preserve features a little-disturbed old-growth forest, some of the best remaining examples of the region's mosaic of dry and upland forest, and such wildlife as wild turkeys, vultures and owls. The area is SW of Story, past the end of Elkinsville Road.

Carnes Mill, 59 acres: The area was named for an old mill built over a natural rock tunnel through which water flowed. It is a geologically, historically and biologically significant area, with a steep old-growth deciduous forest along a rugged outcrop of sandstone overlooking the Little Blue River. Carnes Mill itself is private property, but the rest of the area is open to the public. Among its rare plants are skullcap, barrens strawberry, hairy mint and mountain laurel. The terrain is rough, but visitors can hike the area by parking along Highway 37. It's in the Tell City Ranger District, S of English.

Hemlock Cliffs, 1,500 acres: Described as a "rocky adventureland," this special area encompasses a narrow sandstone canyon, stone cliffs, rushing waterfalls, pools and hemlocks. A rugged hiking trail begins at the parking area. The special area is in the Tell City Ranger District, W of Highway 37 and S of English.

Pioneer Mothers Memorial Forest and Research Natural Area, 253 acres: Designated as a National Natural Landmark, this area contains 88 acres of virgin pre-settlement forest with oak, hickory, sugar maple and American beech. It was preserved because original owner Joseph Cox refused to log it in the 19th century. In 1941, an 89-day fund-raising drive by local preservationists, led by the Meridian Club of Paoli, collected $24,300 to save the trees from being logged. Among its 2,600 trees are some of the finest forest-grown black walnut trees in the United States, as well as a 1-mile trail. There's also a memorial wall commemorating the women who helped settle the region; the forest is named for Pioneer Mothers of Indiana, a group that provided about one-fourth the money needed to protect it. There's a 165-acre buffer in addition to the 88-acre Research Natural Area.

Bill Thomas, in his book Wild Woodlands, calls Pioneer Mothers "one of the most impressive old-growth forests in the entire Midwest. The walnuts tower above the forest floor. To walk the narrow dirt trail leading through the grove is an experience not to be missed."

It's on Highway 37, S of Paoli in the Tell City Ranger District.

Wilderness Area

Charles C. Deam Wilderness, 12,935 acres: Indiana's only designated wilderness is in the northern part of the national forest near Lake Monroe. It was named for Indiana's renowned botanist and forester who collected and catalogued the state's plants for half a century. This was one of the last local areas to be settled because of its marginal soil conditions and steep terrain. By the mid-1800s, 81 small farms and ridgetop fields dotted the landscape within the current wilderness boundaries. A sign informs visitors: "The wilderness contains many material remains of its former residents, old roads, house sites and cemeteries." There are a variety of ponds, hollows and pine plantations within its borders. Hiking, backpacking, fishing, nature study and other low-impact recreational activities are permitted.

Thirty-seven miles of trails are marked, and horseback riders are required to stay on designated trails. Volunteers from Hoosier's Wilderness Ambassador Program travel by horse or by foot through the wilderness to provide help and education to visitors. Passport in Time program participants have conducted a wilderness survey here.

The wilderness is in the Brownstown Ranger District, NE of Bedford. Use Highway 446 to reach it.

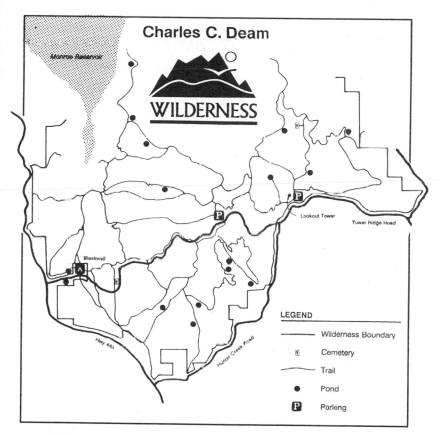

Historic Attractions

Carnes Mill Site: A 19th-century grain mill operated here on the Little Blue River, with help from a dam that is still in use. A natural rock tunnel helped power the wheels. The privately owned site is 1 mile S of Grantsburg near Highway 37 but is accessible only by foot cross-country on national forest land or by canoeing on the river. For natural beauty, mountain laurel, bush honeysuckle and eastern hemlock grow here.

Celina/Rickenbaugh House: Jacob Rickenbaugh, a tanner, designed the house on Lake Celina in 1874. He hired three Belgian immigrant stone masons, who built it of native sandstone

IN THE FOREST
Todd Cemetery and Hickory Ridge Fire Tower

The dead may tell no tales, but their cemeteries do.

So it is at Todd Cemetery, tucked into a forest opening along a gravel road on the edge of the Charles C. Deam Wilderness. Most travelers don't stop and listen.

Todd Cemetery's first tale is of family.

Gravestones show that many folks were named Axsom or Myers or Todd or Harris or Hillenburg. These families grew up together, often intermarried and, when death came, were buried in the same soil.

The second tale is of anonymity.

Many identities remain secret. Inscriptions eroded by harsh winters left us struggling to decipher words and numbers. More unsolvable were grave sites marked only by irregular chunks of stone, anonymous memorials to now-forgotten men, women and children. However, living memorials rather than stone mark some graves, perennial flowers and plants such as iris, peonies and vinca.

Todd Cemetery tells tales of tragedy.

Dates etched into stone illustrate how family after family suffered the loss of a newborn or a child in the rugged southern Indiana hills. Consider the grieving Myers family: Violet, 1910-1911, and Viless, 1915-1916, share a headstone marked with an angel; a lamb adorns the grave of Cleadis Myers, 1899-1904.

Yet others lived long, among them Civil War veteran Robert Hayes, 1826-1902, of Co. C, 32nd Regiment, of the Indiana Volunteers.

Todd Cemetery's final tale is one of transition.

Just as their homes have reverted to the wilds, so, too, is

their final resting place losing the battle of permanence. Relentless weather continues to erase the tombstones. Plastic flower bouquets fade into pale pastels, then crumble. The forest presses in.

Nearby Lake Monroe, Indiana University and the craft shops of Nashville don't matter to these people. But wandering among the graves, we wonder about the parents, wives, children, lovers and dreams they had. We wonder, too, what they would think of the changes, of the disappearance of their community, of their farms swallowed up by national forest, of futures that were not to be.

Hickory Ridge Fire Tower looms a few miles east of Todd Cemetery, also along Tower Ridge Road. Like the cemetery, it, too, is a legacy of the past and an anachronistic part of the present.

The Civilian Conservation Corps built the 100-foot-high tower in 1936; it was actively used from 1937 until the mid-1970s. The last remaining fire lookout in Hoosier National Forest, it now attracts energetic visitors.

Your heart pounds from the exertion of climbing and the exhilaration of being above the treetops as you look down upon a sea of green. This vantage point provides a real sense of the forest's hills, ridges and ravines. What would it be like to be up here when a storm rolls in? When lightning slashes through the sky? When smoke is spotted in the distance?

Evening falls and the wind picks up. The tower seems to tremble. Is it swaying, or just an overactive imagination?

with 3-foot-thick walls. It served as the Rickenbaugh family home, church meeting place and post office. The family cemetery is W of the house. The site is on the National Register of Historic Places. It's near Lake Celina Campground in the Tell City Ranger District, S of I-64 off Highway 37.

Hickory Ridge Fire Tower: Built in 1936 by the Civilian Conservation Corps and used until the mid-1970s, it overlooks the Charles C. Deam Wilderness and Lake Monroe. Visitors can climb to the top of the only fire tower left in the national forest. There's a parking area at the tower base on Tower Ridge Road, E of State Route 446.

Initial Point: A monument commemorates the spot used in 1795 for the federal government's original land survey of Indiana and the Midwest. It also memorializes the surveyors who died on the frontier. The Initial Point is near the trailhead for Youngs Creek Horse Trail, S of Paoli.

More Things To Do & See

Bicycling: A scenic loop that begins and ends in Tell City passes for almost 50 of its 87 miles through Hoosier National Forest. It heads N along Routes 66, 245, 62 and back to 66 through New Boston, St. Meinrad, Sulphur, Oriole, Derby and Cannelton. Although the loop is paved, a largely unpaved 9-mile round-trip spur south of Oriole leads to Buzzard Roost Campground and Overlook, with its view of the Ohio River Valley and nearby Kentucky. William N. Sherwood, author of Old Roads: The Cyclist's Guide to Rural Indiana, recommends mountain bikes for the spur.

A 41-mile loop listed in Sherwood's book starts and ends in Paoli, passing through hilly terrain in the national forest. Pioneer Mothers Memorial Forest, a popular preserve of virgin hardwoods, is along the way. Major roads on the loop are Sandyhook Road, County Road 200N, Route 337, Valeene Road and Route 37; it goes through the communities of Pumpkin Center, Livonia, Hardinsburg and Valeene.

Birding: Among the rich bird life found in the national forest are barred and great horned owls, wild turkey, vultures and whip-poorwills. During spring and summer, the woods vibrate with the songs of neotropical migratory species such as warblers and vireos.

Buzzard Roost Overlook: There's a breathtaking view of the Ohio River bottoms with a hardwood forest backdrop. Its name comes from the hundreds of buzzards or vultures that once soared here and perched atop the 300-foot-high cliff waiting to eat refuse from a now-defunct slaughterhouse along the Ohio River below the cliffs. The overlook is in the Tell City Ranger District.

Gayle Gray Overlook: This scenic spot, 890 feet above sea level near Hemlock Cliffs Recreation Area, offers a great vista. It was named as a memorial to a local teenager who died in a car crash, but the overlook is no longer maintained. It's S of Mifflin in the Tell City Ranger District. There's no sign and the site is difficult to find.

Hill Country Scenic Route: This state route enters the national forest N of Indian Lake on the W and leaves it E of Sulphur. Overall, it runs between Gentryville, near the Lincoln Boyhood National Park, and Corydon on State Routes 62 and 162.

Hoosier Heritage Trail Scenic Route: Part of this state-designated scenic highway crosses Hoosier National Forest along State Route 66. The entire route runs between Newburgh and Sulphur.

Horseback riding: Horses are allowed at some campgrounds and on designated horse trails, but not on hiking trails or in day use areas. Horses should be kept in single file on the trails. At campgrounds, riders should use hitching rails. Horses may safely drink from streams and ponds, but riders should carry water for themselves.

Twin Oaks Visitor Center: At Hardin Ridge Recreation Area in the Brownstown Ranger District, the visitor center offers exhibits, children's activities and ranger-led programs on such topics as endangered species, edible insects and turtles. An interpretive loop trail begins and ends at the center.

Ranger Districts

Brownstown: 608 W. Commerce St., Brownstown, IN 47220; ☎ (812) 358-2675.

Tell City: 248 15th St., Tell City, IN 47586; ☎ (812) 547-7051.

Gateways

Bedford: Bedford Chamber of Commerce, 1116 16th St., Bedford, IN 47421; ☎ (812) 275-4493.

Bloomington: Bloomington Convention & Visitors Bureau, 2855 N. Walnut St., Bloomington, IN 47404; ☎ (800) 800-0037 or (812) 334-8900.

Evansville: Evansville Convention & Visitors Bureau, 623 Walnut St., Evansville, IN 47708; ☎ (800) 433-3025 or (812) 425-5402.

French Lick: French Lick Chamber of Commerce, Box 347, French Lick, IN 47432; ☎ (812) 936-2405.

Nashville: Brown County Convention & Visitors Bureau, Box 840, Nashville, IN 47448; ☎ (800) 753-3255 or (812) 988-7303).

Paoli: Paoli Chamber of Commerce, P.O. Box 22, Paoli, IN 47454; ☎ (812) 723-4769.

Tell City: Perry County Chamber of Commerce, Box 82, Tell City, IN 47586; ☎ (812) 547-2385.

MICHIGAN

Huron National Forest
Manistee National Forest
Hiawatha National Forest
Ottawa National Forest

Lumbermen's Monument, one of the most popular stops along the River Road Scenic Byway, is dedicated to the loggers who cut the trees of what is now Huron National Forest. Photo by Michigan Travel Bureau.

HURON

1755 S. Mitchell St.   432,836 acres
Cadillac, MI 49601
☎ (800) 821-6263 or (616) 775-2421

Lumbering once ruled this land. The pristine Au Sable River was originally called Riviere aux Sables, or River of Sand, and at one point in the late 1800s was little more than an avenue for loggers to ship their timber to mills on Lake Huron.

To meet the timber needs of a growing nation, lumber barons turned Michigan into the country's top producer of white pine, but in the process left little more than a wasteland of stumps. Watersheds were destroyed, soil erosion was rampant and entire species of animals were being obliterated. None of this was more evident than along the Au Sable River.

By the turn of the century, a growing number of conservation leaders, including Theodore Roosevelt, were pushing to retain land in public ownership and manage it for the common good over the long term. In 1909, a presidential proclamation established the Michigan Forest from abandoned farms and lumbered wastelands surrounding the heavily logged areas of the Au Sable River. It was eventually renamed Huron National Forest and since 1945 has been administered jointly with Manistee National Forest, also in Michigan's Lower Peninsula.

During the Depression, the Civilian Conservation Corps had 11 camps in the national forest and enrollees set a record in 1935 when they planted more than 16,000 acres of trees. By the time the camps closed in 1942, the enrollees had planted 485 million trees. Fish also had been extensively stocked in the forest waterways.

Today, trout fishing in the Au Sable is so highly regarded that one stretch is referred to as "the Holy Waters" for fly fishing. The forests also returned and have transformed what was a "wasteland" into a recreational playground for hikers, skiers, campers, canoers and others. Nowhere else is that mix of natural and human influences better evidenced than at Lumbermen's Monument, where on the banks of the Au Sable beneath towering pines a statue honors the lumberjacks who left this land barren.

Among the features of Huron National Forest are extensive trails, including part of the Michigan Shore-to-Shore Trail stretching between Lakes Huron and Michigan, and the Au Sable, today designated a National Scenic River. The forest is dotted with lakes and rustic lakeside campgrounds while every summer birders from around the country arrive at the Ranger District Office in Mio for an opportunity to sight the endangered Kirtland's warbler.

 ## Camping

Prime waterfront locations highlight the national forest's developed campgrounds. The improved campsites, number of sites and locations are:

Harrisville Ranger District
Jewell Lake (32), 1 mile SE of Barton City on Forest Road 4601;
Horseshoe Lake (9), 4 miles NE of Glennie on Forest Road 4124;
Pine River (11), 10 miles E of Glennie on Forest Road 4121 (Rearing Pond Road).

Mio Ranger District

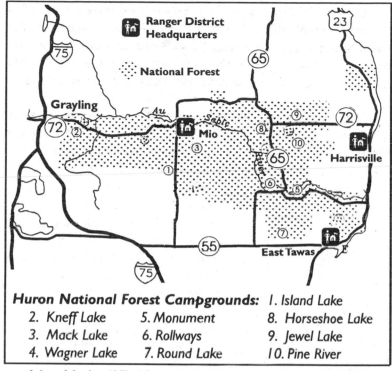

Huron National Forest Campgrounds: *1. Island Lake*
2. Kneff Lake   *5. Monument*   *8. Horseshoe Lake*
3. Mack Lake   *6. Rollways*   *9. Jewel Lake*
4. Wagner Lake   *7. Round Lake*   *10. Pine River*

Island Lake *(17)*, 12 miles S of Mio on County Road 486;
Kneff Lake *(26)*, 8 miles SE of Grayling on Stephan Bridge Road;
Mack Lake *(42)*, 9 miles SE of Mio on County Road 489;
Wagner Lake *(12)*, 8 miles SE of Mio on Wagner Lake Road.
Tawas Ranger District
Monument *(20)*, 13 miles NW of East Tawas on River Road;
Rollways *(19)*, 7 miles N of Hale on Rollways Road;
Round Lake *(33)*, 9 miles NE of East Tawas on Latham Road.
Many hikers and horseback riders who use the Michigan Shore-to-Shore Hiking and Riding Trail stop at one of its three trail camps. Luzerne fills to capacity several times a year with members of the Michigan Trail Riders Association, who help maintain the trail. All three trail camps accommodate individuals, families and groups. They are:

Luzerne *(10 sites)*, in the Mio Ranger District, 3 miles S of Luzerne on Forest Road 4477;

McKinley *(100 sites)*, in the Harrisville Ranger District, 9 miles E of Mio on County Road 602;

South Branch *(15 sites)*, in the Tawas Ranger District, 20 miles NW of East Tawas on Rollways Road.

In addition, there are walk-in campgrounds at Hoist Lake (5 sites) and Reid Lake (6 sites,) both in the Harrisville Ranger District.

 ## Trails

Huron National Forest boasts hundreds of miles of trails for cross-country skiing, snowmobiling, hiking, off-road vehicle and horseback riding across a variety of terrains, from generally flat to sharply sloped. There are self-guided nature trails, such as the Island Lake Nature Trail between Rose City and Mio.

The 91-mile Huron Trail is the longest snowmobile route in the forest. Other major snowmobile routes include two segments of the Oscoda County Trail (78 and 36 miles), Pine River (53 miles), and Ogemaw Hills (7 miles). Snowmobilers also use two-track roads.

Both the Shore-to-Shore Trail and the Michigan Cross Country Cycle Trail traverse the national forest:

Michigan Cross Country Cycle Trail, *29 miles:* Part of this 211-plus mile trail for motorized off-road vehicles runs through Huron. In the Mio district, it passes two creeks and the Kirtland's Warbler Management Area. It weaves through grassy openings and stands of oak, jack pine and aspen, along flat to gently rolling terrain, and over generally sandy soil. Access points include M-72, W of Luzerne; County Road 488, NW of Rose City; Parmalee Bridge State Forest Campground, N of Luzerne; and Luzerne Trail Camp, S of Luzerne.

Shore-to-Shore Trail, *96 miles:* In its entirety, this 220-mile trail for horses, hiking, skiing and snowshoeing runs across the state between Empire on Lake Michigan and Tawas City on Lake

Byron Lake in the Hoist Lakes Foot Travel Area.

Huron. The Huron National Forest segments go through jack and red pine plains, pine plantations, and along high banks with a ridge paralleling the Au Sable River. The Mio district segment crosses two creeks and the Au Sable's South Branch amid a variety of vegetation and morainal hills, which were built of debris left by glaciers. Summer and fall rides are sponsored by the Michigan Trail Riders Association. Horses can be watered at stream crossings;

camping is allowed along the route and at the trail camps. Access spots include the junction of U.S. 23 and First Street in Tawas City; McKinley Trail Camp E of Mio, and Luzerne Trail Camp S of Luzerne. Other popular trails include:

Harrisville Ranger District

Hoist Lakes Foot Travel Area, 20 miles: The steep, rolling land provides scenic vistas and a challenge for experienced skiers and hikers. There are seven small lakes in this 10,000-acre area. A popular viewpoint, overlooking the Au Sable River Valley, is just S of the backcountry campsites on Byron Lake. Other campsites are located along South Hoist Lake. The eastern trailhead is N of Glennie on M-65.

Jewell Lake Trail, 1 mile: Built by the Youth Conservation Corps, this predominantly flat trail follows a portion of the shore of scenic Jewell Lake near Jewell Lake Campground. Observant walkers can spot woodpecker holes, animal dens and other signs of wildlife. The trailhead is SE of Barton City on Forest Road 4601.

Reid Lake Foot Travel Area, 6 miles: This network of trails is popular among hikers and cross-country skiers. The terrain is gently rolling; some trails pass the open fields and old orchards that are a result of the area being farmed until the 1960s. There are several backcountry campsites and two fishing docks on Reid Lake. The trailhead is on M-72 W of Harrisville.

Mio Ranger District

Island Lake Nature Trail, 2 miles: Numbered stops and an informational brochure explain points of interest and the natural history of this area, which was shaped by Ice Age glaciers. The trail is set among hardwoods and glacial hills between Loon and Island lakes. The trailhead is at Island Lake Recreation Site, N of Mio on County Road 486.

Midland-to-Mackinac Pathway, 12 miles: The pathway passes through the national forest on its way to the Straits of Mackinac and is used for hiking and snowshoeing. It was built by the Boy Scouts to simulate the original migratory route used by the Chippewa. Access to the segment within Huron National Forest is on Forest Road 4027, W of Mio.

Wakeley Lake Foot Travel Area: Visitors use an extensive network of trails and non-motorized roads, with walk-in camping. Catch-and-release fishing is allowed on Wakeley Lake, which is a half-mile portage from M-72. Wildlife management techniques are used in this 1,415-acre area to protect loons and eagles; a loon nesting spot on the NE side of the lake is closed to public use from March 1 to July 15. Wakeley Lake is in the Mio Ranger District, with access at M-72, E of Grayling.

Tawas Ranger District

Corsair Trail Complex, 43 miles: This network of trails is in what once was a hunting ground for the Chippewa and Ottawa, and later devastated by forest fire. In the 1850s, lumberjacks who settled here considered the area to be a wasteland of barren land, occasional pines and scattered blueberry patches. The land has been reforested, however, and the trails are used primarily by skiers in the winter. Many believe Corsair offers the best cross-country skiing on the E side of the state as it traverses gently rolling to hilly terrain while passing several creeks and lakes, including Silver Creek, Wright's Lake and Lost Lake. The trail system is NW of Tawas City on Monument Road.

Eagle Run, 7 miles: This generally level cross-country ski trail system is maintained by the Oscoda Chamber of Commerce within the national forest boundaries. The Eastgate Welcome Center serves as the trailhead.

Highbanks Trail, 7 miles: There are panoramic views from the bluffs that overlook the Au Sable River Valley between largo Springs Interpretive Site and Lumbermen's Monument. The trail is used by hikers and skiers.

 Boating & Canoeing

Because most of Huron's lakes are small - 1/2 mile to 2 miles across - the best motorized boating opportunities are for craft under 20 horsepower and shorter than 26 feet. Ponds created by

IN THE FOREST
Kirtland's Warblers

By Ian Freedman

Jack pine forests are found in northern Michigan, including the Huron National Forest, northern Wisconsin and parts of Canada. These trees provide the only suitable nesting habitat for the endangered Kirtland's warbler. In recent years, the warblers have faced loss of habitat.

The birds nest only in the northern Lower Peninsula of Michigan, in regions of young jack pine forests, 6 to 20 years old. Older jack pines are unsuitable for Kirtland's warbler nesting because the birds will not nest under trees with dead lower branches. However, jack pine cones only release their seeds in extreme heat. Ironically, the Forest Service, in its efforts to provide fire protection, has created germination problems by its policy of putting out forest fires.

Cowbird parasitism is the other major problem Kirtland's warblers encounter. Cowbirds lay their eggs in the nests of other birds, including the Kirtland's warbler, and aggressive cowbird hatchlings eat the other birds' food. When settlers came to Michigan, they cleared the land and cut down many forests. The cowbird, originally a Great Plains inhabitant, then had a giant, expanded habitat to plunder.

However, there's hope for the Kirtland's warbler because the Forest Service, Michigan Department of Natural Resources and U.S. Fish and Wildlife Service teamed up to propagate young jack pine forests for these endangered birds to nest in. As part of their recovery plan, areas of jack pine are cleared each year and replanted with seedlings. These young forests provide habitat for Kirtland's warblers, as well as deer, wild turkey and other animals. The government agencies can do this because more than 140,000 acres of jack pine forest are growing in the Huron

A Kirtland's warbler in the Huron National Forest.

National Forest and surrounding state forests. After 50 years, a region is cleared and the wood sold to be made into paper or wood chips. The agencies also monitor cowbird populations to keep them from infesting too many nests.

Because of this government intervention, the Kirtland's warbler is surviving and the number of singing males is increasing. Additionally, programs such as the Forest Service's Plant-A-Tree help create habitat for the Kirtland's warbler to survive. Individuals can show support by touring a warbler habitat or making a Plant-A-Tree donation.

People created this problem when they tampered with the virgin forests. Now, fortunately, they're using forestry management to solve it.

hydroelectric dams allow for slow, lake-like boating. Sailing is limited because of restricted maneuvering space and inadequate wind.

The federal Wild and Natural Rivers program protects miles of rivers and streams here from development, creating canoeing opportunities that might otherwise have been lost or degraded. A number of commercial canoe liveries on the Au Sable River and South Branch of the Au Sable offer rentals; a list is available at national forest offices.

Au Sable River, 68 miles: Canoeists on the Au Sable experience many changes in scenery and river conditions, including high banks, floodplain, waterfowl nesting habitat, ponds, lowland swamps and beaver-dammed bayous. A 23-mile stretch of this major tributary to Lake Huron is a National Scenic River. Water levels fluctuate, and there can be turbulence because of drawdowns at the hydroelectric plants. When canoeing the Au Sable, be alert for submerged deadheads - jammed logs - which are potentially dangerous legacies remaining from the lumbering era of the late 1800s, when the lower Au Sable was the last leg of the great log drives. The marks of logging companies are still visible on the ends of logs embedded along the banks and shallow river areas. The free-flowing section of the Au Sable begins at Foote Dam and continues until the river empties into Lake Huron.

The best canoeing is between early May and early October. There are 15 access points within the national forest, including Mio Bridge and McKinley Bridge in the Mio Ranger District; Bamfield Road Bridge and Bobcat Creek in the Harrisville Ranger District; and the Au Sable boat launch and Hoppy Creek in the Tawas Ranger District. The last exit point in the national forest is at Five Channels Pond.

 Fishing

The Au Sable River is legendary among anglers. Beyond brook, brown and rainbow trout, it's home to coho, Chinook, steelhead and Atlantic salmon. Rivers, ponds and lakes are fine for northern pike, bluegill, muskellunge, sunfish, largemouth and smallmouth bass, walleye and yellow perch. Below Foote Dam, steelhead and salmon are plentiful during seasonal spawning runs and walleyes throughout the summer. Farther upstream, a stretch of river just below Alcona Dam offers brown trout, walleye and northern pike. Between Mio and McKinley is a state-designated "quality fishing area" managed for trophy trout.

A series of ponds along the Au Sable - Loud Dam, Five Channels, Cooke Dam and Foote Dam ponds - hold a variety of warm water species such as panfish, walleye, pike and bass.

The national forest also offers a wide range of "walk-in" fisheries where anglers can escape the outboard motors and crowds found on many other lakes. Wakeley Lake, which can be fished only from June 15 to Aug. 31, is renowned for its trophy bluegills and bass. Several lakes in the Hoist Lakes Foot Travel Area hold bass, bluegill or trout including Byron Lake, South Hoist and North Hoist. Reid Lake has both bluegill and stocked trout and is a walk of less than a mile from the trailhead.

Michigan's only "barrier-free fishing access in a primitive setting" is in the Huron National Forest. O'Brien Lake Fishing Pier features a zigzagging 638-foot ramp down an embankment to a floating pier on the small, remote lake just N of the Au Sable River. O'Brien is stocked with trout and offers a wild, rustic setting for anglers with and without disabilities. The pier is at the end of Forest Road 4838, E of M-32 in McKinley.

Other fishing areas with multiple species within the national forest include the Pine River, Bliss Lake and Buck Creek Pond. Rainbow trout are also stocked at Kneff and Horseshoe lakes, which both feature campgrounds and unimproved boat launches.

 ## Historical Attractions

Lumbermen's Monument: This is a 14-foot-high bronze statue of a sawyer, a river driver, a timber cruiser, and their tools. Their labors "made possible the development of the prairie states," according to the inscription on the 1932 statue by sculptor Robert

Aitken. Exhibits at the adjacent visitor center explain how logs are cut and transported to sawmills; there also are slide shows, a book shop and a huge log pile. Nearby, a 260-step stairway leads down to scenic Cooke Pond, which was formed when the first Au Sable River power plant and dam were completed in 1911. Forest Service interpretive programs are conducted at the visitor center on River Road, W of Oscoda in the Tawas Ranger District. It's open from the third week of May to late October.

Passport in Time: Volunteers have surveyed the Au Sable River's drainage area, looking for prehistoric and historic sites along the river and its tributaries.

Natural Areas

Au Sable River Preserve, 360 acres: Near the nesting area of the endangered Kirtland's warbler, the preserve in the Mio Ranger District was acquired by the Nature Conservancy and turned over to the Forest Service. It includes stands of young jack pines favored by the birds, as well as upland pine-aspen forests and white cedar swamps, which provide watershed protection for the Au Sable. Hill's thistle and Allegheny plum, both rare plants, grow in forest openings. It's S of Frederic on an unmarked gravel road W of Batterson Road.

Iargo Springs: The springs by the Au Sable River are adjacent to River Road National Scenic Byway in the Tawas Ranger District. The Chippewa, who used the site for pow-wows, called it "Many Waters" and believed the springs held curative or mystical powers. Loggers in the 19th century constructed dams on the springs to supply water to nearby logging camps; visitors camped at the top of the bluff in the 1920s-1930s. This is now an interpretive area with displays explaining local geology, history and plant and animal life. Visitors can use an elevated boardwalk and 30-foot-high observation deck.

Kirtland's Warbler Management Area, 4,010 acres: The Kirtland's warbler was first identified in 1851 near Cleveland, Ohio, but its breeding grounds near Mack Lake were not discovered until 1903. As botanist Robert H. Mohlenbrock explains in Natural History magazine: "In modern times, suppression of forest fires has meant that many of the jack pine stands have aged, outgrowing their usefulness to the warblers. To satisfy the warbler, the jack pine stands must not only contain sufficient young trees, but must also cover at least 80 acres and preferably as much as 200. Such stands usually have some deciduous trees such as Hill's oak, red oak, pin cherry and shadbush mixed in, but if the proportion of such trees is too high, the warbler will reject the stand."

American Forest magazine's first Heritage Forest planting project in the United States took place on 100 acres here. Now the Forest Service and Michigan Department of Natural Resources plant more jack pines each year to build habitat for the warblers. The annual Kirtland's warbler census shows a dramatic increase in the number of birds since 1951.

Tuttle Marsh, 700 acres: Once a large peat-filled wetland near Lake Huron, this marsh was logged, drained and planted with blueberries. Later, the wetlands were restored and are now dominated by conifers, particularly tamarack, black spruce and balsam fir. It's surrounded by a forest of quaking aspen, pine, red maple and northern red oak. Wildlife include migrating waterfowl, sandhill cranes, mink, muskrat, shorebirds and bald eagles. It's NE of Tawas City on Forest Road 4546.

More Things To See & Do

Au Sable River Queen: These two-hour paddlewheel boat trips follow the Au Sable along the route of the River Road Scenic Byway in the Tawas Ranger District. Trips run from late May through September, with weekend color tours in October. For information, contact Au Sable River Queen of Oscoda, 7604 W. Wickert Road, Hale, MI 48739; ☎ (517) 739-7351 or (517) 728-5713.

Birding: From osprey and eagles to loons and northern water thrush, from wild turkeys and rails to vireos and bitterns, a myriad of birds are found here. Just to the W of the Lumbermen's Monument Visitor Center is Eagle's Nest Overlook, where bald

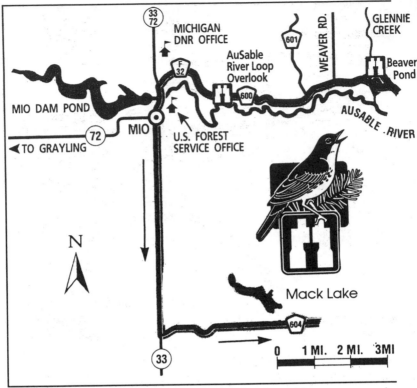

eagles have nested since about 1985. Also found here are northern goshawks, great horned owls and great grey owls. The 5,225-
acre wetland complex known as Tuttle Marsh Wildlife Area N of
East Tawas offers some of Huron's finest birding opportunities;
waterfowl nesting islands lure mallards, wood ducks, Canada geese,
blue-winged teal and black ducks to breed and rear their broods.

Guided tours of Kirtland's warbler nesting areas leave from
Mio and Grayling between mid-May and early July; late May and
June offer the best chances of spotting these rare songbirds, though
there's no guarantee of a sighting. Participants are encouraged to
bring binoculars or spotting scopes. In Mio, the tours begin at U.S.
Forest Service Ranger Station, 401 Court, and are offered Wednes-
day through Friday at 7:30 a.m. and Saturday and Sunday at 7:30
a.m. and 11 a.m. In Grayling, tours depart from the Holiday Inn on

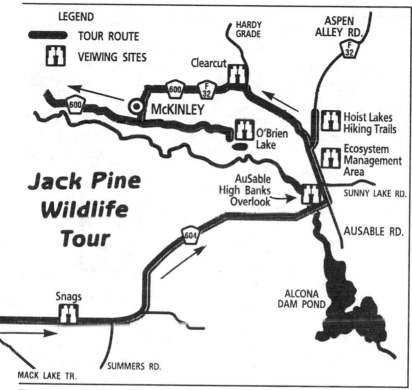

Business Loop I-15 at 7 a.m. and 11 a.m. daily.

For more information, contact the Mio Ranger District, Mio, MI 48647; ☎ (517) 826-3252, or the Michigan Department of Natural Resources Grayling office; ☎ (517) 348-6371.

Canoe Marathon: The annual Au Sable River Canoe Marathon has been a premier competition for more than 45 years. Each July, 30 to 40 crews from the United States and Canada take on the 120-mile Grayling-to-Oscoda challenge. They leave Saturday evening and arrive about 15 hours and 50,000 paddle strokes later. The event is sponsored by Au Sable River International Canoe Marathon Inc.

The marathon and related weekend events draw about 40,000 spectators. The most popular event is the "LeMans" style start of the race when the teams dash several blocks through downtown

Grayling to Ray's Canoe Livery, where they throw their canoe in the Au Sable and begin their all-night paddle to cheers of thousands of spectators. The 9 p.m. start is immediately followed by spectators driving out to a series of bridges along the river to cheer on the paddlers. Some race fans stay up all night, leapfrogging from bridge to bridge, until the teams reach the finish line in Oscoda on Sunday morning.

For a list of activities or a spectators map of the river contact the Au Sable River International Canoe Marathon headquarters at P.O. Box 911, Grayling, MI 49738; ☎ (517) 348-4425. For lodging information, contact the Oscoda Lodging Association, Box 165, Oscoda, MI 48730, ☎ (517) 739-5156; or Grayling Area Visitors Council, 213 James St., Grayling, MI 49738, ☎ (800) 937-8837 or (517) 348-2921.

Canoers' Memorial: Built in the 1950s, the monument honors the marathon canoeists who take part in the annual Grayling-to-Oscoda race. It's at Eagle Nest Overlook and offers a panoramic view of Cooke Dam Pond.

Jack Pine Wildlife Viewing Tour, 48 miles: This self-guided auto tour goes through the Au Sable River Valley and the jack pine ecosystem that is home to the Kirtland's warbler. The loop begins and ends at the Mio Ranger District office. Features include the Au Sable River Loop Overlook; a Wild Turkey side trip to Fairview, which calls itself the "Wild Turkey Capital of Michigan;" a 331-acre area that was clear-cut in 1988 to create Kirtland's warbler habitat; O'Brien Lake; the Hoist Lakes trails; Au Sable High Banks Overlook; and the Mack Lake burn, created by a 1980 fire and now an important nesting area.

Kiwanis Monument: This monument honors Kiwanis clubs in Michigan for donating money in the 1920s-1930s to replant more than 10,000 acres of red pines in the national forest. Chapters across the state provided the rocks and stones, many of which have are carved with the chapters' names or numbers.

Mushroom gathering: This activity is popular from late April through June. Morels, puff balls, and shaggy manes are the most plentiful of the edible ones.

Picnicking and swimming: Day use activities are available at Loon Lake Recreation Area, N of Rose City on Forest Road 4228 in the Mio Ranger District; and Sand Lake Recreation Area, NW of Tawas City on Indian Lake Road in the Tawas Ranger District.

River Road Scenic Byway, 22 miles: The route parallels the S bank of the Au Sable River, going by the Lumbermen's Monument Visitor Center and statue, Eagles Nest Overlook and Canoers' Memorial. As it follows River Road - an old Saginaw-to-Mackinac Indian trail - and Route 65, the byway passes national forest campgrounds and great fishing spots and boat launch sites. Foote Dam, along the way, is a hydroelectric power plant with a 500-foot fishing pier. largo Springs, another stopping place, was a gathering place with mystical waters, according to Native American tradition. Welcome centers at each end provide informational displays: Eastgate, near the Eagle Run Trail system, and Westgate, next to Rollways Picnic Area.

Ranger Districts

Harrisville: U.S. 23, Harrisville, MI 48740; ☎ (517) 724-6471.

Mio: 401 Court St., Mio, MI 48647; ☎ (517) 826-3252.

Tawas: 326 Newman St., East Tawas, MI 48730; ☎ (517) 362-4477.

Gateways

Oscoda: Oscoda/Au Sable Chamber of Commerce, 100 W. Michigan, Oscoda, MI 48750; ☎ (517) 739-7322.

Harrisville: Huron Shores Chamber of Commerce, P.O. Box 151, Harrisville, MI 48740; ☎ (517) 724-5107.

Grayling: Grayling Area Visitors Council, 213 James St., Grayling, MI 49738; ☎ (800) 937-8837 or (517) 348-2921.

Tawas City/East Tawas: Tawas Bay Tourist Bureau, Box 10, Tawas City, MI 48764; ☎ (800) 55-TAWAS or (517) 362-8643.

Fishing for bluegills and other panfish is good at Shelley Lake, a dispersed recreation area that offers walk-in sites and primitive camping. The lake is located 11 miles N of White Cloud near the Loda Lake Wildflower Sanctuary.

MANISTEE

1755 S. Mitchell St.　　　　　　　　　　**531,100 acres**
Cadillac, MI 49601
☎ **(800) 821-6263 or (616) 775-2421**

The Manistee National Forest is known for recreational treasures and environmental gems such as Lake Michigan's Nordhouse Dunes. There are campsites, trails — primarily non-motorized — and gloriously scenic rivers.

The human history of Manistee National Forest includes the legacy of more than 1,000 members of the Civilian Conservation Corps who put up buildings, planted trees and fought hordes of grasshoppers that invaded the forest in 1936; an estimated 37.8 million grasshoppers were found in a single 160-acre pine plantation. Remnants of old sand blowouts are still evident. Established as a national forest in 1938, the Manistee is now administered jointly with Huron National Forest to the east.

 ## Camping

Lakes and rivers highlight the 19 developed campgrounds of Manistee National Forest. The largest is at Lake Michigan Recreation Area, adjoining the Nordhouse Dunes Wilderness Area. Here are the improved campgrounds, number of sites and locations:
Baldwin Ranger District
Bowman Bridge *(20)*, 5 miles W of Baldwin on 52nd Street;

Gleason's Landing (6), 3 miles SW of Baldwin on Brooks Road;

Highbank Lake (9), 2 miles W of Lilley on Roosevelt Road;

Old Grade (20), 11 miles N of Baldwin on Forest Road 5190;

Timber Creek (9), 2 miles E of Branch on Forest Road 5198.

Cadillac Ranger District

Hemlock (15), 5 miles W of Cadillac on Pole Road;

Peterson Bridge (26), 16 miles S of Mesick on M-37;

Ravine (6), 12 miles W of Cadillac on South 17 Mile Road (Forest Road 5334);

Seaton Creek (17), 7 miles SW of Mesick on Forest Road 5993.

Manistee Ranger District

Bear Track (20), 7 miles W of Irons on Forest Road 5202;

Dorner Lake (8), 8 miles SE of Wellston on Synder Road;

Driftwood Valley (21), 4 miles W of Irons on Forest Road 5357;

Lake Michigan (99), 13 miles SW of Manistee on Forest Trail (Forest Road 5629);

Pine Lake (12), 4 miles SW of Wellston on Pine Lake Road;

Sand Lake (45), 1 mile S of Dublin on Forest Road 5728;

Udell Rollways (23), 8 miles NW of Wellston on Horseshoe Bend Road.

White Cloud Ranger District

Benton Lake (24), 4 miles W of Brohman on Pierce Drive (Forest Road 5308);

Nichols Lake (28), 3 miles W of Woodland Park on Forest Road 5140;

Pines Point (33), 9 miles SW of Hesperia on 168th Avenue (Forest Road 5118).

There are primitive camping facilities at a number of locations in the national forest. They include Blacksmith Bayou, W of High Bridge in the Manistee Ranger District; Bear Creek, E of Rainbow Bend in the Manistee Ranger District; Rainbow Bend, NE of Manistee in the Manistee Ranger District; Brush Lake, NE of White

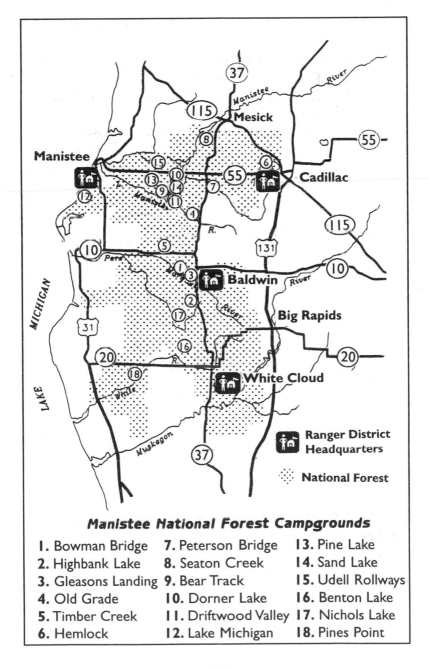

Manistee National Forest Campgrounds

1. Bowman Bridge
2. Highbank Lake
3. Gleasons Landing
4. Old Grade
5. Timber Creek
6. Hemlock
7. Peterson Bridge
8. Seaton Creek
9. Bear Track
10. Dorner Lake
11. Driftwood Valley
12. Lake Michigan
13. Pine Lake
14. Sand Lake
15. Udell Rollways
16. Benton Lake
17. Nichols Lake
18. Pines Point

Cloud in the White Cloud Ranger District; Shelley Lake, E of Woodland Park in the White Cloud Ranger District; and Minnie Pond, NE of Hesperia in the White Cloud Ranger District. In addition, primitive campgrounds are found at the Cedar Creek Motorcycle Staging Area and Horseshoe Lake Motorcycle Staging Area, both in the White Cloud Ranger District.

Three popular dispersed camping areas are in the White Cloud Ranger District: Diamond Point, SW of Hesperia on Forest Road 9304; Indian Lake, SW of Brohman on Pierce Road; and Hungerford Lake, W of Big Rapids on Forest Road 5134.

 ## Trails

An extensive trail system accommodates hiking, snowmobiling, horseback riding, motorcycling, ATVing, cross-country skiing, mountain biking and snowshoeing. The Michigan Cross-Country Cycle Trail and North Country National Scenic Trail cross more than one ranger district.

Michigan Cross-Country Cycle Trail, *211 miles:* Portions of this trail are in the Manistee National Forest. The White Cloud segment provides sections for licensed motorcycles and a loop for non-street-legal motorcycles and ATVs; expect heavy use on weekends and holidays. Along the Baldwin segment are the Big "O" Loop and an ATV loop. There's a combination of single-track and two-track sections on the Cadillac segment, which has flat to rolling terrain. Access sites include M-37, N of Wolf Lake; M-115, S of Mesick; M-20, NW of White Cloud; Timber Creek Campground, E of Branch; and 48 Mile Road, E of Hoxeyville.

North Country National Scenic Trail, *112 miles:* Various segments pass through the Manistee; the longest is the Baldwin segment. The Manistee segment crosses the Little Manistee River and passes through the Udell Hills; much of it follows a ridge paralleling the river. The White Cloud segment is primarily flat to rolling, but has short, hilly stretches; some streams are crossed on logs rather than bridges. Trailheads include Beers Road, NE of Marilla; 40th Street, SW of White Cloud; M-55, W of Wellston;

Freesoil Road, E of Freesoil; Nichols Lake Recreation Area, W of Woodland Park; 76th Street (Big Star Lake Road), SW of Baldwin; Bowman Bridge Campground, W of Baldwin; and Timber Creek Campground, E of Branch.

Other popular trails are:

Baldwin Ranger District

Bowman Lake Trail, I mile: Hikers, skiers and snowshoers can see glacial depressions and unusual vegetation along this short trail circling Bowman Lake. It's within a semi-primitive non-motorized area W of Bowman Bridge Campground and the Pere Marquette River. The trailhead is W of Baldwin on 56th Street.

Honeymoon Lake Snowmobile Trail, 20 miles: Loops follow two-track, Forest Service and county roads. Big Star Lake is the largest body of water on the route. The trailhead is on Birchwood Avenue, SW of Baldwin.

Ward Hills Snowmobile Trail, 40 miles: Forest roads, two-track trails and county roads combine to provide scenic loops for snowmobiling. Park at Timber Creek Campground.

Cadillac Ranger District

Caberfae Way National Snowmobile Trail, 34 miles: One of the state's earliest snowmobile trails, Caberfae Way's trailhead is near the entrance of Caberfae Ski Area. This is one of Michigan's original snowmobile trails and was built by the Forest Service and Job Corps. Loops connect with the Mesick, Wellston, Silver Creek and Cadillac West trails. Caberfae is W of Cadillac on 13 Mile Road.

Manistee River Trail, 12 miles: Limited to non-motorized use, this trail starts at the backwaters of Hodenpyl Dam. Combine ground and water trails by putting in a canoe just S of the dam, canoeing down the Big Manistee to Red Bridge, then hiking back. It's also possible to combine this trail with a portion of the North Country Trail on the other side of the river by crossing over at Red Bridge. This makes an overnight trek of 25 miles through some of the most remote areas of the Lower Peninsula. On both sides of the river are vistas that provide views of the Manistee

River from wooded bluffs. The trailhead for the Manistee River Trail is at Seaton Creek Campground on the backwaters of Hodenpyl Dam.

Manistee Ranger District

Arboretum Trail, 1 mile: This self-guided trail is ideal for a leisurely stroll along Pine Creek. It goes through a number of stands of European, U.S. and Asian trees planted in 1940 to study their growth potential in this climate. Among them are darvian larch, hemlock, Austrian pine, Scotch pine, table mountain pine, black cherry, white spruce, Norway spruce, blue spruce, Douglas fir, pinon pine, Balkan pine, red pine, pitch pine and jack pine. The trail is SW of Wellston on Pine Lake Road.

Udell Hills Snowmobile Trail, 18 miles: The loops run through mixed stands of oak and pine, with a change in elevation of 250 feet. The access site is E of Manistee on Stronach Road.

White Cloud Ranger District

Cedar Creek Motorcycle Trail, 26 miles: The trail is laid out on sandy soils through flat to rolling terrain; there are some low, wet spots. Part of the trail parallels Cedar Creek, with two bridge crossings. The vegetation is primarily oak with a sparse grass and fern undersurface and stands of red and white pine.

Horseshoe Lake Trail, 24 miles: This motorcycle trail offers two loops, mostly single track. There are marshy areas, and crossings of Cushman Creek and numerous lightly traveled public roads. Access is NW of Fremont on 184th Road.

Pines Point Trail, 1 mile: This short trail is generally flat to rolling and passes through a variety of vegetation types in the Pines Point Recreation Area. It's used for hiking and snowshoeing. The trailhead is on Garfield Road, SW of Hesperia.

White River Trail, 12 miles: Starting at the Pines Point picnic area, this trail passes through a semi-primitive area and is used for snowshoeing and horseback riding as well as hiking, biking and cross-country skiing. It is also used by anglers interested in reaching isolated stretches of the White River. The topography is flat to rolling in a terrain that features forested areas and open fields.

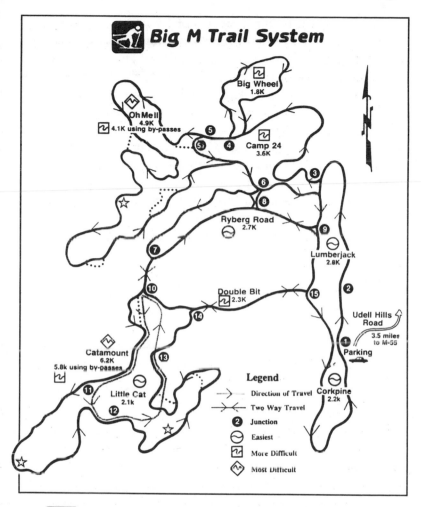

Big M Trail System

Big Wheel
1.8K

Oh Me II
4.9K
4.1K using by-passes

Camp 24
3.6K

Ryberg Road
2.7K

Lumberjack
2.8K

Double Bit
2.3K

Udell Hills
Road
3.5 miles
to M-55

Parking

Catamount
6.2K
5.8k using by-passes

Little Cat
2.1k

Corkpine
2.2k

Legend

→ — Direction of Travel

→← — Two Way Travel

② Junction

⊖ Easiest

♫ More Difficult

◈ Most Difficult

 Cross Country Skiing

These are the trail systems in the Manistee National Forest designed and maintained primarily for cross country skiing:

Big M Ski Trails, *20 miles:* This system of loops is in the Udell Hills. The *Catamount* and *Oh Me II* runs are especially challenging because they include old downhill slopes. Access to the trails is available from Udell Hills Road, W of Wellston. There are also easier runs on the N side of the trail system. Facilities include a warming lodge with a wood-burning stove. The trail system is posted along M-55, halfway between Wellston and Manistee.

Hungerford Ski Trail, 13 miles: This loop trail system traverses open stands of northern hardwoods, pine plantations and thick young aspen. It's also used for mountain biking. The trail system is W of Big Rapids on Forest Road 5134; park by Hungerford Lake.

Mackenzie Ski Trails, 13 miles: Although best known among skiers, mountain bikers have also discovered the allure of Mackenzie. This network of four trails is adjacent to Caberfae, a popular ski resort. (For more information, see In the Forest). Access is available W of Cadillac on Caberfae Road.

 # Boating & Canoeing

Manistee National Forest's eight major rivers, each from 20 to 80 feet wide, provide 246 miles of canoeing. Many have commercial canoe liveries; check with a Forest Service office for a list.

The Manistee River runs 47 miles through the Manistee and Cadillac ranger districts. It offers variety, from wide, slow-moving stretches to the swift, turbulent waters produced by Tippy Dam, a hydroelectric site. Be alert for stump and log jams. Bayous below the dam are exciting to explore. The river is popular among anglers who fish for salmon, steelhead, walleye, trout and pike. The upper segment includes the backwaters behind Tippy Dam and Hodenpyl Dam. The lower segment, which includes access at High Bridge, Blacksmith Bayou, Bear Creek and Rainbow Bend, ends at Lake Michigan.

Other canoe routes include:

Baldwin Ranger District

Pere Marquette River, 44 miles: Designated both a National Scenic River and a State Natural River, the Pere Marquette has a fairly fast current and submerged rocks and logs, but no risky rapids in the national forest. Many banks are steep and eroding. It draws a large number of canoers on summer weekends, as well as anglers and drift boats, causing one outdoor writer to observe, "Pere Marquette is a river in the process of being loved to death." Be alert between Walhalla and Indian Bridge because the river breaks into numerous channels, making it difficult to find a way through. Access sites include Forks Landing, Bowman Bridge, Rainbow Rapids and Indian Bridge.

In 1992, the U.S Forest Service instituted a permit system for paddlers on the Pere Marquette, due to its overwhelming popularity. Daily watercraft permits are required for anyone on the river between May 15 and Sept. 10. There is a small daily fee for the permit; reservations can be made in advance by calling the Forest Service at ☎ (616) 745-3100.

Pere Marquette River, Big South Branch, 15 miles: The river gradually becomes slower, wider and deeper as the area turns swampier, and its banks become less distinct. This is a State Natural River. Campbell Bridge and Riverside Bridge provide access.

Manistee Ranger District

Big Sable River, 37 miles: The Big Sable cuts through the national forest on its way to Lake Michigan. Some canoeists enjoy trout fishing on the upper stretches, and warm water species plus the occasional sturgeon on the lower stretches and in Hamlin Lake. Ten road crossings can be used to launch canoes, including the South Campbell-Yonker Road Bridge and Freesoil Road Bridge.

Little Manistee River, 25 miles: Although the Little Manistee is canoeable, it's better known for its steelhead fishing. Sections are shallow, especially during long dry periods, and impeded by overhanging brush. There also are sharp, horseshoe bends. Oak and white pine cover the high banks. The Link's Ponds area is a series of former fish rearing ponds and now attracts wildlife. It empties into Manistee Lake. Driftwood Valley and Bear Track campgrounds are among the access sites.

Pine River, 33 miles: There are no hazardous rapids, but the current on this pool and riffle stream is swift. Banks are steep, sandy and fragile; some low-hanging branches and popular fishing bridges loom over the river, which is a high-quality trout stream.

You can launch at Elm Flats, Dobson Bridge and Peterson Bridge.

As with the Pere Marquette River, a watercraft permit is required on the Pine for canoers on the water from May 1 through Oct. 1. Reservations can be made in advance by calling the Permit Station on M-55 at ☎ (616) 862-3333. Canoe liveries will obtain the permit for those planning to paddle a rental boat.

White Cloud Ranger District

Little Muskegon River, 26 miles: The river corridor is popular for wildlife viewing, especially deer, rabbit, woodchuck, songbirds, beaver, duck, geese, muskrat and swan. The upper two-thirds is a pool-and-riffle stream, but it widens and slows down near Croton Dam Pond. Bullrushes and slack water are found at the mouth. Water levels are low during mid- to late summer. The first put-in is just below Morley Dam.

White River, 37 miles: This is Michigan's southernmost major trout stream and empties into Lake Michigan. Upstream of Hesperia, the river is floatable but difficult due to a narrow channel, downed trees and occasional log jams. The route downstream of Hesperia to White Lake is bordered by woodlands of hardwood and white cedar. There are some pools and riffles; the course twists and meanders with a steady, moderate current below Pines Point. Banks are steep and eroding along the river. There are flooded tag alder and dogwood marshes. Access sites include the Pines Point Recreation Area.

 Fishing

The Pere Marquette River is highly regarded as one of Michigan's top fishing streams, especially for brown trout, spring steelhead runs and fall salmon runs. In fact, in 1884 it became the first place in North America where brown trout were planted. Today, the most popular stretch of the river is the catch-and-release, flies-only stretch that begins at M-37. The Manistee, Little Manistee and Pine rivers are fished for steelhead, chinook, salmon and coho. Behind the Tippy Dam on the Manistee is an especially popular fishery with shoreline steelheaders from fall through the winter. When the run is at its peak in early spring, anglers are often shoulder to shoulder on the river bank.

Lakes and ponds produce smallmouth and largemouth bass, bluegill, tiger muskellunge, yellow perch, walleye, northern pike, and brown, rainbow and brook trout. Fisheries habitat improvement efforts, such as that of the Fish America Foundation on Bigelow Creek, are ongoing in the national forest.

There are small native brook trout streams, backcountry bluegill and bass lakes and larger lakes for northern pike and walleye. Perch Lake is a walleye rearing pond, and Nichols Lake is stocked with walleye. Some favorite panfishing lakes are Indian, Brush, Shelley, Twinwood, Hidden and Bluegill. Alley Lake Picnic Area is a good spot for bass and panfish. Other popular places include Croton Dam Pond, Diamond Lake and Hamlin Lake for musky, and the Tippy Dam impoundment, Robinson Lake and the Hodenpyl backwaters for northern pike.

The closest Great Lakes fishing is from Manistee on Lake Michigan.

 ## Wilderness Area

Nordhouse Dunes Wilderness Area, 3,450 acres: The irreplaceable and fragile Nordhouse Dunes run along 7,300 feet of undeveloped Lake Michigan shoreline; the dunes extend inland more than a mile. Located in the Manistee Ranger District, these are the state's best example of windblown dunes and the world's most extensive interdunal wetlands adjacent to fresh water. Formed within the past 13,000 years, the dunes reach 140 feet high and surround small parcels and plateaus of woody vegetation. Some are lightly covered by dune grass, with marshes and small water holes found throughout the area.

Pitcher's thistle and spotted wintergreen grow here. As botanist Robert H. Mohlenbrock writes in Natural History magazine, "A number of environmental conditions constrain the growth of vegetation in the various dune communities. The driving winds not only shape the dunes but literally sandblast living and dead

A backcountry campsite in the Nordhouse Dunes Wilderness, the only federally-designated wilderness in the Lower Peninsula of Michigan.

trees. Because of the paucity of vegetation and high exposure, temperatures on the dunes are more extreme than in surrounding areas - higher in summer, lower in winter."

A 10-mile trail system, composed mostly of old logging roads and railroad lines, provides access throughout the N half of the wilderness. Backcountry camping is allowed but campfires are discouraged in open sand areas. Use is heaviest during summer and fall. The Nordhouse Dunes are also adjacent to Ludington State Park, whose N half is a dedicated natural area. Together the two areas preserve Big Sable Point and allow backpackers to trek for miles along an undeveloped Lake Michigan shoreline.

The wilderness is directly S of the Lake Michigan Recreation Area, just S of Manistee and reached from U.S. 31 via Lake Michigan Recreation Area Road. The other trail access is the W end of

206

Nurnberg Road reached by heading S of Lake Michigan Recreation Area Road on Quarterline Road.

 ## Natural Areas

Blue Lakes Barrens, 2,000 acres: This is a biologically rich combination of coastal plain marsh and oak-pine barrens, with a scenic stretch of Burns Lake shoreline. Endangered species include the Karner blue butterfly and purple spike-rush. This plentiful collection of marshland plants is rare in the Great Lakes, according to the Nature Conservancy. It is in the Cadillac Ranger District.

Loda Lake Wild Flower Sanctuary: The sanctuary in the White Cloud Ranger District encompasses a small lake, bog, some high ground and dry areas, with a network of trails. Planning by the Federated Garden Club of Michigan and the Forest Service began in 1938, but World War II interrupted their work. Protected species include trailing arbutus, bird's foot violet, bittersweet, club mosses, flowering dogwood, trillium, Michigan holly, American lotus, native orchids, gentian and pipsissewa. In addition to wildflowers, visitors can see evidence of human presence, including an old orchard and the foundation of an abandoned barn. It is NW of White Cloud on Five Mile Road. At the parking area you can pick up an interpretive brochure that corresponds with numbered posts along the trails.

Newaygo Prairies: The tall grass prairies of mid-America are largely gone, but several environmentally important patches have survived near Newaygo, within the national forest's White Cloud Ranger District. The patches are up to 110 acres each, and as many as 125 species of plants have been identified in the largest one. They include Indian grass, June grass, blazing stars, big and little bluestem, heath aster, prairie cinquefoil and the rare prairie smoke.

Walkinshaw Wetlands, 1,031 acres: This wetlands, crossed by several streams, contains extensive wet meadow and marsh habitat. Greater sandhill cranes - more than 200 at a time in late

IN THE FOREST
MACKENZIE SKI TRAILS

Except for the soft whoosh-whoosh of my skis, all's quiet beneath the pines as a gentle wind dislodges newly fallen snow from the branches above. The gray-white bark of leafless birches contrasts with the glistening whiteness of the surrounding snow.

This is one of four Mackenzie Ski Trails, which stretch almost 13 miles in Manistee National Forest. The Mackenzie trails combine the outdoor experiences, serenity and lack of crowds that make cross-country skiing so appealing, so unstressful, so attuned to the environment. That means most cross-country trails through the national forests don't attract skiers who relish the amenities of convenient hot meals and chalet-style socializing.

Yet unlike most such trails, the luxuries are immediately at hand because the Mackenzie trails are adjacent to Caberfae, the popular downhill ski resort, with its T-bars, chair lifts, rope tows, snow-making equipment and dozens of downhill runs. Free parking is available at Caberfae, as are the resort's cafeterias, snack bar, and restrooms. Cross-country gear is also available for rent.

There are marked trailheads for each of the Mackenzie routes: W of Edelweiss Lodge at the bottom of the beginner downhill slope; N of SkyView Cafeteria; at the SW corner of the Caberfae Way Snowmobile Trail parking lot; and on 38 Road, W of the entrance to the downhill area.

Despite the proximity of Caberfae, you're more likely to spot a deer than a stranger along some stretches of the trail. The solitude provides an opportunity to wonder what makes some translucent dead leaves stubbornly cling to otherwise winter-bare branches, or to fantasize about how far you could go off the trail in some direction before finding a road or house.

To help skiers, the Mackenzie trails are marked for difficulty with diamond-shaped blazers on trees and posts. There's a

The serenity of cross country skiing in the national forests.

"You Are Here" map posted at each intersection, showing your present location and the rest of the trails. If you want to rest or picnic, you'll find benches at several intersections.

It's important to know your own stamina and that of your companions. Sudden bad weather, fatigue, a twisted ankle or changing snow conditions can make a route much longer than it appears on the map. Plan ahead and provide plenty of time to return before darkness sets in. First aid is available at Caberfae.

Use a fanny pack to carry snacks, water, a plastic ski tip, compass, matches, wax for changing snow conditions and extra gloves and socks. Be sure to drink plenty of water: just because it's cold doesn't mean you won't sweat.

September and early October - northern harriers and other marsh birds are found here, along with waterfowl, shorebirds and wetland species that use the marsh and surrounding fields during their migrations. Access is on 198th Avenue, SW of Walkerville.

 ## More Things To See & Do

Birding: More than 150 species of birds have been found in Manistee National Forest, ranging alphabetically from the alder flycatcher to the yellow-throated vireo. Loons, woodpeckers, owls, warblers, ducks, hawks, finches, hummingbirds and geese are among them. So are turkeys, great blue herons, greater sandhill cranes, wood thrush, spruce grouse, belted kingfisher, American kestrels and turkey vultures.

Cadillac Fall Color Tour, 82 miles: Fall foliage is a big draw in northern Michigan, and this self-guided tour focuses on the changing colors. It starts and ends in Cadillac, passing through the national forest and the small communities of Mesick, Harietta and Boon. For maps, contact the Cadillac Ranger District.

Downhill skiing: Caberfae Peaks Resort in the Cadillac Ranger District offers 18 runs, five chair lifts, two T-bars and some of the longest vertical drops in the Lower Peninsula. Cross-country ski trails lead deep into the national forest. Much of the Caberfae Sports Area is a legacy of Civilian Conservation Corps labor. Members built five ski runs, a 15-meter ski jump, toboggan runs, and 6 miles of snowshoe runs. Two CCC buildings are still used. It's on Caberfae Road, W of Cadillac.

Mushrooming: May is morel month in the national forest, although these delicacies can also be found from late April through June in beech-maple forests, oak woods, burned-over meadows, brushy places and around elm stumps. No permit is required to gather them. A free national forest brochure illustrates the differences between the true morel and the inedible false morel. Other edible mushrooms gathered here are the white, black and the rare giant morel.

Manistee National Forest Festival: This annual summer

A young tuber leisurely floats down the White River after departing from Pines Point Campground. She'll also end at the campground, following an oxbow in the river.

gathering features activities in the national forest and in the Lake Michigan community of Manistee. Although events change yearly, they often include foot races, canoeing, fireworks, a parade, arts and crafts, historic building and sawmill tours, entertainment and hikes.

The National Forest Visitor Center is open, and events include a North Country National Scenic Trail hike and a canoe tour of the Big Manistee. For information, contact the Manistee Area Chamber of Commerce, 11 Cypress St., Manistee, MI 49660; ☎ (616) 723-2575.

Picnicking: Apart from the campgrounds with day use picnic facilities, the national forest offers Alley Lake Picnic Area on Echo Drive (Old M-20), SW of White Cloud. Across the road from the picnic area is the W.I. White Memorial Pine Plantation.

Self-guided auto tour: Starting in Cadillac, you can drive 60 miles round trip to the site of the Civilian Conservation Corps' former Camp Axin; Olga Lake and its dam; Caberfae ski area; a pine plantation; and Chittenden Nursery, established to produce Norway and white pine and white spruce.

Tubing: In addition to camping, picnicking, hiking and canoeing at Pines Point Recreation Area, visitors can go tubing on the White River in the White Cloud Ranger District. At the campground, the river forms a huge oxbow so it's possible to put in at the canoe launch, tube for a half hour or so and then depart at the picnic area, eliminating the need for special transportation. Most of the summer the river is shallow with a mild current, making it ideal for families tubing with children.

Ranger Districts

Baldwin: 650 N. Michigan Ave., Baldwin, MI 49304; ☎ (616) 745-4631.

Cadillac: 1800 W. M-55, Box 409, Cadillac, MI 49601; ☎ (616) 775-8539.

Manistee: 1658 Manistee Hwy., Manistee, MI 49660; ☎ (616) 723-2211.

White Cloud: 12 N. Charles St., White Cloud, MI 49349; ☎ (616) 689-6696.

Gateways

Big Rapids: Mecosta County Convention & Visitors Bureau, 246 N. State St., Big Rapids, MI 49307; ☎ (800) 833-6697 or

(616) 796-7640.

Cadillac: Cadillac Area Visitors Bureau, 222 Lake St., Cadillac, MI 49601; ☎ (800) 225-2537 or (616) 775-9776.

Grayling: Grayling Area Visitors Council, 213 James St., Grayling, MI 49738; ☎ (800) 937-8837 or (517) 348-2921.

Ludington: Ludington Convention & Visitors Bureau, 5827 West U.S. 10, Ludington, MI 49431; ☎ (800) 542-4600 or (616) 845-0324.

Manistee: Manistee Area Chamber of Commerce, 11 Cypress St., Manistee, MI 49660; ☎ (616) 723-2575.

National forest campsites are usually wooded rustic with picnic tables, fire rings and often latrine posts.

HIAWATHA

2727 N. Lincoln Road　　　　**880,000 acres**
Escanaba, MI 49829
☎ **(906) 786-4062**

The only national forest to border three Great Lakes -Superior, Huron and Michigan - Hiawatha mixes rugged Upper Peninsula wilderness with scuba diving, canoe routes, trails and dramatic lakeshore vistas. Named for Longfellow's famous poem *Song of Hiawatha*, the forest features more than 30 varieties of trees, hundreds of species of birds, historic sites, and animals ranging from black bear and moose to ruffed grouse and bobcat.

Not surprisingly, with 775 miles of streams and rivers and more than 410 lakes, water provides a major theme for recreational users and tourists, offering waterfalls, Wild and Scenic Rivers, Great Lakes fishing and inland boating. Most campgrounds are on a lake, and there's a scenic byway along the Lake Superior shore.

Hiawatha's Grand Island Recreation Area is across from Pictured Rocks National Lakeshore. Found here are remnants of Indian encampments, two mid-19th-century lighthouses, bears and eagles, towering sandstone cliffs, waterfall-formed winter ice caves, and Echo Lake, believed to be North America's largest lake created by beaver dams. The island, 4 miles wide and almost 8 miles long, boasts a 27-mile coastline.

Camping

Hiawatha has more than 20 developed campgrounds. Their names and locations, with number of camping sites, are:

Manistique Ranger District

Camp 7 Lake (47), 37 miles S of Munising on County Road 442;

Colwell Lake (35), 20 miles S of Munising on Forest Road 2246;

Corner Lake (9), 15 miles S of Munising on Forest Road 2259;

Indian River (12), 20 miles N of Manistique on M-94;

Little Bass Lake (12), 23 miles NW of Manistique on County Road 437.

Munising Ranger District

Au Train Lake (37), 10 miles W of Munising on Forest Road 2596;

Bay Furnace (53), 5 miles W of Munising on M-38;

Hovey Lake (50), 12 miles SW of Munising on Forest Road 2473;

Island Lake (45), 12 miles S of Munising on Forest Road 2268;

Pete's Lake (41), 12 miles S of Munising on Forest Road 2173.

Widewaters (34), 13 miles S of Munising on Forest Road 2262.

Rapid River Ranger District

Haymeadow Creek (15), 11 miles NE of Rapid River on County Road 509;

Little Bay de Noc (38), 7 miles S of Rapid River on County Road 513;

Flowing Well (10), 14 miles E of Rapid River on Forest Highway 13;

Sault Ste. Marie Ranger District

Bay View (24), 27 miles W of Sault Ste. Marie on Lake Shore Drive (Forest Road 3150);

Monocle Lake (44), 7 miles NW of Brimley on Lake Shore Drive (Forest Road 3150);

216

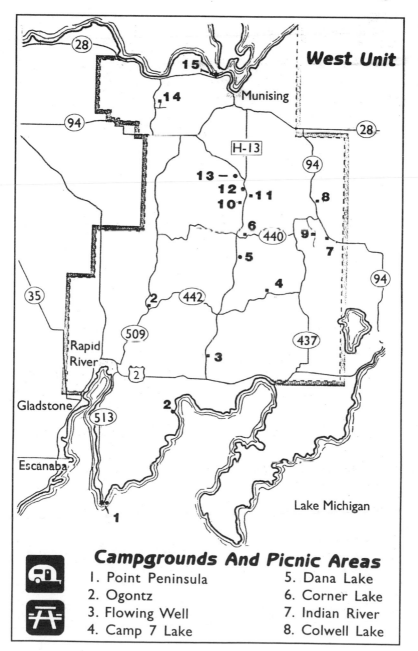

Campgrounds And Picnic Areas

1. Point Peninsula
2. Ogontz
3. Flowing Well
4. Camp 7 Lake
5. Dana Lake
6. Corner Lake
7. Indian River
8. Colwell Lake

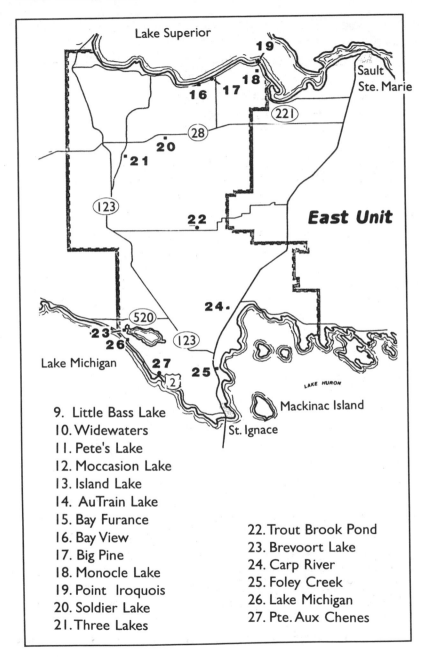

Lake Superior

19

16 17 18

Sault Ste. Marie

221

28

20

21

123

22

East Unit

24.

520

23
26

123

Lake Michigan

27

2

25

LAKE HURON

Mackinac Island

St. Ignace

9. Little Bass Lake
10. Widewaters
11. Pete's Lake
12. Moccasion Lake
13. Island Lake
14. AuTrain Lake
15. Bay Furance
16. Bay View
17. Big Pine
18. Monocle Lake
19. Point Iroquois
20. Soldier Lake
21. Three Lakes

22. Trout Brook Pond
23. Brevoort Lake
24. Carp River
25. Foley Creek
26. Lake Michigan
27. Pte. Aux Chenes

Soldier Lake (55), 30 miles SW of Sault Ste. Marie on Forest Road 3138;

Three Lakes (48), 38 miles W of Sault Ste. Marie on Forest Road 3142.

St. Ignace Ranger District

Brevoort Lake (70), 20 miles W of St. Ignace on Forest Road 3473;

Carp River (44), 8 miles N of St. Ignace on Forest Road 3445;

Foley Creek (54), 6 miles N of St. Ignace on Old Mackinac Trail (H-63);

Lake Michigan (38), 18 miles W of St. Ignace on U.S. 2.

There's a single walk-in developed campsite at *Ewing Point* on McKeever Lake near Bruno's Run Hiking Trail. There also are waterfront spots with primitive campsites: *Triangle Lake* (2); *Toms Lake* (1); *Swan Lake* (4); *Steuben Lake* (4); *Mowe Lake* (2); *Lyman Lake* (10); *Leg Lake* (2); *Jackpine Lake* (2); *Gooseneck Lake* (4); *Ironjaw Lake* (1); *Lake Nineteen* (2); *East Lake* (3); *Crooked Lake* (1); *Chicago Lake* (4); *Carr Lake* (1); *Banana Lake* (1); *Bear Lake* (1); *Camp Cook* (4); *Carr Lake* (1); *Muleshoe Lake* (2); *Square Lake* (1); and *Lake Michigan* (3).

 Trails

Parts of the North Country National Scenic Trail pass through Hiawatha, including 35 miles in the St. Ignace District and 42 miles in the Sault Ste. Marie District.

There are interpretive trails at some campgrounds, including Brevoort Lake's Ridge Trail and Camp 7 Lake's 3-mile Van Winkle Nature Trail. Colwell Lake Campground is the starting point for the 2-mile Stutts Creek Nature Trail. At Camp Round Lake, an interpretive trail traces the history of the Civilian Conservation Corps and explains what life was like for the young men in the camps. Maywood History Trail on Little Bay de Noc explains life for the Noquet Indians and for early 20th-century travelers who arrived by steamer.

Other campgrounds offer access to short trails. At Monocle

Lake, a 2-mile trail includes a boardwalk across a beaver dam and wetlands; it leads to a high bluff overlooking the lake, the Canadian hills and the St. Marys River shipping channel. At Haymeadow Creek, a winding path crosses small bridges through the forest to a high-quality trout stream and waterfalls. And from Foley Creek, it's a 2-mile round trip on the Horseshoe Bay Hiking Trail through northern white cedar lowlands, past ponds frequented by great blue herons and then to a secluded, sandy Lake Huron beach.

Popular trails include:

Bay de Noc-Grand Island Trail, *40 miles*: It parallels the Whitefish River along the approximate route of an ancient Chippewa portage trail in the Rapid River and Munising Ranger Districts. Parts are relatively flat, while other sections have random, short rounded hills created by glaciation. The trail is open to horseback riders as well as hikers. The trailhead is on County Road 509.

Bruno's Run Trail, *7 miles*: Hikers, snowshoers and experienced cross-country skiers use this loop. It traverses a glacial plain, passes small lakes and crosses Hemlock Cathedral, a dense grove of mature hemlock. A segment follows an old logging grade. To reach it, take Forest Highway 13 in the Munising Ranger District.

Maywood History Trail, *0.6 miles*: Twelve interpretive panels cover the rich history of the area, which was used as a summer campground by Noquet Indians traveling to Lake Superior to trade fur. Until the early 1920s, the Maywood Hotel catered to visitors from as far away as Chicago. To reach the trail, take County Road 513 from Rapid River.

Nahma Grade Snowmobile Trail, *31 miles*: It follows an abandoned roadbed that was part of 75 miles of track of the Nahma & Northern Railway. Track construction began in 1901, but logging trucks started to make the steam locomotive obsolete after World War I; the first of the tracks were removed in 1947. This groomed and marked trail traverses lowlands, sand flats, cedar swamps, bogs, sand dune ridges and rolling hardwood hills. It crosses Mormon Creek and the Sturgeon River. The trailhead is

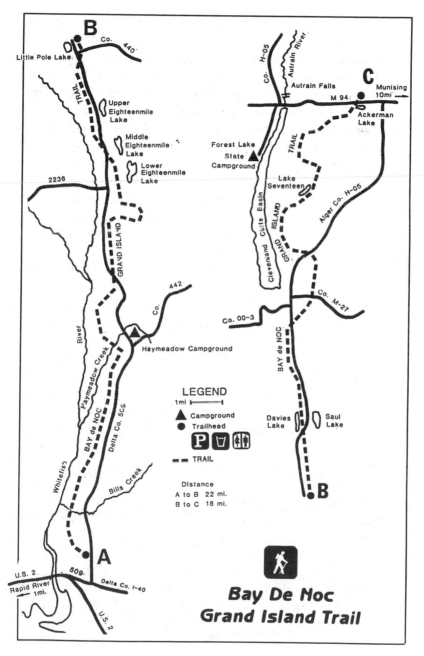

B

Little Pole Lake

Co. 440

TRAIL

Upper
Eighteenmile
Lake

Middle
Eighteenmile
Lake

Lower
Eighteenmile
Lake

2236

GRAND ISLAND

Co. 442

River

Paymeadow Creek

BAY de NOC

Delta Co. 5CS

Whitefish

Bills Creek

509

A

U.S. 2

Rapid River
1 mi.

Delta Co. I-40

U.S. 2

Co. H-05

Autrain River

Autrain Falls

M 94

C

Munising
10mi

Ackerman
Lake

Forest Lake
State
Campground

Lake
Seventeen

Cleveland Cliffs Basin

GRAND ISLAND

Alger Co. H-05

TRAIL

Co. M-27

Co. 00-3

BAY de NOC

Davies
Lake

Saul
Lake

B

Haymeadow Campground

LEGEND

1mi ├────┤

▲ Campground

● Trailhead

🅿 ⛺ 🚻

▬ ▬ TRAIL

Distance
A to B 22 mi.
B to C 18 mi.

**Bay De Noc
Grand Island Trail**

on County Road I-40 E of Rapid River.

Pine Marten Run Trail, 26 *miles:* This trail network, open to both hikers and horseback riders, is in the Ironjaw Semi-Primitive Area, NW of Manistique. Accessible from County Roads 440 and 437 and Forest Road 2258, Pine Martin Run is composed of five loops with interconnecting spurs that wind around a dozen lakes and the Indian River. Camping is permitted throughout the area but permits are needed to camp at Sawn, Triangle, Ironjaw and Lake Nineteen. There are also Adirondack shelters with fire rings at Rim and Rumble lakes.

 ## Cross Country Skiing

Hiawatha National Forest offers the best variety of cross country ski trails in Michigan, particularly around Munising, which, thanks to Lake Superior, receives close to 200 inches of snow a year. Most trails in this area are groomed on a regular basis and many feature warming huts at the trailheads. For more information or a location map of these trails call the Munising Ranger District (☎ 906-387-2512). Here are the popular ski trails throughout the national forest:

McKeever Hills Ski Trail, 8 *miles:* Located south of Munising, McKeever Hills offers a three-loop trail system that includes many hills, long downhill runs and scenic vistas. The 4.7-mile B Loop is a particularly scenic route that passes the shorelines of three lakes. Also located with the trail system is a rustic log cabin that overlooks McKeever Lake and can be rented as overnight accommodations. The trailhead is located on Forest Highway 13 S of Munising. Call the Munising Ranger District to rent McKeever Lake Cabin.

Buckhorn Ski Trail, 17 miles: Located near McKeever Hills, this extensive trail system features gently rolling hills and five loops that range from "easiest" to "most challenging." Several loops wind past Hovey Lake or cross Indian River and are particularly good places to spot wildlife in the winter. The trailhead is on Buckhorn Road, W of Forest Highway 13.

The McKeever Cabin located along the McKeever Hills Ski Trail can be rented year-round.

Christmas Ski Trail, *2 miles:* Come winter Bay Furnace Campground is transformed into this easy but delightful ski trail. Loop B skirts Lake Superior while Loops C and D are lit for night skiing. Rental equipment is available near the trailhead, located on M-28 in the town of Christmas.

Valley Spur Ski Trail, *12 miles:* Inland from Lake Superior in the Munising Ranger District, Valley Spur features loops that range from a mile to a 7-mile skating loop. This is one of the best cross country ski systems in the Upper Peninsula and some sections are especially hilly with runs named *Catapult Hill, Slingshot, Devil's Hole, Bigfoot's Revenge* and *Stairway to Heaven.* The trailhead is on M-94 and features a warming hut with tables and a wood-burning stove inside.

Hiawatha Ski Trail, *8 miles:* Extending from the parking area of the Hiawatha Slopes Ski Hill is four-loop trail system. Hiawatha Ski Trail is not groomed and offers skiers more of a backcountry

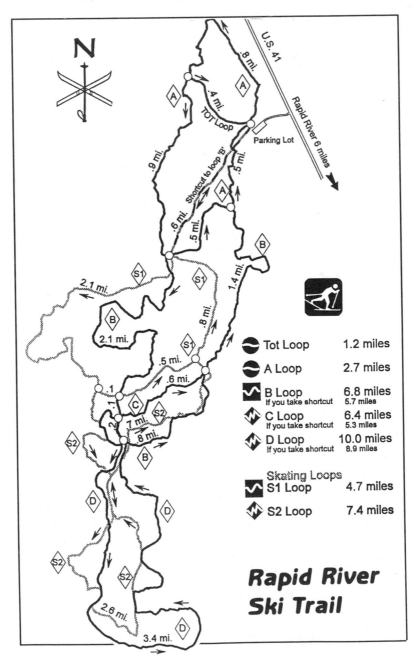

N

U.S. 41

.8 mi.

TOT Loop

.4 mi.

A

A

Rapid River 6 miles

Parking Lot

.9 mi.

Shortcut to loop 'B'

.5 mi.

A

.6 mi.

.5 mi.

B

2.1 mi.

S1

S1

1.4 mi.

.8 mi.

B

2.1 mi.

S1

.5 mi.

.6 mi.

.1

C

S2

.2 mi.

7 mi.

S2

8 mi.

B

D

D

S2

S2

2.6 mi.

D

3.4 mi.

	Tot Loop	1.2 miles
	A Loop	2.7 miles
	B Loop If you take shortcut	6.8 miles 5.7 miles
	C Loop If you take shortcut	6.4 miles 5.3 miles
	D Loop If you take shortcut	10.0 miles 8.9 miles
	Skating Loops S1 Loop	4.7 miles
	S2 Loop	7.4 miles

Rapid River
Ski Trail

experience. Hiawatha Slopes is reached from Chatham by turning N on Forest Road 2483.

Rapid River Ski Trail, 39 miles: Passing through flat bottom-lands and steep pine-covered ridges, the trail offers different levels of challenge. Easy sections have names such as *Slowpoke* and *Easy Rider;* expect more difficulty on *Herringbone Hill, Pike's Peak, Buzz's Bounce* and *Highrise.* The trailhead is on U.S. 41 in the Rapid River Ranger District.

Sand Dunes Ski Trail, 8 miles: The trail goes over and around old Lake Michigan dunes, now extinct because they are no longer moved by the wind. The trailhead is at the site of a former 1930s CCC camp. There are optional bypasses around some big hills, so less experienced skiers can skirt them while advanced skiers can go over them. The trail is off Brevoort Lake Road (H-57), just N of U.S. 2 in the St. Ignace Ranger District, and features a warming hut.

McNearney Ski Trail, 9 miles: This trail system is designed primarily for skiing and offers easy loops as well as *Forester's Loop,* a "most difficult" 3-mile run that includes several steep hills. The loops pass through the site of an early 20th-century logging camp, a white spruce plantation, the Hemlock Cathedral grove, nine lakes and ancient sand dunes. The trailhead is on Salt Point Road in the Sault Ste. Marie Ranger District.

St. Martin Ski Trail, 3 miles: Completed in 1992, this "figure 8" trail is rated easy to moderate and offers a good opportunity to spot bald eagles while skiing as the birds often winter here. The trail also passes through a deer yard. From M-134, head S on Forest Road 3436 to reach the trailhead.

Boating & Canoeing

With abundant inland lakes and rivers, and with frontage on Lake Michigan, Lake Huron and Lake Superior, Hiawatha offers a cornucopia of boating and canoeing opportunities, and ample boat launch sites. For a lake country canoe experience, paddle Big Island Lake Wilderness, an area of 23 lakes connected to each

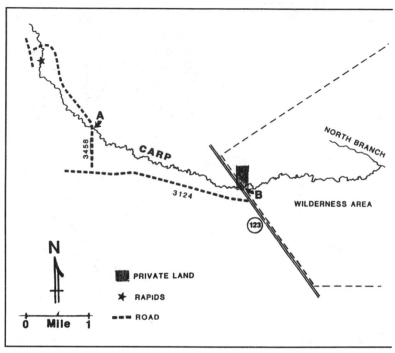

other by a system of portages (see Wilderness Areas).

These are the popular canoeing rivers:

Carp River, 28 miles: The route ends at Lake Huron's St. Martin Bay in the St. Ignace Ranger District. The river was used for 19th-century log drives and is rated as a second-quality trout stream. Portages are necessary. The start is at Forest Road 3458 at St. Martin's Bay on Lake Huron.

Indian River, 36 miles: Starting at the Fish Lake access site in the Manistique Ranger District, the route runs to Indian Lake. Some spots requiring portaging or maneuvering to avoid logs and shallow, maze-like braids.

Sturgeon River, 41 miles: Although this stretch of the Sturgeon is relatively slow moving with many meanders, there are two areas of rapids and riffles that can be swift, deep, cold and hazardous for inexperienced canoeists in early spring. For the best canoeing, the water is high between April 30 and the end of June, or

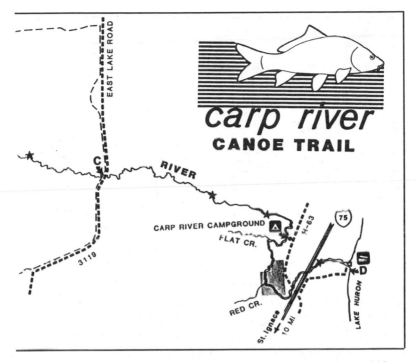

after mid-September. The first access is on County Road 440 in the Rapid River Ranger District.

Whitefish River, 28 miles: Canoeing routes exist on the river's East and West Branches in the Rapid River Ranger District. Prime season is from the end of April until the end of June. East Branch access begins on County Road H-03 at Trout Lake; West Branch access begins on County Road 444.

Au Train River, 10 miles: This slow-moving river offers an easy paddle to Lake Superior, a four- to six-hour trip. Once a run for loggers, the river now is an ideal family trip due to the lack of rapids and portages. Canoes can be rented from area resorts and you can access the river from either the national forest boat launch at Au Train Campground on the lake or from a bridge where County Road H-03 crosses the river.

Fishing

Anglers have the benefit of three diverse fishing options in Hiawatha: Great Lakes, inland lakes and ponds, and rivers and streams. The vast majority of lakes in the national forest support a warmwater fishery that includes largemouth bass, panfish, perch, crappies and walleyes. One of the best walleye lakes in the eastern half of the Upper Peninsula is Brevoort, site of the a national forest campground and boat ramp at its W end. The 4,233-acre undeveloped lake features a 2,100-foot long walleye spawning reef that was constructed in 1985 and has since enhanced the fishery. Other noted walleye lakes in the national forest include Au Train just W of Munising, Corner and Moccasin off of County Road H-13, and Gooseneck and Thunder lakes in the Manistique Ranger District.

Petes Lake off County Road H-13 features a campground and boat ramp and is fished for smallmouth bass and bluegill while nearby McKeever Lake is popular for pike. Other recommended lakes include Lyman in the Manistique Ranger District for bluegills, Camp 7 (campground and boat launch) off County Road 442 for large perch, and Jackpine in the Manistique Ranger District for smallmouth bass.

There is also an excellent coldwater fishery throughout the national forest with anglers targeting rainbow trout, brook trout and brown trout in particular. Some of the best brook trout fisheries are smaller streams in the Manistique Ranger District and include Kilpecker Creek, Carr Creek, the lower half of Little Murphy Creek and Little Indian River. Good brown trout fishing occurs in Indian River upstream from County Road 449 and in the Sturgeon River between County Road H-13 and U.S. 2.

 Wilderness Areas

Big Island Lake Wilderness, 5,856 acres: Old stumps, railroad grades and roadbeds, as well as an abandoned homestead

An angler holds a walleye taken from AuTrain Lake. Hiawatha National Forest offers a variety of angling opportunities.

229

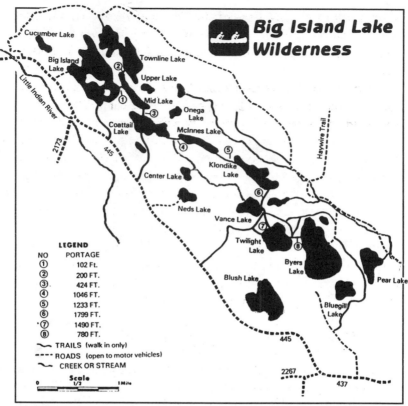

Big Island Lake Wilderness

LEGEND

NO	PORTAGE
①	102 Ft.
②	200 FT.
③	424 FT.
④	1046 FT.
⑤	1233 FT.
⑥	1799 FT.
⑦	1490 FT.
⑧	780 FT.

∼ TRAILS (walk in only)
---- ROADS (open to motor vehicles)
∼ CREEK OR STREAM

Scale
0   1/2   1 Mile

and the sites of former logging camps are legacies of the period from the 1890s until the 1930s, when this area was heavily logged. Today the wilderness is a popular canoeing destination that features hardwood forests, rolling hills and 23 lakes linked by portage trails. Because the lakes are relatively sterile and low in fish production, special regulations limit the types and size of fish that can be taken and ban the use of live bait. Visitors may see beaver, bald eagles, loons, great blue herons, pine martens, bobcats and sandhill cranes. Big Island Lake is in the Munising Ranger District and reached from County Road H-13 and County Road 445.

Delirium Wilderness, *11,870 acres:* This area, part of the Sault Ste. Marie Ranger District, was formed from old glacial lakes. Evidence exists of past strip cutting of cedars. The thickly forested swamps are the headwaters of the Pine and Waiska rivers. Also here are Delirium Pond and Sylvester Pond. The wilderness is home to beaver, bobcat, loon, duck, whitetail deer, otter and black bear.

Horseshoe Bay Wilderness, 3,790 acres: There's been little human activity here since logging ended in the early 20th century. This wilderness features 7 miles of Lake Huron frontage; the terrain ranges from low ridges covered by balsam and cedar to marshes and narrow, shallow swamps. Wildlife includes otter, mink, muskrat, beaver, black bear, whitetail deer, great blue heron, gulls, eagles, coyotes, fox and snowshoe hare. Foot travel is rugged due to wet cedar swamps in the interior, but a 1.5-mile trail connects Foley Creek Campground to a Lake Huron beach.

Part of Horseshoe Bay along the Lake Huron shore has been proposed for Research National Area status because it's one of the state's best remaining large examples of wooded dune and swale habitat. It's in the St. Ignace Ranger District just off I-75 on County Road H-63.

Mackinac Wilderness, 12,230 acres: Ridges, forests, marshes and shallow bogs define the area, as do at least seven major beaver ponds. The second-growth forest is 60 to 80 years old. Within the wilderness, the Carp River is marked by oxbows and water-cut riverbanks. In addition to beaver, wildlife includes black bear, ruffed grouse, mink, muskrat, raccoon, osprey, black bear and pileated woodpeckers. The main recreation use is by canoeists paddling the Carp River. The area is in the St. Ignace Ranger District and its SW border lies on M-123.

Rock River Canyon Wilderness, 4,640 acres: This area in the Munising Ranger District was cut over between the late 19th century and the 1920s; old skid trails, railroad grades and logging roads remain evident. It's best known for the Rock River and Silver Creek canyons, each about 150 feet deep and separated by a broad, flat ridges. Erosion by weather and water carved caves 10 to 40 feet deep into the sandstone outcroppings. In the winter, water seeping over the canyons forms ice curtains and ice caves that are favorites among by ice climbers equipped with ropes, axes and crampons. Remote Rock River Falls is a favored destination in the spring, when water cascades over a ledge into a pool 15 feet below.

There are 18 species of fish in the stream system, including brown, rainbow and brook trout, coho salmon and northern pike. Because the sandstone walls are fragile, climbing is discouraged. Although there are no posted trails in the wilderness, old roads provide access. Keep in mind, however, foot travel along the canyon floors and steep walls is rough; it's easier to hike the high grounds. Rock River Canyon is 15 miles W of Munising and 4 miles NW of M-94. Forest Road 2276 provides access into the area.

Round Island Wilderness, 378 acres: The island known as Nissawinagong to the local Indians is in the Straits of Mackinac, E of the Mackinac Bridge between Mackinac Island and Bois Blanc Island. It has been free of logging and other commercial activity since the early 20th century. Limestone bedrock outcroppings are present, and there's a 76-foot-high limestone cliff on the NE side. The island, part of the St. Ignace Ranger District, is accessible only by boat or over the ice. The three-story Round Island Lighthouse is not part of the wilderness.

 # Grand Island

This 21-square-mile island recreation area is located less than a mile from the mainland near Munising and is a destination in itself. A recent Forest Service management plan allows limited commercial development and motorized transportation but the number of off-road vehicles, cars and trucks on the island at any one time is strictly regulated.

The island, however, is already a paradise for mountain bikes and hikers who explore a 122-mile network of roads, mostly two-tracks and old logging roads. Although many old roads are starting to brush in, the main ones are easy to follow and marked at the intersections with maps. There are three rustic campsites on

Two campers walk the Lake Michigan shoreline near the Sand Dunes Special Management Area of the national forest.

the beaches of Murray Bay and three more on Trout Bay; backcountry camping is permitted elsewhere on the island. Anglers venture to Duck and Echo lakes for bass and northern pike.

The other users of Grand Island are kayakers who can depart from Bay Furnace Campground and paddle across well-protected Grand Bay to the island. Parts of Grand Island's shoreline are steep rock cliffs and sea caves similar to those found in nearby Pictured Rocks National Lakeshore. Other stretches of shoreline feature sandy beaches, sheer cliffs and an historic lighthouse. Paddling Grand Island has become so popular in recent years, the Forest Service has plans to install "paddle-in" campsites at Bay Furnace Campground.

There is regular public transport to Grand Island throughout the summer. Ferry service is provided by Pictured Rocks Cruises of Munising (☎ 906-387-2379) which makes three runs a day after July 1. Many mountain bikers make Grand Island a day trip and skip the overnight camping. For more information call the Munising Ranger District (☎ 906-387-3700).

 ## Natural Areas

Dukes Research Natural Area, 231 acres: Three white cedar-mixed conifer swamps within its borders are among the few such undisturbed swamps in the Great Lakes region. The swamps are surrounded by northern hardwoods such as basswood, yellow birch, sugar maple and white ash. It's a National Natural Landmark. The area is E of Skandia in the Munising Ranger District.

Pointe aux Chenes, 4,000 acres: This area on Lake Michigan is being studied for protection as a possible Research Natural Area due to its swale and wooded dune habitat. It's home to migratory songbirds, ospreys, eagles, shorebirds and rare Great Lakes endemic plants. The area is W of St. Ignace on U.S. 2.

Purple Coneflower Plant Preserve, 21 acres: Hiawatha surrounds this Michigan Nature Association sanctuary near the ghost town of Kenneth. The purple coneflower, a Great Plains native, is the main attraction, especially when it blooms in early August; other wildflowers and grasses grow here too. The area is W of the ghost town of Kennedy in the the St. Ignace Ranger District.

Sand Dunes Special Management Area: Fragile sand dunes are found NW of St. Ignace along U.S. 2 on Lake Michigan. While some are along the shore, others are farther inland because they date back to a time when the Great Lakes were higher. Some 5,000- to 7,000-year-old dunes are stable and covered by soil and forests. Others are fragile, with dune sand that moves with high winds, especially when the covering vegetation is damaged or disturbed by people or bad weather. Motor vehicles and off-road vehicles are banned from the dunes. The Nature Conservancy has helped acquire and protect some dunes that are home to rare plants. Eagles and osprey nest within wooded dunes.

Shingleton Bog, 5 square miles: This area combines fens, white cedar swamps and peatland with a variety of plant life. Among them are royal and cinnamon ferns, pink lady's-slipper orchids, evergreen club mosses, shrubby cinquefoil, wintergreen, starflower, mountain holly, red chokeberry and bog rosemary. Several arctic species are botanical legacies of receding Ice Age glaciers. The area is SE of Munising.

Squaw Creek Old Growth Area, 65 acres: Fast-moving Squaw Creek divides this area. Red pine, white pine, northern red oak and white birch are predominant N of the creek; eastern hemlock, red pine and white pine dominate to the S. A stroll shows what northern forests were like a century ago: natural reproduction is evident and fallen trees are allowed to decay rather than being removed. It's on County Road 513 in the Rapid River Ranger District.

Sturgeon River Preserve, 3,215 acres: Acquired by the Nature Conservancy and now part of the national forest, the preserve includes part of the Sturgeon River before it empties into Big Bay de Noc on Lake Michigan. There are northern white cedar swamps, black spruce bogs, habitat for migrating waterfowl, and forests of jack pines and northern hardwoods.

Summerby Fen, 1,700 acres: Michigan's leading example of a northern fen community, with its wetlands and open forest, has been proposed for Research Natural Area status. It combines fen and cedar swamp zones, with such plants as Labrador tea, wintergreen, wood lily, Indian paintbrush, arrowgrass, cranberry, goldthread and bunchberry. The area is E of Allenville in the St. Ignace Ranger District.

 ## Historical Attractions

Bay Furnace: All that remains of Onota, a once-prosperous iron smelting town founded in 1869, are the ruins of an iron kiln. The community was abandoned after an 1877 fire destroyed the town. The furnace ruins have been stabilized and interpreted. Markers are posted at Bay Furnace Campground and Picnic Area on the shore of Lake Superior, on M-38 W of Munising.

Peninsula Point Lighthouse: Now part of a picnic area on the Stonington Peninsula, the 40-foot tower is easy to climb, providing a Lake Michigan panorama. Keepers and their families lived in an attached brick home from 1865 until 1922, when the hand-operated oil light was automated. The lighthouse ceased operation in 1936; the keeper's house burned down in 1959. It's at the end of Forest Road 2204 on the Stonington Peninsula. A mile-long interpretive trail leads from the parking area to the light-house.

Point Iroquois Lighthouse: Now a museum, the 1870 Point Iroquois Light Station portrays lighthouse history and technology, as well as daily life of lightkeepers and their families. Named for a 1600s battle between the Chippewa and Iroquois, it marks the transition between the St. Marys River and Lake Superior's White-fish Bay. As the museum brochure notes: "Despite hard work and long hours, life at Point Iroquois had its advantages. Compared with more isolated stations, Point Iroquois offered space and a homelike atmosphere. With increased water traffic, it was necessary to expand personnel. By 1908, the light station housed a head keeper, two assistants and their families. They formed their own self-sustaining community complete with a schoolhouse and a teacher for their children."

The light was replaced in 1962 by an automatic signal beacon across Whitefish Bay at Gros Cap, Ontario. Visitors can climb 72 steps to the top of the 65-foot brick tower for a view of Lake Superior, and can walk wildflower-lined paths to a stony beach. Listed on the National Register of Historic Places, the Point Iroquois Lighthouse is open daily May 15 to Oct. 15. To reach it, take Lake Shore Drive N from Bay Mills.

Round Island Lighthouse: Built in 1895-1896 in the Straits of Mackinac, it was abandoned in the late 1940s when a channel light was installed closer to Mackinac Island. The lighthouse was preserved and restored in the late 1970s. It's not open to the public, but can be seen by boat, ferry and from Mackinac Island.

📷 More Things To See & Do

Auto tours: Self-guided tours take you back to the

The Point Iroquois Lighthouse was built in 1870 and now is a maritime museum on the shores of Lake Superior.

Depression's Civilian Conservation Corps era. The routes pass CCC camps and project sites, including pine plantations and nurseries, stream improvement structures, campgrounds, fire towers and a dam. Ask at the national forest supervisor's office, ranger district offices, Point Iroquois Lighthouse or the visitor centers for maps and information.

Big Pine Picnic Area: With its red pine, birch and maples, this is a great spot to watch tankers and freighters on Whitefish Bay heading to and from the Sault Ste. Marie locks. The beach is a popular place for collecting agates. A short distance to the W lies Salt Point, where salt barges under tow from Detroit and Port Huron washed ashore during storms; on calm days, the shattered ribs of one sunken barge are visible offshore from the mouth of Grants Creek. It's on Forest Highway 42, W of Monocle Lake Campground.

Birding: More than 300 species of birds have been identified at Hiawatha and nearby Pictured Rocks National Lakeshore, Seney National Wildlife Refuge and the Audubon Society Whitefish Point Bird Observatory N of Paradise; some species are uncommon or rare. Annual breeding bird surveys assess general population trends and the effects of management practices on avian populations. The surveys are part of the "Partners in Flight" Neotropical Migratory Bird Conservation Program studying birds that winter in Central and South America but return north to breed. A Hiawatha National Forest field checklist is available, with information on each bird.

Enjoy the 2-mile Au Train Songbird Trail, beginning at Au Train Lake Campground in the Munising Ranger District. From Au Train Grocery and A&L Grocery in Au Train you can rent a songbird kit that includes a cassette player, 28-minute audio tape keyed to color plaques on the trail, binoculars, trail map and Peterson's bird guide. The trail then takes through a wooded and open terrain where you pass through the habitats of 20 songbirds.

Diving: Alger Bottomland Preserve, 113 square miles in size, lies between Hiawatha's Grand Island Recreation Area and Pictured Rocks National Lakeshore. Divers can explore eight major wrecks at depths of 12 to 100 feet, underwater caves and rock cliffs in the state-operated preserve. Wrecks include the schooner *Burmuda*, lost at the S end of Grand Island in 1868; the schooner *George*, lost N of Miners Castle in 1893; the steamer *Herman H. Hettler*, lost off the E end of Trout Point on Grand Island in 1926; the steamer *Kiowa*, lost S of Au Sable Point in 1929; the steamer *Manhattan*, lost near the south end of Grand Island in 1903; and the steamer *Smith Moore*, lost in the East Channel of Munising Bay in 1889.

Most of the 148-square-mile Straits of Mackinac Bottomland Preserve is not directly off Hiawatha's shores, but wrecks of the schooner *M. Stalker* and the freighter *Cedarville* are between Round Island and Mackinaw City. *M. Stalker* sank in 1886, when it was hit by a tow barge. The *Cedarville* was struck by another ship in a 1965 fog, losing 10 crew members and a load of limestone. An unnamed dump barge sank in shallow water in the NW section of the preserve.

Downhill Skiing: The Chatham Hill Ski Area, W of Munising, has two rope tows. It's also the site of the Hiawatha Ski Trail.

Hiawatha National Forest Visitor Center: The center, at 400 E. Munising Ave. in Munising, contains audio visual displays, natural history exhibits and a bookstore.

Fish Hatcheries: On the S shore of Lake Superior, the U.S. Fish & Wildlife Service manages Pendills Creek and Hiawatha Forest National Fish hatcheries, which produce more than 2 million lake trout a year. Inch-long fry from other hatcheries are reared here for about a year until they're 5 to 8 inches long and ready for stocking in the Great Lakes.

Pendills Creek Hatchery is on the site of an 1849 sawmill, W of Brimley on Lake Shore Drive; (906) 437-5231. Hiawatha Forest Hatchery is on M-28 near Raco; (906) 248-5231. Their mailing address is RR No. 1, Box 420, Brimley, MI 49715. Both are open to visitors seven days a week year round, but the Pendills Creek visitor center is open only weekdays from 8 a.m. to 4 p.m. Fish can be seen from the outside raceways at both hatcheries until dusk.

Spectacule Lake Overlook: S of Monocle Lake Campground, there's a spectacular view of Lake Superior, Sault Ste. Marie, Ont., the Soo Locks, Point Iroquois Lighthouse and Spectacle Lake. A memorial plaque is dedicated to Herman and Frances Cameron: "The quiet beauty of this overlook provided inspiration and spiritual strength to this Chippewa couple who lived in the Bay Mills Indian Community. It was their special place for contemplation and renewal."

Whitefish Bay Scenic Byway, 27 miles: Whitefish Bay is the site of many shipwrecks, including that of the famous but ill-fated *Edmund Fitzgerald.* Starting at Monocle Lake Campground the two-lane road, with its "Highway to the Past" theme, follows the shore past sites of historic significance and natural beauty, and provides an opportunity to see ore boats and other freighters on Lake Superior. Most of the route follows Forest Roads 3150 and 42 across public land. One stop provides a vista of Tahquamenon Bay and Emerson Point, as well as access to the North Country Trail; this section of trail winds through old growth forest and over boardwalks to the Naomikong ("where the breakers strike the shore" in Ojibway) Creek Swinging Bridge. Other stops include the Point Iroquois Lighthouse Museum, Pendills Creek National Fish Hatchery, and Bay View and Monocle Lake campgrounds.

Ranger Districts

Manistique: 400 E. Lakeshore Drive, Manistique, MI 49854; ☎ (906) 341-5666.

Munising: 400 E. Munising Ave., Munising, MI 49862; ☎ (906) 387-2512.

Rapid River: 8181 U.S. 2, Rapid River, MI 49878; ☎ (906) 474-6442.

Sault Ste. Marie: 4000 I-75 Business Spur, Sault Ste. Marie, MI 49783; ☎ (906) 635-5311.

St. Ignace: 1498 West U.S. 2, St. Ignace, MI 49781; ☎ (906) 643-7900.

Gateways

Escanaba: Delta County Tourist & Recreation Bureau, 230 Ludington St., Escanaba, MI 49829; ☎ (906) 786-2192.

Manistique: Manistique Area Chamber of Commerce, Box 72, Manistique, MI 49854; ☎ (906) 341-8433.

Munising: Munising Visitors Bureau, Box 310, Munising MI, 49862; ☎ (906) 387-4864.

Sault Ste. Marie: Sault Ste. Marie Tourism Bureau, 2581 I-75 Business Spur, Sault Ste. Marie, MI 49783; ☎ (906) 632-3301 or (800) 647-2858.

St. Ignace: St. Ignace Area Tourism Association, 11 S. State St., St. Ignace, MI 49781; ☎ (800) 338-6660 or (906) 643-6950.

IN THE FOREST
World War II POW Camps

History sometimes hides, and the vast forests of Michigan's Upper Peninsula shroud most of the evidence of more than 1,000 German prisoners of war who labored in the vast northern woods during World War II.

Trees, brush and even wildflowers have reclaimed five Depression-era Civilian Conservation Corps (CCC) camps that housed enemy prisoners. Now they are little visited and nearly forgotten places of memories and imagination.

Hiawatha National Forest archaeologist John Franzen attempts to find whatever is left to be found, whether fence posts or caved-in cellar walls or weathered sheet metal. Clutching an old site plan for long-abandoned Camp Evelyn, he plunges into the trees and locates four concrete blocks and rusting iron anchors - all that's left of an Army guard tower - obscured by the greenery.

Among the native hardwoods grows a wild apple tree, perhaps germinated from a seed spit out long ago by an American soldier or German prisoner.

Relentless time and the area's harsh weather pose the greatest threats to the identification and preservation of cultural resources in the northern forests, including the remains of POW camps, Paleo-Indian sites and 1800s logging camps.

Changes and further deterioration are inevitable, archaeologist Franzen admits. "It's a dynamic thing, you can't stop it. You can't save and restore everything."

Camp AuTrain, another one-time POW facility, presents an unusual memento of the 1944-1946 era. Graffiti is carved into a concrete platform: "Const. by J.B. Brown June 12th, 1945, Sgt. Shows, Cpl. Kornoelje."

Visible remains at AuTrain, organized for CCC Co. 3607 in 1935, and Evelyn, established for CCC Co. 3613 in 1935, include pieces of crumbled shingles, concrete platforms and pads, stove pipes, fence posts, sheet metal and galvanized nails. Yet remnants of only a few structures still stand. Among them are a concrete motor vehicle grease pit at Evelyn.

At AuTrain, a bathhouse trench and part of a stone-walled root cellar are evident. So is a below-ground stone building with two rusty, double-barrel stoves that had heated an overhead garage, preventing truck cable brakes from freezing in the bitterly cold winter nights. Although the stairs are solid and rusty hinges still hang from the door frame, the door and the garage itself disappeared decades ago.

Why were the POW camps placed here, so far from the battlefields of North Africa and Europe where the Germans were captured?

Well, the war drew Upper Peninsula loggers to military duty or essential civilian jobs elsewhere. Timber was still important, however, so the Army Corps of Engineers converted former CCC camps to facilities for 1,098 POWs who would help make up for the American labor shortage. Two hundred Army officers and soldiers were assigned guard duty.

In addition to Evelyn and AuTrain, POWS were housed at Camp Raco, also within Hiawatha National Forest, and further W at Camps Pori and Sidnaw in Ottawa National Forest. After the war, Pori and Sidnaw were used a while for a college summer forestry program, but the buildings were dismantled in the mid-1950s. The Sidnaw site is no longer owned by the government.

The Army rented the POWs to private timber and paper companies. They labored year-round in the woods - cutting and peeling logs, building bridges and loading pulpwood. The pay was as high as 80 cents an hour, paid on release after the war ended.

Security was tight and visitors were few, so records of the POW era are limited. A few Signal Corps photos of Camp Evelyn have been found, though. In one, the commander inspects crafts made by the prisoners, with a framed picture of Hitler on the wall. Another shows smiling POWs in "a moment of relaxation" at the canteen, where they used scrip to buy two bottles of beer each night.

Former U.S. Army Staff Sgt. Albert Dobrenz wrote in a 1983 remembrance letter about guarding the Camp Evelyn POW kitchen: "These POWs weren't the tough Hitler type, they were the younger troops, when Hitler was running short of men. Some of them would have liked to have stayed in the United States because they had no one to go back to in Germany. All in all they were pretty good POWs."

The Evelyn and Au Train sites are in remote spots and diffi-cult to find. But intrepid visitors can feel both the history and the transience of these remote spots, where wild strawberries and reindeer moss cover ground where guards and prisoners once marched.

A Forest Service sign marks the site of Camp Au Train, in the North Country National Scenic Trail, the 3,200-mile hiking route between New York and North Dakota. The sites of Camp Evelyn and other ex-CCC camps, whether or not used for POWs, are unmarked, but still open to the public. Visitors are welcome to poke around and explore, but may not destroy, damage or take artifacts.

Viewing waterfalls is one of the favorite activities for travelers in Ottawa National Forest and throughout much of the western half of Michigan's Upper Peninsula.

OTTAWA

E. U.S. 2   **953,600 acres**
Ironwood, MI 49938
☎ **(906) 932-1330 or (800) 562-1201**

A cornucopia of delights can be found in Ottawa National Forest, the largest of Michigan's national forests and the furthest from major cities. Ottawa's offerings range from waterfalls and black bears to chilly Lake Superior and remote gorges. More than 500 lakes and 2,700 miles of streams and rivers fit within its borders. Parts of six river systems - Black, Ontonagon, Paint, Presque Isle, Sturgeon and Yellow Dog - are protected under the National Wild and Scenic River System. Pine, maple, fir, spruce and birch are the dominant trees. The terrain was shaped by retreating glaciers and is often rugged, with sharp changes in elevation. Some areas are reachable only on foot or water.

Human involvement included prehistoric Native American settlements, logging and mining, as well as privately owned hunting and fishing camps and clubs. Ottawa was established as a national forest in 1931.

There's good reason for residents of the western Upper Peninsula to call this Big Snow Country: parts of Ottawa get more than 200 inches of snow each year.

 Camping

There are 27 developed campgrounds in Ottawa, ranging in

size from three to 40 sites with most on a river or lake.

The three most developed campgrounds are Lake Ottawa, Clark Lake within Sylvania Recreation Area and Black River. Backcountry camping is also an attraction, especially in the three wilderness areas (special rules apply in Sylvania Wilderness).

Here are the improved campgrounds, the number of sites each and their locations by ranger district.

Bessemer Ranger District

Black River Harbor *(40)*, 15 miles N of Bessemer on County Road 513;

Bobcat Lake *(12)*, 3 miles SE of Marenisco on Forest Road 8500;

Henry Lake *(11)*, 10 miles SW of Marenisco of Forest Road 8100;

Matchwood Tower *(5)*, 4 miles SW of Bergland on Matchwood Tower Road;

Moosehead Lake *(13)*, 16 miles SE of Marenisco on Forest Road 8500;

Pomeroy Lake *(13)*, 15 miles SE of Marenisco on Forest Road 6828;

Langford Lake *(11)*, 20 miles SE of Marenisco on County Road 531.

Iron River Ranger District

Block House *(2)*, 10 miles E of Gibbs City on Forest Road 2180;

Golden Lake *(22)*, 14 miles NW of Iron River on Forest Highway 16;

Lake Ottawa *(32)*, 7 miles W of Iron River on Lake Ottawa Road;

Paint River Forks *(4)*, 1 mile W of Gibbs City on County Road 657.

Kenton Ranger District

Lake Sainte Kathryn *(25)*, 8 miles S of Sidnaw on Sidnaw Road;

Lower Dam *(7)*, 7 miles SE of Kenton on Forest Road 3500;

Norway Lake (28), 8 miles S of Sidnaw on Forest Road 2400;

Perch Lake West (20), 11 miles S of Sidnaw on Winslow Lake Road;

Sparrow Rapids (6), 4 miles NW of Kenton on Forest Road 1100;

Sturgeon River (9), 5 miles N of Sidnaw on Forest Road 2200;

Tepee Lake (17), 7 miles S of Kenton on Forest Road 3630.

Ontonagon Ranger District

Bob Lake (17), 18 miles SE of Greenland on Forest Road 1960;

Courtney Lake (21), 8 miles E of Greenland on Forest Road 1960.

Watersmeet Ranger District

Burned Dam (6), 7 miles NE of Watersmeet on Forest Road 4500;

Imp Lake (22), 6 miles SE of Watersmeet on Forest Road 3978;

Marion Lake (39), 5 miles E of Watersmeet on Forest Road 3980;

Paulding Pond (4), 8 miles N of Watersmeet on U.S. 45;

Robbins Pond (3), 9 miles NW of Watersmeet on Forest Road 5230;

Sylvania-Clark Lake (35), 8 miles SW of Watersmeet on Forest Road 6360;

Taylor Lake (6), 8 miles E of Watersmeet on Forest Road 3960.

 Trails

From easy interpretive nature walks to a stretch of the North Country National Scenic Trail, there are thousands of miles of forest roads and trails for hikers, snowmobilers, cross-country skiers, snowshoers, mountain bikers and horseback riders. More than 1,000 miles of snowmobile trails crossing national forest and private land alone are groomed. There also are short trails to

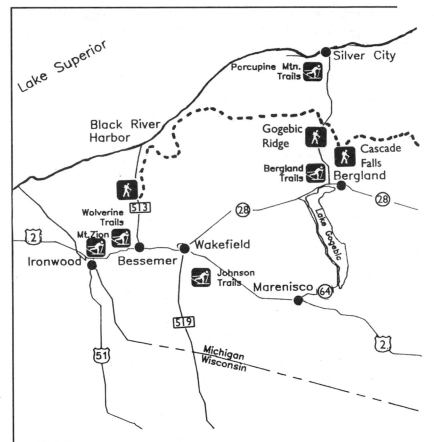

Ottawa National Forest Trails

 Hiking Trails

Black River Drive Trails
North Country Trail
Gogebic Trail
Cascade Falls Trail
Sylvania Wilderness
Bob Lake Trail

 Sking Trails

Berland Trails
Wolverine Trails
Ge-che Ski Trail
Old Grade Ski Trail
Sylvania Wilderness

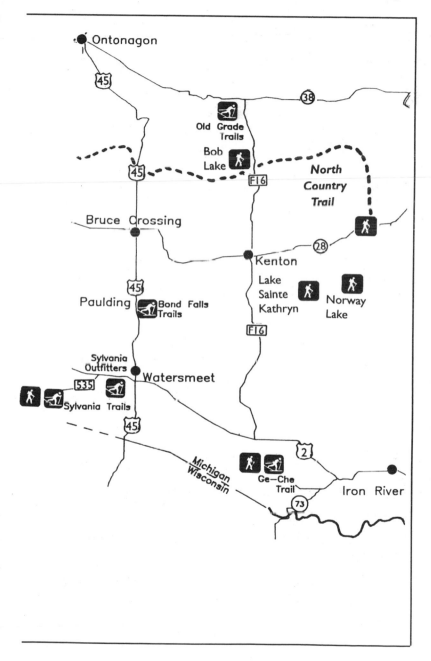

scenic vistas and waterfalls at Silver Mountain, Wolf Mountain, Sturgeon Falls, Yondota Falls and Kakabika Falls, as well as non-strenuous lakeshore trails at several campgrounds. Some of the most popular, and most interesting, are:

North Country National Scenic Trail, 118 miles: Ottawa offers some of the most difficult, challenging terrain found along this 3,200-mile national trail which crosses the forest W to E. There are no bridges over the majority of stream crossings and often stretches of the trail are overgrown with brush. Hiking too close to the edge of the cliffs and escarpments can be dangerous. The Black River segment, which parallels the river and passes several waterfalls (see In The Forest), is the best developed and most popular stretch. The Bergland segment includes high ridge lines and scenic vistas. The Victoria segment offers several river crossings and a view of O-Kun-De-Kun Falls; the Sturgeon River segment passes through the remote Sturgeon River Gorge Wilderness.

Bergland Ranger District

Cascade Falls Trail, 2 miles: There are two alternative routes from the same trailhead. Both lead to a small waterfall on Cascade Creek. The mile-long Twin Peaks route climbs a bluff to an overlook with a good view of the Trap Hills and the West Branch of the Ontonagon River. The Valley route stays in the forest with little climbing involved. The trailhead is NE of Bergland at the junction of Forest Roads 400 and 468.

Gogebic Ridge Trail, 9 miles: This spur of the North Country Trail follows the shore of Weary Lake to a ledge overlooking Lake Gogebic. It then skirts ridge lines, passes through bogs and follows portions of the Lake Gogebic-Iron River Indian Trail, a historic route more than 125 years old. One trailhead is along Forest Road 250, N of M-28 at Merriweather. The other is on M-64, N of Bergland.

Kenton Ranger District

Deer Marsh Interpretive Trail, 3 miles: This nature route is not strenuous, although longer than most national forest interpretive trails. It's at Lake Sainte Kathryn Campground, S of Sidnaw on Sidnaw Road.

Ontonagon Ranger District

Beaver Lodge Interpretive Trail, 2 *miles:* This easy nature trail is at Bob Lake Campground, SE of Greenland on Forest Road 1960.

Watersmeet Ranger District

Consider The Connections Interpretive Trail, 0.25 *miles:* At the Watersmeet Visitors Center, just W of Watersmeet on U.S. 2. This short trail has displays on ecosystem management.

 # Boating & Canoeing

There is a first-come, first-served transient docking and fuel facility run by a concessionaire from Memorial Day through September at Black River Harbor on Lake Superior. It's one of only two harbors within the national forest system. Canoeing opportunities fall into two basic categories. In the southern part of Ottawa, rivers range from flat water with moderate current to small rapids. Beaver dams and a thick overgrowth of tag alder are found on many smaller streams. To the north, expect fast water, waterfalls and rock ledges as the rivers head for Lake Superior. There also are seasonal variations, with fast water and potentially hazardous torrents during spring run-off; water levels are low in the summer.

Some favorite canoeing streams and their navigable lengths are:

Bergland Ranger District

Ontonagon River, South Branch, 42 *miles:* The river starts wide and slow but changes to a narrower, rocky-bottomed channel as it heads N. A 2-mile stretch of rapids W of the end at Reservoir Landing can be difficult during medium to high water. The river can be paddled from County Road 527 at Sucker Creek to Reservoir Landing.

Ontonagon River, West Branch, 7 *miles:* This part of the river is heavily affected by a power dam; released water comes

A canoer paddles into a backcountry campsite on Clark Lake of Sylvania Wilderness and Recreation Area.

suddenly, while closing the dam suddenly stops the flow. Most shoreline is forested, and, in places, the W bank features rock escarpments 200 feet high. Access is off M-28 and Norwich Road.

Bessemer Ranger District

Black River, 10 miles: The river varies along its course from a narrow stream valley to open areas. During low water, expect shallows and shoals where wider, flat stretches flow over conglomerate rock. The northernmost section is not runable because of numerous rapids and seven major waterfalls. Access sites include Black Jack Mountain Ski Area; Moore Street Bridge, Narrows Wayside; and Copper Peak Ski Flying Hill on County Road 513.

Presque Isle River, 17 miles: Although starting wide and flat with some small rapids, the current becomes swifter and banks more pronounced as the river heads N toward rapids and falls.

Some Class IV white water will be encountered near South Boundary Road. Most canoeists paddle the stretch from the headwaters at Marenisco to M-28. The stretch above M-28 is for experienced paddlers only. Expect flat, shallow water and sections of shoals during periods of low water.

Presque Isle River, East Branch, 11 miles: Flat terrain and a mix of spruce, fir, aspen and hardwoods dominate. There are some narrow tag alder and shallow shoal sections. River access is available at Moosehead Lake and Pomeroy Lake campgrounds.

Presque Isle River, South Branch, 4 miles: This branch offers easy paddling through slow-moving water and no rapids. There are some narrow, tag alder shallow shoals. The river is floatable from Mallard canoe landing on Forest Road 8100 to a wayside area on M-64.

Presque Isle River, West Branch, 8 miles: This branch runs through relatively flat country with low stream banks and some marshy areas. Some sections have shallow shoals, but there are no rapids. The river is floatable from Teal canoe landing on Forest Road 8100 to Presque Isle Flowage Dam on M-64.

Iron River Ranger District

Brule River, 25 miles: Separating Ottawa National Forest in Michigan from Nicolet National Forest in Wisconsin, the Brule runs through some shallow rapids before joining the Menominee River, which continues to Green Bay on Lake Michigan. The river is floatable from Highway 73 Bridge to Pentoga Bridge, with access at Brule River Campground on the Wisconsin side of the border.

Paint River, 6 miles: There are shallow riffles, and some large rocks are found in the upper 5 miles of the river. In the national forest, the river is floatable from Paint River Forks Campground to Block House Campground. Beyond that, the river is easily paddled for another 33 miles before encountering Class III rapids and Horse Race Rapids, which cannot be run.

Paint River, North Branch, 13 miles: It runs through a mix of northern hardwoods and conifers. Portaging may be required around beaver dams, even in peak flow seasons. The river is canoeable from Forest Highway 16 to Paint River Forks Campground.

Paint River, South Branch, 19 miles: The adjacent countryside is dominated by conifers and northern hardwoods. The river can be paddled from Forest Highway 16 to Paint River Forks Campground.

Kenton Ranger District

Ontonagon River, East Branch, 16 miles: This river is only canoeable in the northern-most sections as downed trees, beaver dams, long rock stretches and thick vegetation make the rest impassable. The river is floatable from Onion Creek, S of Mass City, to Middle Branch.

Sturgeon River, 27 miles: Spring and fall along the Sturgeon are especially challenging as it cuts through Sturgeon River Gorge Wilderness. High flow is mid-April to June; most of the river is not canoeable any other time of the year due to large, heavy rocks in the river bed, treacherous falls and rock outcroppings. Cliffs, bluffs and scenic views interlace the hilly terrain. The river is run from East Forest Boundary at Sturgeon River Campground to North Forest Boundary.

Ontonagon Ranger District

Ontonagon River, 29 miles: Intermediate-level canoeing is available, with best conditions during fall and spring high water. In some spots, steep banks rise to 200 feet above the river while most of the shoreline is privately owned timberland of hardwoods, spruce, fir and hemlock. The river is floatable from Military Hill Bridge to Ontonagon.

Watersmeet Ranger District

Ontonagon River, Middle Branch, 19 miles: There are several log jams along the canoeable stretches and Mex-i-min-e Falls must be portaged. Otherwise, there are no major rapids on the Middle Branch, a river for intermediate paddlers. The river is floatable from Forest Road 378 (Russes Road, W of Watersmeet) to Bond Falls Flowage.

Sylvania Wilderness: Portage trails link 36 pristine lakes within the wilderness area for excellent lake canoeing opportunities. One route travels the length of Clark and Loon lakes to Deer Island, Cub, Big Bateau, Florence and Fisher lakes before looping back to Loon Lake.

 ## Fishing

Ottawa National Forest has more than 500 named lakes and almost 2,700 miles of rivers and streams open to fishing. River anglers will find opportunities throughout the forest, but lake fishing is concentrated in the southern half.

Brook trout is the predominate species sought in the rivers and streams but anglers also stalk rainbow trout, brown trout, steelhead and smallmouth bass. In the larger rivers such as the Ontonagon and its branches, walleye are common. Lake trout are occasionally hooked in the Black River, and salmon at the mouth of the Presque Isle and the East Branch of the Ontonagon, as well as the Black River.

Lakes range from the 4,260-acre Lac Vieux Desert and the 2,118-acre Bond Falls Flowage to 12-acre ponds. Smallmouth bass, bluegill and other panfish species are the predominate catch, with walleye and northern pike also common. Dozens of lakes hold trout or muskies.

 ## Wilderness Areas

McCormick Wilderness, 16,850 acres: This was once "the oldest and possibly grandest of all the secluded private estates in the Upper Peninsula" when it belonged to Cyrus McCormick, whose father had invented the reaping machine harvester. Three generations of McCormicks used the area as a wilderness retreat until Gordon McCormick donated the land to the U.S. Forest Service in 1967.

There are glacier-scoured hills, rugged stone outcroppings, isolated waterfalls and 18 small lakes. The wilderness includes the headwaters of the Yellow Dog, Dead, Peshekee and Huron rivers, as well as the divide between the Lake Michigan and Lake Superior watersheds.

The area is laced with old roads and logging tracks that are difficult to find and easy to lose. A 3-mile foot trail is posted along County Road 607, N of its junction with M-28 near Champion. The trail ends at White Deer Lake, site of the McCormick family lodge and camp which has long since been removed. It's in the Kenton Ranger District.

Sturgeon River Gorge Wilderness, 14,139 acres: Steep gorges up to 300 feet deep, waterfalls, rapids, ponds and oxbows mark this area in the Kenton Ranger District. Sturgeon Falls, 40 feet high, was formed by volcanic outcrops. The terrain is rugged and rolling, and forested in a mix of conifers and hardwoods. Bald eagles and osprey feed in the Sturgeon River and its tributary trout streams while black bears are common in the area. Challenging canoeing and kayaking opportunities are found on the Sturgeon River. There are outstanding panoramas from overlooks on the eastern rim of the 13-mile-long gorge - billed as the "deepest readily accessible gorge east of the Mississippi."

The rim is accessed along Sturgeon Gorge Road (Forest Road 191), W of Baraga. The main access to the wilderness area is on Forest Road 2200. Within 11 miles, the road swings close enough to the rim to see from your car. The best view can be found by following the signs to Silver Mountain. The 1,312-foot peak, at one time the site of a fire tower, is a 250-step climb, but the view from the top is stunning.

The North Country Trail also passes through the wilderness area, while just outside the boundary and along the river is Sturgeon River Campground, a nine-site unit on Forest Road 2200.

Sylvania Wilderness, 18,327 acres: Once the privately owned Sylvania Club, this is where founder and timber baron A.D. Johnston and his friends built fishing and hunting lodges and cabins. President Dwight Eisenhower fished for northern pike and smallmouth bass here. In *Wild Woodlands*, Bill Thomas dubs Sylvania "the crown jewel of Ottawa National Forest" and recalls a Christmas morning

Hikers climb the long staircase to the top of Silver Mountain near the Sturgeon River Gorge Wilderness. The view from the top of the scenic lookout includes much of the wilderness.

there:

"The skies were clear, and the trees were popping like the sharp report of a gun from the bitter cold. It was just 20 below zero with 42 inches of snow on the ground. But that was cold enough, and we certainly needed no more snow."

Sylvania features 4,000 acres of clear lakes, some sporting such alluring names as Devil's Head, Glimmerglass, East Bear and Golden Silence. The area is home to black bears, old growth forests, bald eagles, rare orchids, loons and osprey. The Sylvania Recreation Area is adjacent to the wilderness and features a developed campground. Use of backcountry campsites is by permit only, and reserving a permit in advance is strongly recommended since the area is popular from mid-June through mid-August.

Fishing is excellent in the wilderness area due in part to special regulations of catch-and-release and artificial lures only. Canoeing opportunities are not extensive but there are several natural lake loops with most portages under a half-mile long. It is in the Watersmeet Ranger District. Access is available from County Road 535, W of Watersmeet. For a permit or more information, contact Sylvania Wilderness Permits, Watersmeet Visitor Center, Box 276, Watersmeet, MI 49969; ☎ (906) 358-4724 or (906) 358-4834.

 Waterfalls

Welcome to Waterfall Country. There are almost 200 falls in the Upper Peninsula with the vast majority in the western half and many of those in Ottawa National Forest. The Black River National Scenic Byway alone features five that are easy to drive to and can be reached from parking lots along short access trails (see In The Forest).

Here are the falls in Gogebic, Houghton and Ontonagon counties; most are on national forest land:

Gogebic County
Superior Falls, Montreal River, 14 miles NW of Ironwood.
Saxon Falls, Montreal River, 11 miles NW of Ironwood.

Interstate Falls, Montreal River, 12 miles NW of Ironwood.

Rocky Forty Falls, Siemens Creek, 3 miles NW of Bessemer.

Manakiki Falls, Maple Creek, 11 miles NE of Bessemer.

Rainbow, Sandstone, Gorge, Potawatomi, Conglomerate, Algonquin and Chippewa Falls, Black River, 8 to 13 miles N of Bessemer.

Granite Rapids Falls, Black River, 3 miles SE of Bessemer.

Yondota Falls, Presque Isle River, 4 miles N of Marenisco.

Nelson Canyon Falls, Nelson Creek, 2 miles S of Lake Gogebic.

Judson Falls, Slate River, 6 miles E of Marenisco.

Kakabika Falls, Cisco Branch of Ontonagon River, 3 miles SE of Gogebic Station.

Ajibikoka Falls, Brush Lake, 5 miles NW of Watersmeet.

Mex-i-min-e Falls, Middle Branch of Ontonagon River, 7 miles NE of Watersmeet.

Houghton County

Sturgeon Falls, Sturgeon River, 10 miles NE of Sidnaw.

Onion Falls, East Branch of Onion Creek, 7 miles NE of Trout Creek.

Jumbo Falls, Jumbo River, Forest Highway 16, 3 miles SW of Kenton.

Duppy Falls, Jumbo River, Forest Highway 16, 5 miles south of Kenton.

Vista Falls, North Branch of Sturgeon River, Forest Highway 16, 6 miles SW of Nisula.

Hogger Falls and West Branch Sturgeon Falls, the West Branch of the Sturgeon River, 3 miles S of Nisula.

Sparrow Rapids Falls, East Branch of Ontonagon River, 3 miles NW of Kenton.

Nokomis, Abinodji, Ogimakwe and Ogima Falls, Copper Creek, County Road 519, N of M-28 in Wakefield.

Lepisto Falls, Presque Isle River, County Road 519, N of M-28 in Wakefield.

Ontonagon County

Nimikon and Minnewawa Falls, Presque Isle River, 5 miles

IN THE FOREST
Black River Waterfalls

It's waterfall after waterfall as the Black River makes its final 3-mile run northward to chilly Lake Superior. With names such as Conglomerate and Potawatomi and Rainbow, the falls conjure up the human and natural history of the Great Lakes.

The headwaters of the Black River are in Wisconsin, and the river drops nearly 1,000 vertical feet in 30 miles before it empties into Lake Superior.

The falls owe their existence to geology. "The river is almost as ancient as the hills it cuts through," an Ottawa National Forest interpretive sign explains. "It's held its course through the centuries while the bedrock was gradually being raised and tilted." Harder layers of ancient bedrock are more resistant to stream erosion than softer ones, so uneven erosion produces a series of falls.

There are two ways to reach the five falls. The first is by driving along the U.S. Forest Service's Black River National Scenic Byway. The road begins in Bessemer next to an oversized, brightly colored - and kitschy - statue of a skier. The byway follows a route used by copper prospectors of the Chippewa Mining Co., according to an 1847-1848 survey.

Each waterfall has a well-marked, paved parking lot and a short, but sometimes steep, trail that usually involves a great many steps. These access trails, all less than a mile long, pass through hardwood forest. Moss grows on the bark of the birches and on the stumps of trees cut long ago. When nearing the river, the sounds of rushing water become louder and more alluring.

The other way to reach the falls is by hiking the 3-mile stretch of the North Country National Scenic Trail along the river. You'll find a combination of dirt paths and wooden boardwalks and steps, some of which detour to fenced, scenic overlooks.

Conglomerate Falls (also known as Great Conglomerate Falls) is the southernmost of the five and a 0.75-mile hike from the road. A huge chunk of conglomerate rock sits in the middle of the river, splitting the water as it plunges 30 feet into a gorge, foaming with a yellowish hue as it hits bottom. The falls are named for a common sedimentary rock in the area, called conglomerate.

Driving along the scenic byway, the first glimpse of Lake Superior comes just N of the Conglomerate parking area. A half mile downriver is Potawatomi Falls, named for a Native American tribe that lived in southwestern Michigan and northern Indiana. The cascade is 130 feet wide and features a 30-foot drop.

Nearby the river narrows at Gorge Falls, where the 24-foot cascade thunders into a steep gorge. At the bottom, water-carved caves flank both sides. The river becomes much quieter below the falls, where powerful flows have lifted giant logs and wedged them between boulders as if they were so many match sticks. A steep set of wooden stairs allows access down to the riverbank and to a walking path covered with red-brown conglomerate rocks.

From the driving route, rather than the North Country Trail hike, Sandstone Falls is the most strenuous of the five to reach. The access trail is only one-quarter mile long but drops sharply; there are about 200 stairs before reaching the overview for the 25-foot cascade.

Finally comes Rainbow Falls, reached from the road by a half-mile trail. The falling water from this 45-foot cascade creates a mist that often produces a rainbow effect when the sun is at the right angle.

The scenic byway ends a short distance away at the mouth of the Black River, spanned by a wooden suspension bridge.

Hundreds of years ago, explorers, fur traders and missionaries made brief stops at the river mouth. The 1847-1848 survey reported a "good harbor for small craft, a wharf and a storehouse."

NW of Tula.

Deer Creek Falls, *Deer Creek*, 7 miles NW of Bergland.
Rapid River Falls, *Rapid River*, 5 miles NW of Bergland.
Nonesuch Falls, *Little Iron River*, 5 miles SW of Silver City.
Bonanza Falls, *Big Iron River*, 1 mile S of Silver City.
Pewabeck Falls, *Little Iron River*, 2 miles SW of Silver City.
Little Trap Falls, *Anderson Creek*, 11 miles S of Silver City.
Cascade Falls, *Cascade Creek*, 7 miles NE of Bergland.
Wolverine Falls, *Cisco Branch of Ontonagon River*, 8 miles W of Paulding.

18 Mile Rapids Falls, *South Branch of Ontonagon River*, 6 miles S of Ewen.

Flannigan Rapids Falls, *South Branch of Ontonagon River*, 5 miles N of Ewen.

Sandstone Rapids Falls, *Skranton Creek*, 9 miles N of Ewen.

Irish Rapids and Grand Rapids Falls, *Ontonagon River*, 5 miles NW of Rockland.

Gleason Creek Falls, *Gleason Creek*, Victoria Road, 6 miles W of old Victoria.

O-Kun-De-Kun Falls, *Baltimore River*, 8 miles N of Bruce Crossing.

Little Falls, *Middle Branch of Ontonagon River*, 5 miles SW of Paulding.

Bond Falls, *Middle Branch of Ontonagon River*, 4 miles E of Paulding.

Three Rapids Falls, *Middle Branch of Ontonagon River*, 7 miles NE of Bruce Crossing.

Agate Falls, *Middle Branch of Ontonagon River*, 4 miles W of Trout Creek.

 ## Historical Attractions

Stateline Historic Treaty Tree Site: An interpretive sign at the picnic area explains how surveyors laid out the boundary between Wisconsin and Michigan near the headwaters of the Brule River. From the picnic area, the short Stateline National Recreation Trail leads to the Mile Zero survey monument and the Treaty Tree site. Another sign and a tree stump mark where native tribes agreed not to harm the surveyors running the boundary line. The site is in the Iron River Ranger District.

 ## More Things To See & Do

Birding: More than 240 species of birds have been spotted within the national forest, from bald eagles, green-backed herons and tundra swans to sandhill cranes, Broad-winged hawks and turkey vultures. Songbirds such as vireos and warblers can often be heard while camping or hiking. Migratory waterfowl are common as well. Owl enthusiasts may spot the great horned, snowy, barred, boreal and long-eared owls. Among other bird species making the forest home are the common loons, sharp-tailed and ruffed grouse and a number of sandpipers, plovers, yellowlegs and woodpeckers.

In addition, the peregrine falcon is returning, thanks to a release program developed by the Michigan Department of Natural Resources, with U.S. Forest Service and National Park Service cooperation. This bird of prey is endangered and in its spectacular dive has been clocked at speeds of 180 mph.

Black River Harbor: Here the Black River flows into Lake Superior at the end of the Black River Scenic Byway. The park provides boat docks, a campground, picnic areas, access to the North Country National Scenic Trail, a playground, beach, agate collecting, waterfall observation facilities, a wooden suspension bridge and an enclosed pavilion of native stone. Because Lake Superior warms the area around Black River Harbor, vivid foliage colors may continue until mid-October - several weeks longer than elsewhere in the Upper Peninsula. The harbor is in the Bessemer Ranger District.

Black River Scenic Byway, 12 miles: Heading N from the outskirts of Bessemer to Lake Superior, the byway provides convenient access to a series of waterfalls and the North Country National Scenic Trail along the Black River. It also passes an eques-

Conglomerate Falls along Black River Drive in Ottawa National Forest. All The falls are a short hike from the road, a designated national scenic byway.

trian school and the Copper Peak ski flying facility - the only ski flying hill in the Western Hemisphere - before reaching Black River Harbor. The route passes stands of old growth northern hardwoods, eastern white pine and hemlock as it follows a wagon road and supply trail originally built for the iron mines of the Gogebic Range. The byway is in the Bessemer Ranger District.

J. W. Toumey Nursery: Established in 1935, the nursery can produce up to 10 million seedlings a year for planting in Ottawa and other Great Lakes national forests. The nursery is N of Watersmeet off U.S. 45.

Passport in Time projects: Little remains of Norwich Mine, a mid-1800s complex of four copper mines and two towns. Only a collapsed log barn, beams, shafts, foundations and a few artifacts are left. Volunteers have mapped and excavated the site to help develop a plan for further research and interpretation.

At Lake Ottawa Recreation Area, Timid Mink and Bleat Creek sites along Lake Ottawa and Hagerman Lake, volunteers have mapped, excavated and screened sites used by nomadic families during their seasonal rounds 3,500 to 10,000 years ago. Artifacts include pottery, stone tools and spruce root cordage. Evidence of the only known prehistoric house in the western Upper Peninsula was found at Timid Mink.

Picnicking: In addition to areas at campgrounds, there are picnic facilities at these non-camping recreation sites: Hagerman Lake and State Line, both in the Iron River Ranger District; Perch River in Kenton Ranger District; Potawatomi & Gorge Falls in Bessemer Ranger District; and Sparrow-Kenton Wayside in the Kenton Ranger District.

Watersmeet Visitor Center: Exhibits trace the history of settlers in the region, including how they survived and used natural resources. Other displays cover wildlife and the management of healthy ecosystems. A multi-media slide show and interpretive programs are conducted in the auditorium. Summer programs and nature films cover natural and human history topics such as wildflowers, loons, bluebirds, waterfalls, wolves and archeology.

The center (☎ 906-358-4724) is accessed from U.S. 2 and U.S. 45.

 Ranger Districts

Bergland: M-28, Bergland, MI 49910; ☎ (906) 575-3441.

Bessemer: 500 N. Moore St., Bessemer, MI 49911; ☎ (906) 667-0261.

Iron River: 801 Adams St., Iron River, MI 49935; ☎ (906) 265-5139.

Kenton: M-28, Kenton, MI 49943; ☎ (906) 852-3500.

Ontonagon: 1209 Rockland Rd., Ontonagon, MI 49953; ☎(906) 884-2085.

Watersmeet: Old U.S. 2, Watersmeet, MI 49969; ☎ (906) 358-4551.

 Gateways

Bessemer: Bessemer Chamber of Commerce, 1006 E. Silver St., Bessemer, MI 49911; ☎ (906) 663-4542.

Iron River: Iron County Tourism Council, 1 E. Genesee St., Iron River, MI 49935; ☎ (906) 265-3822.

Ironwood: Gogebic Area Convention & Visitor Bureau, 126 W. Arch, Ironwood, MI 49938; ☎ (906) 932-4850.

Lake Gogebic: Lake Gogebic Chamber of Commerce, 5600 N. M-64, Bergland, MI 49910; ☎ (906) 575-3265.

Marquette: Marquette County Convention and Visitor Bureau, 501 S. Front St., Marquette, MI 49855; ☎ (800) 544-4321 or (906) 228-7740.

Ontonagon: Ontonagon Tourism Council, Box 266, Ontonagon, MI 49953; ☎ (906) 884-4735.

OHIO

Wayne National Forest

A rushing creek in spring time at Wayne National Forest, the only national forest in Ohio.

WAYNE

219 Columbus Road
Athens, OH 45701
☎ **(614) 592-6644**

214,916 acres

Stretching through the Appalachian foothills of southern Ohio, the area that is now Wayne National Forest was heavily forested before European-American settlers arrived in 1788. Timbering peaked shortly before the Civil War, and the area was completely cut over by 1920. The 19th century was also a time of farming, oil drilling, coal mining, charcoal making and iron mining.

Although the federal government began to buy land here in 1935 and although the Civilian Conservation Corps performed reforestation during the Depression, Wayne did not become a national forest until 1951. It was jointly administered with Indiana's Hoosier National Forest until 1984.

 ## Camping

Wayne National Forest's largest established camping areas are at Vesuvius Recreation Area and at Burr Oak Cove. Both have picnic facilities, while at Vesuvius there's also a beach, launch area and boat rentals. The newest campground is Leith Run, which also features a picnic area.

The developed campgrounds and their number of sites are:

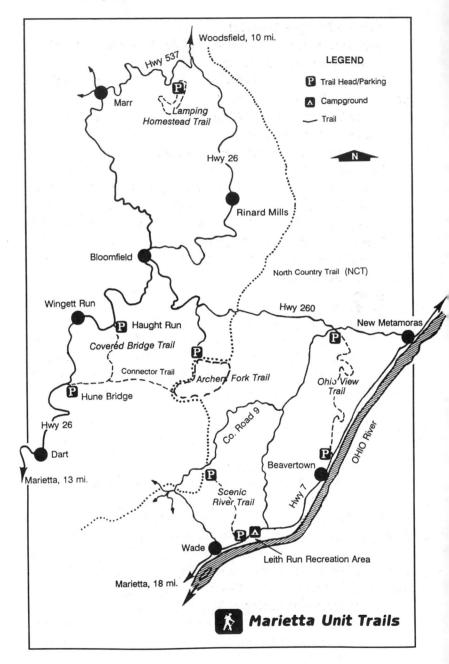

LEGEND

P Trail Head/Parking

⚑ Campground

— Trail

N

Woodsfield, 10 mi.

Hwy 537

Marr

P Lamping Homestead Trail

Hwy 26

Rinard Mills

Bloomfield

North Country Trail (NCT)

Wingett Run

Hwy 260

New Metamoras

P Haught Run

Covered Bridge Trail

P

Ohio View Trail

Connector Trail

P Archers Fork Trail

P Hune Bridge

Co. Road 9

Hwy 26

Dart

Beavertown

P

Marietta, 13 mi.

OHIO River

P Scenic River Trail

Hwy 7

Wade

P ⚑

Leith Run Recreation Area

Marietta, 18 mi.

🚶 Marietta Unit Trails

Athens Ranger District
Burr Oak Cove (19), 13 miles N of Athens on Route 13.
Ironton Ranger District
Iron Ridge (41), 7 miles NE of Ironton on County Road 29 in Lake Vesuvius Recreation Area;
Oak Hill (24), 7 miles NE of Ironton on County Road 29 in Lake Vesuvius Recreation Area.
Marietta, Athens Ranger District
Leith Run (18), 21 miles N of Marietta on State Route 7.
In addition, there are four small camping areas at canoe access points in the Marietta Unit. They are *Haught Run* (4 sites); *Hune Bridge* (3 sites); *Lane Farm* (4 sites); and *Ring Mill* (3 sites). In the Ironton Ranger District, group camping is available at Two Points in the Lake Vesuvius Recreation Area, 7 miles NE of Ironton on County Road 29.

 Trails

Crossed by the North Country National Scenic Trail and the Buckeye Trail, which run together in the Athens Ranger District, Wayne National Forest offers opportunities for hikers, horseback riders, mountain bikers and ORVers.
The principal trails are:
Athens Ranger District
Lake View Trail, 1 mile: This easy trail from Burr Oak Cove campground provides access to Burr Oak Reservoir. It's NE of Athens, with the trailhead at Burr Oak Cove Campground on Route 13.
Monday Creek ORV Area, 60 miles: This network includes Main Corridor, Dorr Run, Long Ridge and Snake Hollow trails. There are access sites NW of Nelsonville on Forest Roads 1980 and 1985; NE of Nelsonville on County Road 24 and Forest Road 758; and SE of New Straitsville on Forest Road 595.
North Country National Scenic Trail, 65 miles: This stretch winds and zigzags through a variety of terrain, including land used for gas wells and strip mines. It begins at Lane Farm and ends at

Ring Mill, with other access sites at Knowlton Bridge, Haught Run and Hune Bridge.

Stone Church Horse Trail, *22 miles:* This loop trail crosses many oil and gas roads. Along the way, riders can see the stone ruins of a 19th-century church and cemetery. The community that built them was wiped out by plague after the Civil War, and the church was abandoned. It's W of Shawnee, with access on County Road 38.

Wildcat Hollow Trail, *15 miles:* This hiking trail is in the national forest adjacent to Burr Oak State Park. The route encompasses a variety of terrains from stream bottoms to ridgetops, and crosses open meadows and white pine plantations. There are stream crossings, rock outcroppings, switchbacks, small gullies, oil pipelines and former oil well sites, plus an abandoned farmhouse and the ruins of a one-room schoolhouse. It's a favorite route for spotting wildflowers and wildlife. Take Irish Ridge Road and Dew Road to reach the trailhead, which is SE of Corning.

Ironton Ranger District

Hanging Rock ORV Trail, *26 miles:* It runs through scenic forested hills. The loops have such names as Gas Well, High Knob, Hanging Rock, Copperhead, Lakeview, Sawmill, Power Line and Oak Spur. The trailhead is on Forest Road 105, NW of Ironton.

Lake Vesuvius Horse Trail System, *33 miles:* These trails wind their way through some of southern Ohio's most scenic landscapes, including brushwood, open fields and new and mature forests. Loops range from less than a mile to 31 miles, with difficulty levels from easy to difficult. Access points are NE of Ironton along County Road 29, Township Road 245 and County Road 4.

Lakeshore Trail, *8 miles:* With gentle grades, the trail loops around Lake Vesuvius, crosses streams by foot bridges, and passes scenic rock formations, pine woodlands and sandstone outcroppings in Lake Vesuvius Recreation Area. It intersects Vesuvius Backpack Trail at the N end of the lake.

Morgan Sisters Trail, *8 miles:* This trail includes three loops

Lake Vesuvius Recreation Area

NORTH

Big Bend Overlook

Two Points Group Area

Big Bend Beach

Pine Knob Picnic Ground

Rock House Picnic Ground

Lake Vesuvius

Whiskey Run Trail

Rock House Trail

Oak Hill Campground

Iron Ridge Campground

Vesuvius Boat Dock

Roadside Picnic Area

⟵ ½ Mile to St. Rt. 93

Furnace Picnic area

Restored Iron Furnace

0   ¼ Mile

near Symmes Creek through Morgan Sisters Woods, a hardwood forest believed to contain virgin timber. The loops are named Coal Branch, Ridge and Schoolhouse, and the sites of a former schoolhouse and homes are along the trails. Access is available off Route 141, between Cadmus and Gage, and at Kenton Lake, S of Gallia on Pumpkintown Road.

Pine Creek ORV Trail, 20 miles: This one passes through hilly, wooded terrain, N of Ironton. The main trailhead, Telegraph, is N of Ironton on County Road 193. There's also parking at Lyra and Wolcott trailheads.

Rock House Hollow Trail, 1 mile: This pavement and boardwalk trail passes a natural rock shelter, large boulders and various formations. The trailhead is at the Lake Vesuvius boat dock parking area, NE of Ironton on County Road 29.

Symmes Creek Trail, 6 miles: Located near Symmes Creek, this hiking trail runs through young and mature forests and along ridges with overlooks. Abandoned farm fields and home sites can be seen. A short connector trail links it with Morgan Sisters Trail on the other side of the creek. The principal trailhead is between Cadmus and Gage along Route 141, S of Gallia.

Vesuvius Backpack Trail, 16 miles: Ralph Ramey's *Fifty Hikes in Ohio* rates this as "one of Ohio's best trails for a one- or two-night trek" and notes: "It crosses brushwood, mature forest, new forest and open fields; it winds along the Lake Vesuvius shore; and it cuts across the ridgetops of the lake basin. Along the way are wildlife ponds, scenic views, creek crossings, stands of pine and the sites of the former Kimble fire tower and the stone fireplaces and chimneys of a former CCC-built shelter house."

The trail briefly joins the Lakeshore Trail and there is parking where the trails intersect at the N end of the lake.

Whiskey Run Trail, 1 mile: This short trail passes an abandoned whiskey still and charcoal pits. The hollow was named for the remnants of the still and barrels that were once found here. The loop begins and ends at Iron Ridge Campground in Lake Vesuvius Recreation Area, NE of Ironton on County Road 29.

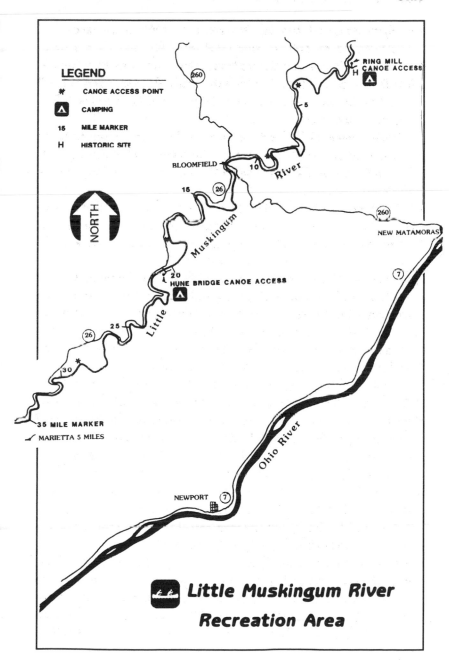

LEGEND

*	CANOE ACCESS POINT
🔺	CAMPING
15	MILE MARKER
H	HISTORIC SITE

NORTH

RING MILL CANOE ACCESS

BLOOMFIELD

New Matamoras

Hune Bridge Canoe Access

Muskingum River

Little

35 MILE MARKER

MARIETTA 5 MILES

NEWPORT

Ohio River

Little Muskingum River
Recreation Area

Marietta, Athens Ranger District

Archers Fork Trail, *10 miles:* The best-known point along this rugged trail is Irish Run Natural Bridge, carved through the sandstone by erosion and weather. It's one of only seven natural bridges in the state. The trail, part of the North Country National Scenic Trail, also passes rock shelters, outcroppings and vintage oil and gas wells. Parking is off Ohio 260, W of New Metamoras.

Covered Bridge Trail, *5 miles:* Two classic century-old covered bridges mark the beginning and end of this route. The trail follows the upland hills above the Little Muskingum River, with parking at Haught Run, E of Wingett Run, and at Hune Bridge, S of Wingett Run.

Lamping Homestead Trail, *5 miles:* There are two loops at the site of the Lamping family's 19th-century homestead. Along the way are a pond, big pines, Clear Fork Creek and old forest stands. The trailhead is along Ohio 537, E of Marietta.

Ohio View Trail, *7 miles:* Passing through second-growth forest, the trail drops, climbs and twists. Hikers can see a wildlife pond, rock outcroppings and the hollows of Collins Run. There are scenic vistas of the Ohio River and West Virginia on the other side. The trailheads are N of Beaverton on Ohio 7 and on Ohio 260 in Yellow House.

Scenic River Trail, *4 miles:* The trail wanders through an Ohio River bottomland field with yellow poplar, blackberry thickets and walnut trees. The route offers steep climbs, switchbacks, river overlooks and rock bluffs. The trailhead is NE of Wade at Leith Run, along Ohio 7.

 # Boating & Canoeing

Canoes, rowboats and pedal boats can be rented at Vesuvius Recreation Area. Wayne National Forest has one boat launch on the Ohio River, located at Leith Run, 21 miles N of Marietta on Ohio 7.

Ironton Ranger District

Symmes Creek: This slow-flowing creek runs for 70 miles

Among the species anglers target in Wayne National Forest are bluegills and other panfish.

through SE Ohio. The Wayne segment passes farmland, forests and rock outcrops. The creek separates Symmes Creek Trail and Morgan Sisters Trail.

Marietta, Athens Ranger District

Little Muskingum River, *35 miles:* The canoe route starts at Ring Mill in covered bridge country and ends upstream of Marietta. Boat access and camping are available at Lane Farm, Hune Bridge, Haught Run and Ring Mill.

In their book *Canoeing and Kayaking Ohio's Streams,* Rick Combs and Steve Gillen describe the route as cutting "through a small, intimate valley in the heart of Wayne National Forest. Although the banks are low, there is little to intrude on your solitude apart from an occasional farm building, and even the nearly constant presence of the infrequently traveled Ohio 26 is not offensive. The unchallenging nature of this stream is not a drawback because it affords time to sit back, drift along and enjoy the incomparable scenery."

Access is also available at Low Gap Road NE of Rinard Mills; Rinard on County Road 406; and Hills on County Road 333.

 Fishing

Both river and lake fishing are popular in the national forest. Species found here include channel catfish, panfish, smallmouth and largemouth bass, spotted bass, muskellunge, bluegill, crappie and sauger.

The Little Muskingum River is home to largemouth, smallmouth and spotted bass, sauger, crappie, catfish and bluegills. There's also pond fishing at Utah Ridge and Sand Run in the Athens Ranger District and at Lamping Homestead in the Marietta Unit.

 Natural Areas

Buffalo Beats, *14 acres:* A remnant of ridge-top prairie remains amid a predominantly oak forest in the Athens Ranger District. The original prairie opening may have been twice its size. Named for the bison that once roamed wild in southern Ohio, this piece of prairie that is closed to public visits supports plants such as rattlesnake-master, hairy sunflower, stiff goldenrod, golden Alexander, blazing-star, big bluestem and Indian grass.

"The existence of a virgin patch of prairie in this region is remarkable, considering that all other tillable tracts have at least been tried for agriculture," botanist Robert H. Mohlenbrock observes in Natural History magazine. "There is renewed hope that the tiny prairie will be preserved for future generations."

Reas Run Research Natural Area, *77 acres:* About half this area is mature Virginia pine that straddles ridge tops and upper slopes. The area is named for a small drainage emptying into the Ohio River, which is called Reas Run. Oak-hickory and maple-beech forests cover the remaining area. It is E of Marietta in the Marietta unit.

Historic Attractions

Covered bridges: Ohio once had more than 2,000 covered bridges, the most of any state. They were built with roofs to protect the main structural timbers from rotting, not to protect travelers. Several historic ones can be seen along the Covered Bridges National Scenic Byway in the Marietta Unit. They are Hills Covered Bridge (built in 1887); Hune Covered Bridge (1879); Rinard Covered Bridge (1876); and Knowlton Covered Bridge (1887).

Ring Mill House: The building, a former grist mill, is on the Little Muskingum River and along the Covered Bridge Scenic Byway in the Marietta Unit. An interpretive sign at the Ring Mill canoe launch, picnic and canoe area talks about the four generations of millers - starting with Walter and Margaret Ring - who lived in this sandstone house from 1846 until 1921, when the mill was damaged by floods. The house is listed on the National Register of Historic Places.

Vesuvius Furnace: This was one of the first iron blast furnaces in Ohio's famous Hanging Rock Iron District. Built in 1833 and used continuously until 1906, it has been restored and stands by the dam in the Ironton Ranger District's Lake Vesuvius Recreation Area. An iron-working village of about 300 residents was swallowed up when Storms Creek was dammed by the Civilian Conservation Corps to create Lake Vesuvius. The furnace is NE of Ironton on County Road 4.

 More Things To Do & See

Birding: Species spotted at Wayne include Canada geese, great blue herons, sharp-shinned and red-tailed hawks, king rails, vireos and warblers. Monitoring of neotropical migratory birds - ones that winter in Central and South America - and landscape analysis are underway as part of research into bird occurrence and distribution in the national forest.

Covered Bridge Scenic Byway, *44 miles:* Four covered bridges

IN THE FOREST
Covered Bridge
Scenic Byway

Covered bridges were once common in the Midwest. In their day, they were nicknamed "kissing bridges" because the dark interiors were suitable for "spooning." Other people called them "wishing bridges," hoping wishes made there would come true. The remaining bridges are cherished for their historic value and for the nostalgia they evoke for the slower-paced, horse-drawn traffic that characterized the era before autos.

The 44-mile Covered Bridge Scenic Byway along Ohio 26 winds along the Little Muskingum - meaning muddy - River between Marietta and Woodsfield. There are four covered bridges in between. The longest at 195 feet long is Knowlton Covered Bridge. Built in 1887, it's also the newest. Hills Covered Bridge is 112 feet long and dates to 1878. Hune Covered Bridge, 128-feet long, has stood since 1879. And Rinard Covered Bridge, 137 feet, was built in 1876.

But the byway's theme goes beyond bridges. It centers on how small rural communities have struggled to survive using the area's limited resources. One indicator of that struggle is the 1865 William Hune Farmstead in Lawrence. As the Ohio Historic Preservation Office observed when the farm was added to the National Register of Historic Places:

Settlements like Lawrence were once common in Ohio and played a leading role in the growth of rural areas. Like many other hamlets, Lawrence had a fourth-class post office, making it a center of communication for the area. Lawrence and places like it declined in importance after the post office introduced Rural Free Delivery in the 1890s.

Another symbolic stop is at the Ring Mill House, a national historic site. In 1840, Walter and Margaret Ring bought this land and built a stone house, grist mill and sawmill. Their family oper-

One of several covered bridges in Wayne National Forest.

ated the mills until a 1921 flood damaged the buildings.

The Lamping Homestead site is another telling 19th-century legacy. Although only part of the stone foundation remains, a small family cemetery testifies to the dangers of illness, drought and crop failure faced by early settlers.

"New beginnings were a lot of hard work and not always successful," the Forest Service tells us.

General stores survive along the byway. Biehl's Store, opened in the 1860s, and has been a general store, pharmacy and funeral parlor. Meyers General Store, which doubles as a post office, is also more than a century old.

For folk art fans, there are Mail Pouch chewing tobacco signs painted on barn walls. The petroleum industry is represented along the byway, too, an indication of how oil and natural gas affected local economic history.

In 1814, oil was accidentally discovered in the area by drillers looking for brine. In the 1820s, oil produced here was marketed for medicinal purposes as well as for lighting. Now, visitors can see active wells - some 2 miles deep - wellhead pumps and pumping systems known as Schackle lines.

give the byway its name, and the development of small rural communities gives the byway its theme. This hilly route - Ohio 26 - winds along the Little Muskingum River in the Marietta Unit. In addition to bridges, visitors can see birds and other wildlife, rock formations, historic buildings, a stone bridge, classic Mail Pouch chewing tobacco signs and evidence of the local oil and gas drilling industry.

Capitol Christmas Tree Picnic Area: The 1987 U.S. Capitol Christmas Tree was cut at what is now Capitol Christmas Tree Picnic Area and shipped to Washington, D.C. The area is N of Leith Run on Ohio 7 in the Marietta Unit. Other picnic facilities include Sand Run in the Athens Ranger District and Lane, Hune, Haught Run, Lamping Homestead, Leith Run and Ring Mill in the Marietta Unit.

Rock climbing: Although rock climbing is allowed at Wayne, no spots are designated for this activity. Two nearby state parks have specific climbing and rapeling areas.

Swimming: Swimming is available at Big Bend Beach in Lake Vesuvius Recreation Area.

Ranger Districts

Athens: 219 Columbus Road, Athens, OH 45701; ☎ (614) 592-6644.

Ironton: 6518 State Rte. 93, Pedro, OH 45659; ☎ (614) 532-3223.

Marietta Unit, Athens Ranger District: Rte. 1, Box 132, Marietta, OH 45750; ☎ (614) 373-9055.

Gateways

Athens: Athens County Convention & Visitors Bureau, Box 1019, Athens, OH 45701; ☎ (800) 878-9767 or (614) 592-1819.

Ironton: Lawrence County Convention & Visitors Bureau, 101 San Solida Road, Southport, OH 45680; ☎ (614) 894-3838.

Marietta: Marietta Area Convention & Visitors Bureau, 316 Third St., Marietta, OH 45750; ☎ (614) 373-5178.

PENNSYLVANIA

Allegheny National Forest

One of the best birding spots in Allegheny National Forest is at the Mead Run Duck Ponds.

ALLEGHENY

222 Liberty Street
Warren, PA 16365
☎ (814) 723-5150

513,000 acres

Allegheny National Forest offers more than 640 miles of trails and 500 miles of fishing streams, as well as access to the 12,080-acre Allegheny Reservoir. The flat-top mountains are part of the Allegheny Plateau, and the forest is dominated by such hardwoods as northern red oak, maple and black cherry. The national forest nestles up to New York; its Kinzua Dam-created Allegheny Reservoir provides recreational opportunities on both sides of the border. Snowmobile trails cross between Pennsylvania and New York as well. As a result of the reservoir, boating, fishing and waterfront camping are major draws, but the national forest has quieter, more remote places as well, including Hickory Creek Wilderness and Allegheny River Islands Wilderness, the smallest federally-designated wilderness in the United States.

The Seneca, the westernmost tribe of the Iroquois Confederation, hunted and fished here before 19th-century settlers started farming and intensive logging of white pine and hemlock stripped the forest. The Allegheny River, which traverses the national forest, was a significant shipping route in the era before railroads. The first oil well was drilled in nearby Titusville in the 1860s and significantly changed the local economy, as well as the world's, as oil replaced coal as a primary source of energy.

Allegheny National Forest was established in 1923 when heavy logging, forest fires and erosion had left most of the area as a wasteland of brush. Local landowners welcomed the chance to sell their "worthless" land to the government, but they retained mineral rights to 94 percent of the subsurface oil, gas and minerals. Oil and gas drilling continues in the national forest.

Camping

Allegheny has 16 developed campgrounds, several of which rank among the largest in number of sites among national forests in the Great Lakes states. Two of them, Hooks Brook and Pine Grove, are accessible only by boat. Three others - Handsome Lake, Hopewell and Morrison - can be reached only by foot or boat. Group camping is available at Buckaloons, Tracy Ridge and Twin Lakes campgrounds. Here are the improved campgrounds, number of sites and locations:

Bradford Ranger District

Dewdrop (74), 3 miles S of Kinzua Point on Forest Road 262 (Longhouse National Scenic Byway);

Handsome Lake (10), on the E shore of Allegheny Reservoir, NE of Bradford and accessible only by foot or boat;

Kiasutha (92), 10 miles NW of Kane on Forest Road 262 (Longhouse National Scenic Byway);

Hooks Brook (20), on the W shore of Allegheny Reservoir, NW of Warren and accessible only by boat;

Hopewell (8), on the E shore of Allegheny Reservoir, NW of Bradford and accessible only by foot or boat;

Morrison (32), on the E shore of Kinzua Bay, SW of Bradford and accessible only by foot or boat;

Pine Grove (28), on the E shore of Allegheny Reservoir, W of Bradford and accessible only by boat;

Red Bridge (55), 9 miles NW of Kane on Route 321;

Tracy Ridge (120), 2 miles E of Allegheny Reservoir on Route

321;

Willow Bay (72), 15 miles NW of Bradford on Route 346.
Marienville Ranger District
Beaver Meadows (37), 5 miles N of Marienville on Forest Road 128 (Township Road T-358).
Ridgeway Ranger District
Loleta (32), 6 miles SE of Marienville on Route 27027;
Twin Lakes (51), 8 miles SE of Kane on Forest Road 191.
Sheffield Ranger District
Buckaloons (51), 6 miles SW of Warren on U.S. 6;
Hearts Content (26), 15 miles SW of Warren on Forest Road 193;
Minister Creek (6), 15 miles SW of Sheffield on Route 666.

 ## Trails

There are more than 225 miles of hiking trails while horseback riding is permitted on any forest road and railroad grade. Interpretive trails in the national forest total 14 miles.

An 88-mile segment of the North Country National Scenic Trail traverses Allegheny National Forest. This section includes rock outcroppings, streams, waterfalls and stands of mountain laurel. Although solitude and wildlife are the prime attraction for hikers, oil jacks are visible where drilling is permitted. Highlights along the route include the ghost town of Braceville, stands of virgin trees, the scene of a 1985 tornado blow down, Tionesta Scenic Area and a mineral spring popular as a deer lick. From N to SW, it passes close to Willow Bay, Handsome Lake, Red Bridge, Minister Creek and Hearts Content campgrounds.

Other popular trails are, by ranger district:
Bradford Ranger District
Johnnycake/Tracy Ridge Trail, 6 miles: Beginning at Tracy Ridge Recreation Area, it drops about 900 feet as it passes through the roadless Allegheny National Recreation Area. There are steep slopes, with large boulders and rock ledges on some hillsides. By joining with the North Country National Scenic Trail, it forms a

9-mile loop. Access the trail from Route 321, W of Bradford.

Morrison Trail, 15 miles: Stretching along Kinzua Creek near the Allegheny Reservoir, this trail has steep slopes; with waterfalls and small streams. The land is heavily forested, with abundant wildlife and scattered virgin white pines. Mountain laurel blooms in early to mid-June. There are two loops, Morrison and Rimrock. The trailhead is E of Warren on Route 59.

Westline Ski Trail, 10 miles: The system follows pipelines, forest roads and logging trails with scenic vistas. One stopping spot provides a view of Thundershower Run flowing into Westline, a village that once was home to a sawmill, two railroads and a chemical wood factory. Loop names include *Boo-Boo's Delight, Ledges* and *Inside-Out.* The access point is S of Bradford on Forest Road 455.

Marienville Ranger District

Beaver Meadows Trail System, 7 miles: Five interconnecting trails make up this network, which winds through the forests around Beaver Meadows Lake. Hikers are welcome to pick blueberries in a half-acre patch along Seldom Seen Trail. Beavers are sometimes seen in Salmon Creek along Salmon Creek Trail. Stumps along Penoke Path serve as reminders of early 1900s logging. Beaver Meadows Loop crosses the lake on a floating boardwalk, and Lakeside Loop passes close to the lake for wildlife viewing. The trailhead is on Forest Road 282, N of Marienville in the Beaver Meadows Recreation Area.

Buzzard Swamp Trail Area, 12 miles: These interconnecting loops of trails and old roads lie within the Buzzard Swamp Wildlife Management Area. Among the loops are Turkey Track, Woodman's Way, Beaver Pond, Pipeline, Deer Run and Canada Goose. The name Buzzard Swamp refers to an early 20th-century logger, not to the bird. Access the trail S of Marienville on Forest Road 157 or E of Marienville on Forest Road 376.

Songbird Sojourn Interpretive Trail, 2 miles: This nature trail is part of the Buzzard Swamp trail system. Pamphlets avail-

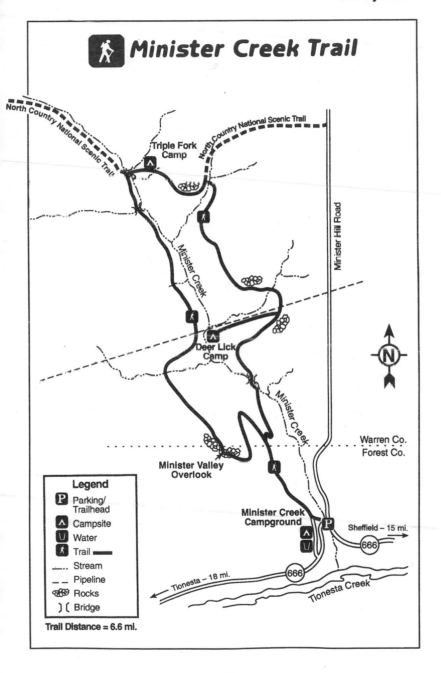

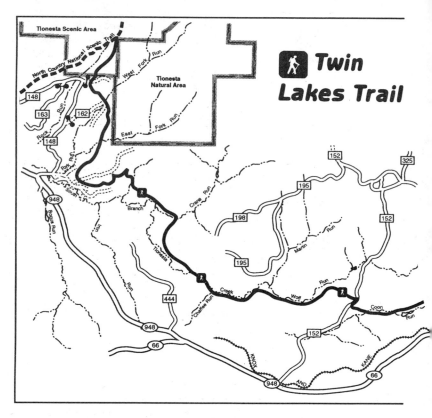

able at the trailhead explain the natural sights. Access to the trail is S of Marienville from Forest Road 157.

Ridgeway Ranger District

***Black Cherry National Recreation Trail,** 2 miles*: This interpretive trail is adjacent to Twin Lakes Recreation Area and focuses on aspects of the forest community. The trailhead is along Forest Road 191.

***Laurel Mill Trail Area,** 11 miles*: Used for hiking and skiing, the trail system through the Clarion River Undeveloped Area has scenic views and ski runs with names such as *Suicide Slide* and *Sam's Slide.* There's a warming hut with a wood-burning stove. The trailhead is W of Ridgway on Township Road 307 (Spring Creek Road).

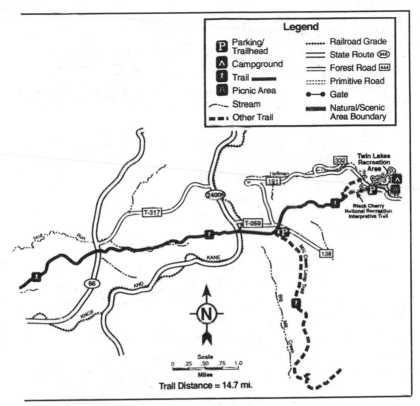

Trail Distance = 14.7 mi.

Loleta Trail, 3 miles: Along this loop trail you'll see pine plantings, hardwood groves and a rock overlook amid rhododendron and mountain laurel. Get there from Forest Road 27027, SE of Marienville.

Mill Creek Loop Trail, 17 miles: It meanders through gently rolling terrain and fern-carpeted open areas, with some challenging climbs. Portions follow old railroad grades; signs of early logging activity are visible. It runs through Mill Creek Semi-Primitive Non-Motorized Area, which provides bear and turkey habitat, and passes the Kane Experimental Forest. Access sites are S of Kane at Twin Lakes Recreation Area and N of Ridgway on Forest Road 185.

Twin Lakes Trail, 15 miles: The trail climbs from Hoffman

Run in Twin Lakes Recreation Area and drops into the headwaters of Wolf Run. Along the route are "tornado swath" overlooks, the Tionesta National Scenic Area, Tionesta Creek and Crane Run. It starts at the far end of the Black Cherry National Recreation Trail, within Twin Lakes Recreation Area at Forest Road 191, and connects with the North Country National Scenic Trail.

Sheffield Ranger District

Buckaloons Seneca Interpretive Trail, 1 mile: An interpretive trail named for the Native American tribe that once inhabited the area, this one circles Buckaloons Campground. It is SW of Warren on U.S. 6.

Deer Lick Ski Trail, 9 miles: It follows roads, old railroad grades and pipelines along terrain that offers a variety of difficulty levels. Access is near the Sheffield Ranger Station at the intersection of U.S. 6 and Tollgate Road.

Hearts Content Ski Trail, 7 miles: The trail cuts through old stands of hemlock, beech and white pine, amid abundant wildlife. There are three loops: Ironwood, Tom's Run and Hearts Content. The trailhead is at the picnic area in Hearts Content Recreation Area, SW of Warren on Hearts Content Road.

Hickory Creek Trail, 11 miles: This trail loops through Hickory Creek Wilderness, an area characterized by gentle to moderate terrain and a lack of steep slopes. Along the way are a red pine plantation, meadows and the remains of a logging camp along Jacks Run. Access the trail from the adjacent Hearts Content Recreation Area, SW of Warren on Forest Road 193.

Minister Creek Trail, 7 miles: Part of this loop follows abandoned logging railroad grades. Wildlife includes pileated woodpeckers, flying squirrels and barred owls. Hikers can find cliffs, wildflowers, a natural overlook and fossilized shells in exposed layers of shale. Its northernmost segment joins the North Country National Scenic Trail. The trailhead is on Route 666, W of Minister Creek Campground.

Tanbark Trail, 9 miles: This area, once home to tanneries, is the site of Sandstone Spring, well known for its pure drinking

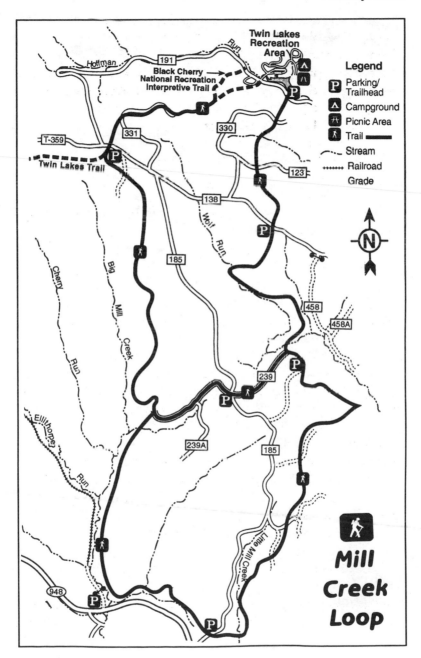

Twin Lakes Recreation Area

Black Cherry National Recreation Interpretive Trail

Legend

- 🅿 Parking/Trailhead
- ⛺ Campground
- 🛆 Picnic Area
- 🚶 Trail ▬▬
- Stream --·--
- Railroad ·····
- Grade

Hoffman

191

T-359

Twin Lakes Trail

331

330

123

138

185

458

458A

239

239A

185

948

Mill Creek Loop

IN THE FOREST

Beaver Meadows Lake

By Scott & Linda Shalaway

Beaver Meadows Lake was constructed in the 1930s by the Civilian Conservation Corps, as were many northern Pennsylvania lakes. Most, Beaver included, are converted wetlands. Years ago, before people understood the biological and ecological importance of marshes, swamps, bogs and other wetlands, they viewed such areas as wastelands and converted them to croplands or dammed them to form lakes.

From its dam at the west end, Beaver Meadows Lake extends due east to shallow headwaters and a series of tiny "islands" of cut-grass. Cut-grass, with its serrated edges that "cut" when touched, rings almost the entire shoreline, while conifers border the shores.

From the launch on the north shore, near the dam, we paddled across the lake and explored the south shore as we headed east. We found two beaver lodges, and beaver paths and channels cut into the banks at regular intervals.

In July, thick beds of water shield cover the lake's east end. Paddling though this area is like paddling through thick green pea soup. Wood duck boxes dot the shore. At this time of year, water level determines how far you can paddle.

Beaver Meadows is a beautiful, isolated area surrounded by national forest.

From **Quiet Water Canoe Guide: Pennsylvania,** *copyright 1994, published by Appalachian Mountain Club, Boston MA, used with permission.*

water. There are other interesting geological features along the trail, part of which was once a railroad grade. A short stretch crosses a corner of Hickory Creek Wilderness; elsewhere the trail intersects the North Country National Scenic Trail, SE of Hearts Content Recreation Area.

Tidioute Riverside Recreation Trek Trail, 5 miles: A scenic hiking, biking and cross-country ski trail, it follows an abandoned railroad grade along a stretch of the Allegheny River that has Wild and Scenic status. The trailhead is in Tidioute.

ATV Trails

There are more than 350 miles of snowmobile trails and 106 miles of ATV trails within the national forest. Here are the more popular off-road trails for all terrain vehicles:

Marienville ATV & Bike Trail, 37 miles: These interconnecting trails offer varying levels of difficulty. Although the western part is designated for bike trails and the eastern part for ATVs, there's no prohibition against ATVs in the bike area or the other way around. The bike area features a narrow, winding, serpentine layout with a narrower treadway and more hill climbs, mud holes and switchbacks; the ATV area is more scenic, with wider riding surfaces. Parking for the main trailhead is NF of Marienville on Route 66. Other trailheads are on Forest Roads 221, 395, 401 and 521.

Timberline ATV Trail, 38 miles: Much of this trail for ATV and snowmobile use is along old roads and former railroad grades. The principal parking area is on Forest Road 232, NW of Highland. There's also parking on Township Road 458 (Forest Road 136) near Beuhler Corner and Township Road 322 at Pigs Ear.

Willow Creek ATV Trail, 11 miles: This trail offers two loops through scenic, forested hills. The trailhead is W of Bradford on Forest Road 137.

Rocky Gap ATV Trail, 21 miles: These loops near Chapman State Park are for intermediate and expert ATV and motorbike riders. The terrain is forested hills; the trail crosses Grunder

Run, Elkhorn Run and several oil fields. Trailhead parking is S of Warren at the intersection of Tidioute to Warren Road and Forest Road 155.

 ## Boating & Canoeing

Boaters can access the Allegheny Reservoir at five Forest Service launches, including Elijah Run. Concessionaire Kinzua-Wolf Run Marina is a full-service marina 4 miles E of Kinzua Dam. It has dockage for 300 boats, a bait-and-tackle store and excursion rides aboard the Kinzua Queen paddle wheeler. The marina also rents canoes, rowboats, motor boats, deluxe pontoon boats and jet skis. For more information, contact Kinzua-Wolf Run Marina, Box 825, Warren, PA 16365; ☎ (814) 726-1650. There's also a small marina on 480-acre Tionesta Lake.

For canoeing and kayaking, the Allegheny River, Clarion River and Tionesta Creek are used most. Some canoeists also enjoy Beaver Meadows Lake because of its waterfowl viewing opportunities. Some popular routes are:

Allegheny River, 43 miles: Below Kinzua Dam, it offers long, placid float trips adjacent to the national forest. Eighty-five miles of the 128-mile-long Allegheny are classified as recreational in the National Wild and Scenic Rivers System. Within the national forest, there's a launch site at Buckaloons Recreation Area, SW of Warren; another well-used public access point is the ramp below Kinzua Dam.

Beaver Meadows Lake: Visitors to the Beaver Meadows Recreation Area can combine canoeing on this 34-acre lake with hiking and waterfowl viewing. The launch ramp is N of Marienville along Forest Road 128 (Township Road T-358).

Clarion River, 104 miles: Adjacent to Allegheny National Forest, the Clarion includes four classified rapids along a 19-mile stretch. This river offers the best canoeing opportunities in the national forest and travels through scenic river corridors that offer semi-primitive recreational experiences. There are no developed launch facilities, but there's access at bridge sites in Sheffield,

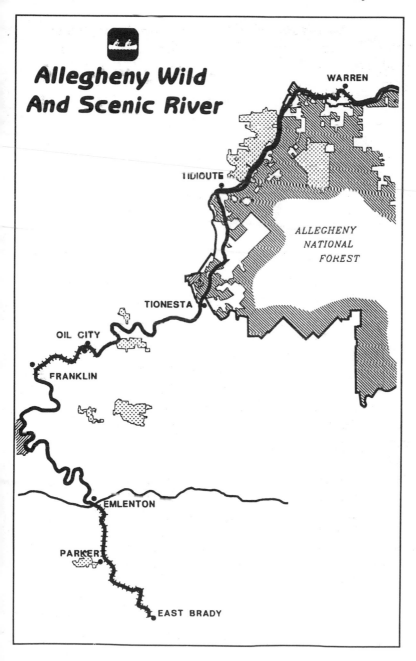

Allegheny Wild And Scenic River

WARREN

TIDIOUTE

ALLEGHENY
NATIONAL
FOREST

TIONESTA

OIL CITY

FRANKLIN

EMLENTON

PARKER

EAST BRADY

Lynch, Mayburg and Kellettville.

Tionesta Creek, 45 miles: This route runs through scenic country, ending at Tionesta Dam. Because of water levels, it's usually floatable only in early spring through May.

 Fishing

Seventy-one species of fish have been caught in national forest waters. Muskellunge, walleye, smallmouth and largemouth bass, brown and brook trout, rock bass, yellow perch, crappie, brown bullhead, channel catfish, carp, white bass, sunfish and northern pike are found in Allegheny's rivers, streams, lakes and in Allegheny Reservoir. To improve fisheries habitat in the reservoir, tire reefs are installed to provide cover; discarded Christmas trees are anchored with cement blocks to attract panfish.

Allegheny Reservoir has produced the Pennsylvania record walleye and northern pike. If you plan to fish at the reservoir, a 24-hour-a-day recorded Fishing Hotline provides information about hot spots, success reports, depths, daily lake conditions, baits, lures and techniques; call ☎ (814) 726-0164. The Army Corps of Engineers also publishes a free, detailed Allegheny Reservoir Fisheries Guide; to get a copy, write to the Army Corps of Engineers, Box 983, Warren, PA 16365.

Crane Run is a state-designated wilderness trout stream; Minister Creek, Tionesta Creek and some tributaries of Big Mill Creek are also home to trout. Other fishing opportunities include Beaver Meadows Lake, which offers bluegill, pumpkinseed, yellow perch and bullhead. More than a dozen ponds in Buzzard Swamp Wildlife Viewing and Hiking Area have smallmouth and largemouth bass, perch, crappie, catfish and bluegill.

 Natural Areas

Hearts Content Scenic Area, 120 acres: The virgin forest here contains huge white pine more than 400 years old and slightly shorter hemlock more than 350 years old; they grow atop a plateau 1,800 feet above sea level. In the natural course of events, shade-tolerant hemlock are gradually replacing the dead and dying white pine. Other tree species include red and white oak, red and sugar maple, cucumber magnolia, yellow birch and black cherry. There's a 1-mile interpretive trail through this designated National Natural Landmark. The area is in the Sheffield Ranger District, adjacent to Hearts Content Recreation Area.

Tionesta Forest, listed on the National Register of Natural Landmarks, has long been studied by biologists. Nearly 75 wildflower species, abundant ferns, 125-foot-tall eastern hemlock and a variety of hardwoods abound here, as do whitetail deer, porcupine and other animals. Trees felled and shattered by a May 1985 tornado were left in place, allowing natural succession to run its course. The forest is divided between the Tionesta Research Natural Area and the Tionesta National Scenic Area. The forest is W of Kane on Forest Road 133.

Tionesta National Scenic Area, 2,018 acres: With its virgin hemlock and hardwoods, this high plateau features one of the largest tracts of virgin forest in the eastern United States. It was dedicated in 1940 as a living natural museum for public enjoyment and study. Two interpretive trails, a mile long and the other less than a mile, allow self-guided tours.

Tionesta Research Natural Area, 2,113 acres: Climax hemlock, beech and sugar maple present opportunities for scientists to study the dynamics of forest succession.

 # Wilderness Areas

Allegheny River Islands Wilderness, 368 acres: The seven islands that make up the wilderness were formed by water carried deposits of mud, clay and sand. They're characterized by river-bottom trees such as sycamore, silver maple and willow. Thompson's Island was the site of the only Revolutionary War battle in NW Pennsylvania. Parts of Crull's Island - the largest - and Courson Island were once farmed, but the forest is reclaiming the abandoned fields. A section of the river between Tionesta and

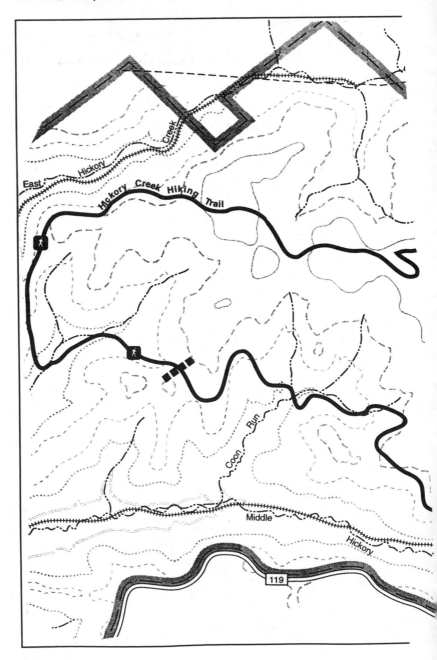

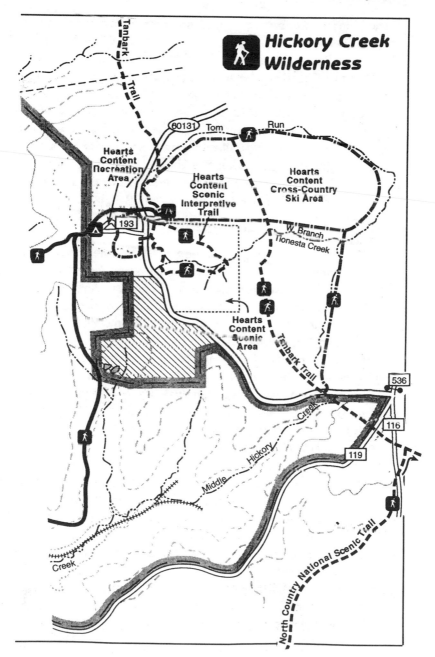

Hickory Creek Wilderness

60131 Tom Run

Hearts Content Recreation Area

Hearts Content Scenic Interpretive Trail

Hearts Content Cross-Country Ski Area

193

W. Branch Tionesta Creek

Hearts Content Scenic Area

Tanbark Trail

536

116

119

Hickory

Middle

Creek

North Country National Scenic Trail

Buckaloons is home to two endangered species of freshwater mussels. The wilderness is in the Sheffield Ranger District, W of Kane. Boat launches are along U.S. 62.

Hickory Creek Wilderness, *8,663 acres*: Much of the area in the wilderness is heavily wooded. East Hickory Creek and Middle Hickory Creek drain this gentle-to-moderate terrain, which is marked by bogs, beaver ponds, meadows, hemlock groves and scattered white pine. Old railroad grades and evidence of small farms abandoned in the 1930s are the only visible signs of past commercial activities here. Hickory Creek Trail climbs in and out of the valleys. It's W of Kane in the Sheffield Ranger District.

 ## Historic Attractions

CCC Monument: A granite monument at Loleta Recreation Area commemorates the Civilian Conservation Corps for providing forest fire protection, planting trees and building recreation sites in the national forest. At Loleta, CCC members constructed the dam, bathhouse and picnic pavilions. The monument is S of Marienville in the Ridgway Ranger District.

Hearts Content Memorial: This is a memorial to two local logging families whose company, Wheeler and Dusenbury, donated some land now within the Sheffield Ranger District's Hearts Content National Scenic Area. Their mill specialized in long logs for bridge timbers, ship spars and masts.

Pennzoil Powerhouse: Passport in Time professional staff and volunteers have worked on restoration of an old oil and gas powerhouse, including putting the equipment back in working order. In the 1920s, this was an important facility for the oil fields. To supplement the physical remains, oral histories from engine operators and oil field workers have been compiled. The powerhouse serves as an information center about the history of oil, gas and related equipment in the area. The structure is on the Longhouse National Scenic Byway (Forest Road 262) in the Bradford Ranger District.

Red Bridge Recreation Area: This area includes the site of a

Depression-era Civilian Conservation Corps camp that later housed World War II German prisoners of war. Camp #3 stood from 1933 to 1946. The location is NW of Kane on Forest Road 321 in the Bradford Ranger District.

Twin Lakes Recreation Area: This area encompasses the former location of a wood alcohol factory, stores and company row houses owned by McKean Chemical Co.; the factory closed in the 1920s. The company's splash dam once stood at the site of the present dam on Hoffman Run. The area is in the Ridgway Ranger District, SE of Kane.

More Things To Do & See

Allegheny National Fish Hatchery: Operated by the U.S. Fish & Wildlife Service, it rears more than 1.2 million fingerling trout for stocking in the Great Lakes and produces 3 million eggs each year. The hatchery is open to the public daily from 9 a.m. to 3 p.m. Group tours can be arranged. The hatchery is on the N bank of the Allegheny River immediately below the Kinzua Dam. For information, contact Allegheny National Fish Hatchery, R D. 1, Box 1050, Warren, PA 16365; ☎ (814) 726-0890.

Birding: Great blue herons, osprey, bald eagles and red shouldered hawks are among more than 200 bird species found in Allegheny National Forest. So are turkey vultures, ruby-throated hummingbirds, kestrels, common loons, whistling swans, Canada geese, red-tailed hawks, warblers, green herons and mallards. Buzzard Swamp and Owl's Nest are favored places for spotting waterfowl and songbirds.

Songbirds are abundant on the seven islands that make up Allegheny River Islands Wilderness. Other favorite bird watching spots include Mead Run Duck Ponds, Tionesta Scenic Area and stretches of the Allegheny and Clarion rivers.

Buzzard Swamp Wildlife Viewing Area: This area provides some of Allegheny's best wildlife viewing opportunities. Thanks to marshlands and grassy meadows, the area attracts 20 to 25 species of waterfowl during spring migration; it's along the Atlantic flyway. There also are deer, beaver, coyote, snapping turtles, eagles, osprey and turkey. Within its borders are a 12-mile network of interconnecting trails, 15 ponds built in the 1960s and the 2-mile self-guided Songbird Sojourn Interpretive Trail. Boating without motors is allowed on the ponds. It's in the Marienville Ranger District. Access is available S of Marienville on Forest Road 157 and E of Marienville on Forest Road 376.

Forest Fest: This celebration each June features interpretive programs, guided hikes and races, nature walks and music programs. During the festival, there's free camping for one night at Allegheny National Forest's developed recreational facilities.

Grand Army of the Republic Highway: Part of U.S. 6, and named in tribute to Civil War veterans from the North, this highway crosses Allegheny National Forest. The renaming followed years of lobbying by Sons of the Union Veterans. The Pennsylvania section is rated one of America's most scenic highways.

Interpretive programs: Forest Service staff present interpretive programs at Kiasutha, Loleta and Twin Lakes recreation areas. The programs cover such topics as wildlife viewing, songbird identification, a day in the life of a ranger and nature walks.

Kinzua Dam: Built and operated by the Army Corps of Engineers, the dam created the Allegheny Reservoir and opened a variety of recreational opportunities in northwestern Pennsylvania. In addition to Forest Service waterfront facilities, there are campgrounds, beaches, trails, boat launches, rental cabins and picnic areas operated by other agencies such as the Corps of Engineers, Cattaraugus County (N.Y.), Allegany State Park (N.Y.) and the Seneca Nation of Indians. Big Bend Visitor Center is just down river of the dam, with fish and wildlife displays, exhibits and slide programs. For information, contact the Army Corps of Engineers, Box 983, Warren, PA 16365.

Kinzua Point Visitor Center: Interpretive displays explain the history of the area, Allegheny Reservoir and the natural resources of the national forest. The center is at the junction of Route 59 and Longhouse National Scenic Byway; ☎ (814) 726-

Enjoying breakfast outdoors in a national forest campsite.

1291.

Kinzua Queen: On weekends and holidays from Memorial Day through Labor Day, this 20-passenger paddle-wheel boat offers 45-minute narrated cruises on the Allegheny Reservoir. Trips depart from Kinzua-Wolf Run Marina.

Longhouse National Scenic Byway, *29 miles:* The winding, hilly byway in the Bradford Ranger District passes Jake's Rocks and Rimrock scenic overlooks along Forest Road 262 and Routes 321 and 59. Both overlooks provide vistas of the Allegheny River Valley; from Jake's Rocks, you can also see Dewdrop Recreation Area and Kinzua Dam. Other stops along the byway include the Pennzoil Powerhouse, Morrison Bridge, the Allegheny Reservoir's

Chappel Bay and the Kinzua Point Information Center. The byway provides access to Morrison Hiking Trail and the North Country National Scenic Trail; to Red Bridge, Kiasutha and Dewdrop recreation areas; to Kinzua-Wolf Run Marina; to Elijah Run boat launch; and to Kinzua Beach.

Otters: Otters have been reintroduced on Tionesta Creek, thanks to cooperation from Pennsylvania State University, Wild Resource Conservation Fund and the Pennsylvania Game Commission. They're expected to disperse into other nearby watersheds. Visitors spotting an otter are asked to call ☎ (814) 723-5150.

Passport in Time Program: In addition to restoration work on the Pennzoil Powerhouse, PIT participants have helped map, photograph and record some of the several dozen prehistoric rock shelters found on national forest land. These are significant archaeological sites.

Tornado Damage Overlook: On May 31, 1985, two tornados tore through a 21-square-mile chunk of the national forest; they destroyed a great blue heron rookery and $10 million worth of timber. As the Sierra Club's Allegheny National Forest Hiking Guide notes:

Some of the swaths are about a mile wide, and trees in the middle were literally ripped to shreds. Trees a few yards away from the swath edges appeared virtually untouched, while trees a few yards into the swaths exist only as stumps topped by ragged splinters where the tornado plucked off the top like someone might pluck a flower.

These swaths can still be seen as areas of young tree growth in the forest.

🏚 Ranger Districts

Bradford: Route 1, Box 88, Bradford, PA 16702; ☎ (814) 362-4613.

Marienville: SR 66, Marienville, PA 16239; ☎ (814) 927-6628.

Ridgway: Montmorenci Road, Ridgway, PA 15853; ☎ (814)

776-6172.

Sheffield: Kane Road, Route 6, Sheffield, PA 16347; ☎ (814) 968-3232.

 ## Gateways

Custer City: Seneca Highlands Tourist Association, Drawer G., 10 E. Warren Road, Custer City, PA 16725; ☎ (814) 368-9370.

Ridgway: Elk County Recreation & Tourist Council, Box 35, Ridgway, PA 15853; ☎ (814) 772-5502

Warren: Travel Northern Alleghenies, Box 804, Warren, PA 16365; ☎ (800) 624-7802 or (814) 726-1222.

NEW YORK

Finger Lakes
National Forest

Searching, finding and picking wildberries. Among the campgrounds in Finger Lakes National Forest is Blueberry Patch Recreation Site.

FINGER LAKES

4588 State Road 224   **14,583 acres**
Montour Falls, NY 14865
☎ (607) 594-2750

Although Finger Lakes National Forest is among the nation's smallest national forests, it offers a variety of recreational opportunities in one of the most scenic areas of the Great Lakes states. Located between glacier-gouged Cayuga and Seneca lakes, it's the only national forest in New York and is administered by Green Mountain National Forest in Vermont.

Just a short drive from some of the Finger Lakes' chic wineries, this unit is an area of intermingled woods and fields, which are used as pastures by grazing cattle from May 15 to Oct. 15. The terrain includes steep gullies, as well as hills with overlooks of the lakes. Spots within the national forest's borders carry such intriguing names as Bumpus Corners, Butcher Hill, Peach Orchard Gulley, Sassafras Pond, Hector Backbone and Chicken Coop Road.

Members of the Iroquois Indian Confederacy, which became the Six Nations, were believed to have been the first human users of the Hector Hills area. In 1790, the area was divided into 600 single acre lots and distributed among military veterans as payment for their services. "The government couldn't afford to pay them cash," a ranger explained. But farming here proved unprofitable as the soil became depleted by the early 1900s, giving the growing number of Midwest farmers a competitive edge.

When the Depression came, the federal government started buying up the property - more than 100 farms between 1938 and 1941 - and relocating their owners. Under Soil Conservation Service management, emphasis was placed on converting cropland for livestock grazing and on stabilizing the soil. By the late 1950s, the emphasis shifted to multiple use management, and the land was transferred to the U.S. Forest Service. It was officially added to the national forest system in 1983.

 Camping

There are three developed campgrounds at Finger Lakes. All of them are NE of Bennettsburg. Despite its small size, backcountry camping is allowed as well.

Blueberry Patch Campground (9 sites) is part of the Blueberry Patch Recreation Site, which includes Interloken Trail and Burnt Hill Trail. Access is along Picnic Area Road.

Potomac Group Campground is a group area and has a picnic shelter. It's along the Potomac Trail, E of Potomac Road.

Backbone Horse Camp is a rustic facility designed for overnight and day use by horseback riders and features hitching rails. It is N of Picnic Area Road.

 Trails

There are more than 25 miles of marked, interconnected trails for hiking, cross-country skiing, horseback riding and snowmobiling. Always close all gates so the beef and dairy cattle won't get loose.

Interloken Trail, 12 miles: This trail runs N-S through Finger Lakes National Forest and is part of the North Country National Scenic Trail. There's a trail shelter a mile before the southern boundary of the national forest.

Finger Lakes Trail System, 2 miles: A portion of the 800-mile Finger Lakes Trail System crosses the southern end of the forest.

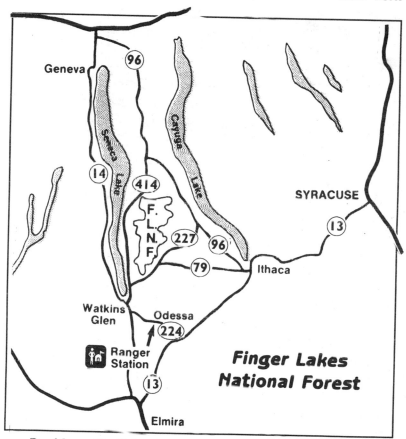

Finger Lakes National Forest

Backbone Trail, *5 miles*: This horseback trail is served by the Backbone Horse Camp.

There are short trails as well: *Potomac* (2 miles); *Ravine* (1 mile); *Southslope* (1 mile); *Gorge* (1 mile); and *Burnt Hill* (3 miles).

Fishing

.Fishing is permitted in scattered wildlife ponds. Ballard, Potomac and Foster ponds are stocked annually with brook and rainbow trout while many ponds have been stocked with large-mouth bass. A few ponds also contain brown bullhead, yellow perch and sunfish. Projects to improve habitat, angler access and

IN THE FOREST

Hiking Finger Lakes National Forest

Wild blueberries tempted, and delayed, us for a few moments as we set off along the Interloken Trail. Interloken means "between the lakes" and like Finger Lakes National Forest itself, the trail is between Cayuga and Seneca lakes.

The hike was planned to be 5 miles through the southern part of the national forest, but those blueberries would prove to be only the first of several reasons why the hike took longer, and went farther, than expected.

Along the way, there would be a stop to examine a fire-scarred maple with a distinctive off-white fungus climbing up its trunk that resembled ladder rungs or barnacles arranged vertically on a pier post.

There would be a break to examine dozens of curious-looking, opaque plastic tubes sticking up from the forest floor like 5-foot-high ventilator shafts. As a Forest Service information sign explained, the tubes were developed in England and were part of a tree shelter experiment on accelerating the growth of oak seedlings and protecting young trees from browsing animals.

There also was more time added and more distance hiked when we got lost, but more about that mild embarrassment in a moment.

Hiking is more than a way to move from place to place, from a starting point to a destination. It's an avenue for observations large and small. Our observations included blueberries and blackberries, streambeds dry in late summer, hoof prints drying in the mud, ferns along a swampy area, wild apple trees, a toad on a dead oak leaf and dead pine needles carpeting a steep downhill slope. We headed through a gorge where enough water trickled to satisfy our companion, a cairn terrier hot and thirsty after snuffling at unfamiliar forest scents.

We began at one of the Interloken Trail trailheads, next to the Blueberry Patch Recreation Site campground. We cut east onto Gorge Trail, then N along the gravel Mark Smith Road, intending to take Burnt Hill Trail back to our starting point.

To understand how our plans went awry, you need to know that Finger Lakes National Forest includes wooded areas and rolling pastures. The fields are leased to farmers for grazing cattle from mid-May to mid-October, so hikers must be careful to close and secure the gates behind them.

Our problem? The trails through the woods were well-marked and well-worn by human feet and, especially noticeable, by hoof prints that made it impossible to get lost. However, trail markers were missing in the fields, where tall grasses, purple clover and bountiful wildflowers such as black-eyed susans and Queen Anne's lace obscured most of the footpath.

So we wandered, and wandered, and wandered some more. We had no compass, and I repeatedly studied my map, hoping vainly for inspiration. As we changed angles in search of the gate leading to Burnt Hill Trail, birds nesting in the high grasses flushed at our approach. A landmark radio tower seemed to change locations. We followed a rusting barbed wire fence line to no avail. At one point, a pale yellow butterfly flew ahead of us. A beacon? A favorable omen? No, a tease. The butterfly apparently didn't know where it was going either.

Finally, we came across what looked like a path. It was - a cow path. Soon we met up with several Holsteins enjoying the shade of a copse of evergreens. "Lost in a field! That's pitiful," my teenage son said.

It was. So we backtracked to the gravel road, walked a short distance west and picked up the Interloken Trail we had started our hike along. As we neared the Blueberry Patch Recreation Site after a 5-mile hike that stretched to more than 7, it was time to pause again. Wild blueberries were a well-deserved reward.

fishing opportunities had been implemented throughout the forest, including South Burnt Hill, Burdick, Sassafras and Potomac ponds.

📷 More Things To See & Do

Auto touring: Forest roads along the ridge top provide many scenic vistas.

Birding: More than 150 species of birds, including game and song birds, have been identified in Finger Lakes. Among them are the great blue heron, Canada goose, ruby-throated hummingbird, wild turkey, ruffled grouse, osprey, turkey vulture and great horned owl. A variety of species of warblers, hawks, finches, swallows, flycatchers, ducks, sandpipers, wrens, woodpeckers and vireos have been spotted here, according to a tally by the Cornell University Laboratory of Ornithology, Partners in Flight and the Ruffed Grouse Society. Nest boxes have been erected as part of a wildlife habitat improvement program.

The Partners in Flight program, a joint effort of the U.S. Forest Service, Cornell University and the U.S. Fish and Wildlife Service, has established two permanent breeding survey plots for neotropical migratory birds at Finger Lakes. They are part of a 10-state network to monitor productivity of the birds, which winter in Central America and South America, then return to North America to breed.

Berry picking: Blueberries are the most popular, with five acres of bushes adjacent to the Blueberry Patch Campground. Blackberries and raspberries grow in scattered parts of the national forest, as do apples.

Gateways

Seneca Falls: Seneca County Chamber of Commerce, Box 294, Seneca Falls, NY 13148; ☎ (315) 568-2906.

Watkins Glen: Schuyler County Chamber of Commerce, 100 N. Franklin St., Watkins Glen, NY 14891; ☎ (607) 535-4300.

Additional Reading

These books provide additional information about the national forests of the Great Lakes states:

Allegheny National Forest Hiking Guide by Bruce Sundquist, Carolyn Weilacher Yartz and Jack Richardson (Allegheny Group, Sierra Club).

Backpacking Loops and Long Day Trail Hikes in Southern Ohio by Robert H. Ruchhoft (Pucelle Press).

Canoe Country Camping: Wilderness Skills for the Boundary Waters and Quetico by Michael Furtman (Pfeifer-Hamilton Publishers).

Canoe Country Wildlife: Field Guide to the Boundary Waters and Quetico by Mark Stensaas (Pfeifer-Hamilton Publishers).

Canoeing and Kayaking Ohio's Streams by Rick Combs & Steve Gillen (Backcountry Publications).

Canoeing Guide to Western Pennsylvania and Northern West Virginia by Roy R. Weil and Mary M. Shaw (Pittsburgh Council, American Youth Hostels).

Canoeing Michigan Rivers by Jerry Dennis & Craig Date (Friede Publications).

Divers Guide to Michigan by Steve Harrington (Maritime Press).

Exploring Superior Country by Craig Charles (NorthWord Press).

Fifty Hikes in Ohio by Ralph Ramey (Backcountry Publications).

Fifty Hikes in Western Pennsylvania by Tom Thwaites

(Backcountry Publications)

Fifty Hikes In Lower Michigan by Jim DuFresne (Backcountry Publications).

Guide to Michigan Waterfalls by Laurie Penrose (Friede Publications).

Guide to Minnesota Outdoors by Jim Umhoefer (NorthWord Press).

Guide to Wisconsin Outdoors by Jim Umhoefer (NorthWord Press).

Hiking Ohio by Robert Folzenlogen (Willow Press).

Lower Michigan's Best 75 Campgrounds by Jim DuFresne (Pegg Legg Publications).

Michigan Free by Eric Freedman (University of Michigan Press).

Michigan's Best Outdoor Adventures With Children by Jim DuFresne (Mountaineer-Books).

Nature Walks in Southern Indiana by Alan McPherson (Hoosier Chapter, Sierra Club).

More Natural Michigan by Tom Powers (Friede Publications).

Natural Michigan by Tom Powers (Friede Publications).

National Forest Scenic Byways by Beverly Magley (Falcon Press).

National Forest Scenic Byways II by Beverly Magley (Falcon Press).

Old Roads: The Cyclist's Guide to Rural Indiana by William N. Sherwood (Sherwood Press).

On the Water, Michigan: Your Comprehensive Guide to Water Recreation in the Great Lake State by Eric Freedman (Huron-Superior-Michigan Press).

Quiet Water Canoe Guide: Pennsylvania by Scott & Linda Shalaway (Appalachian Mountain Club Books).

Superior National Forest: A Complete Recreation Guide by Robert Beymer (Mountaineers-Books).

Travels in Canoe Country by Paul Gruchow (Bulfinch Press).

Wild Woodlands by Bill Thomas (Taylor Publishing Co.).

About The Author

Eric Freedman is a reporter for the Detroit News and a Pulitzer Prize winner in 1994. He writes widely on travel and recreation and is the author of three other books: *Pioneering Michigan; On The Water, Michigan: Your Comprehensive Guide To Water Recreation in the Great Lake State;* and *Michigan Free.* He also teaches journalism at Michigan State University and is a member of Outdoor Writers Association of America.